IMAGES
of America

UNITED STATES AIR FORCE ACADEMY

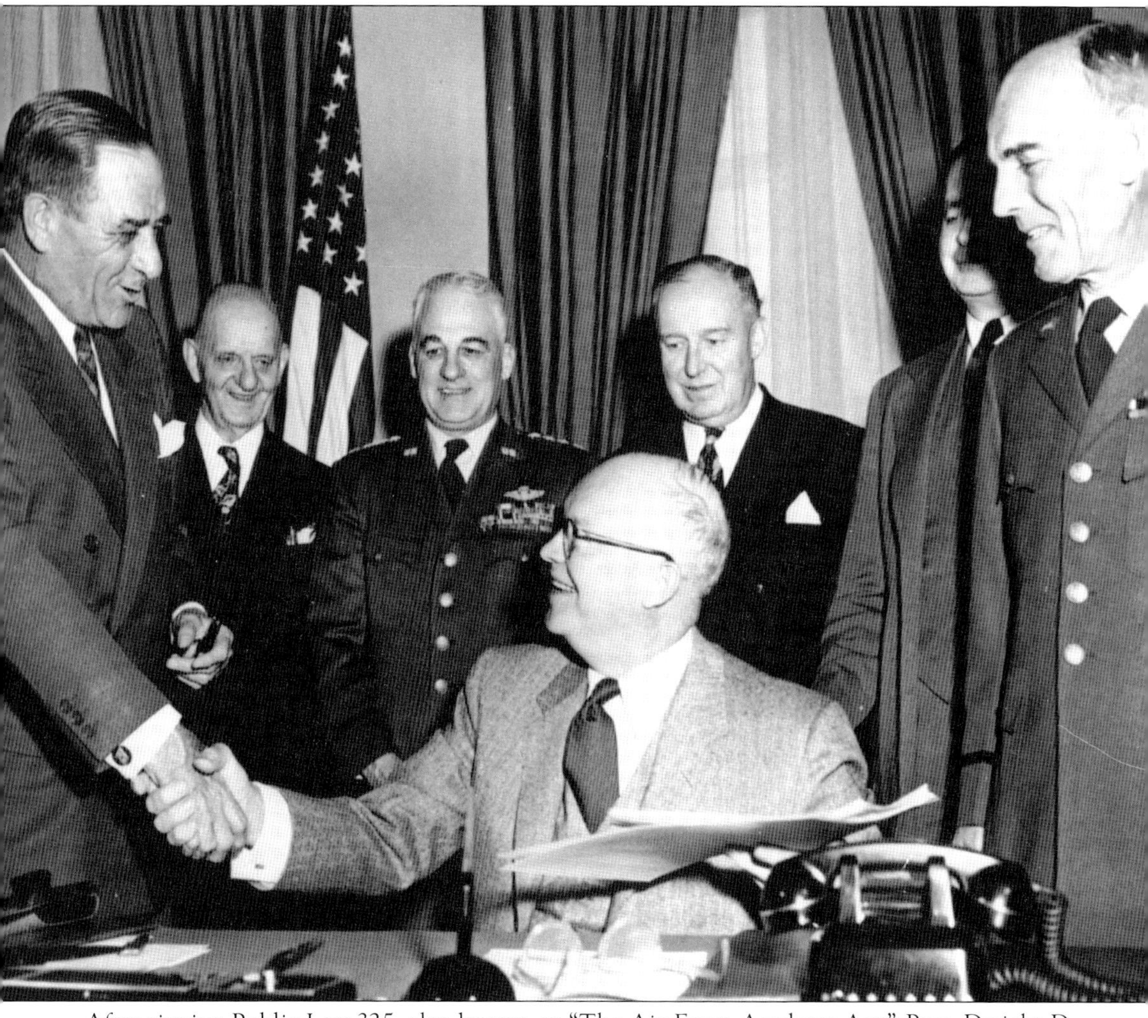

After signing Public Law 325, also known as "The Air Force Academy Act," Pres. Dwight D. Eisenhower shakes the hand of Harold E. Talbott, secretary of the Air Force, on April 1, 1954. (Courtesy of Special Collections, McDermott Library.)

On the Cover: The class of 1960 throws their parade service caps into the air as they celebrate their graduation on Wednesday, June 8, 1960. The Air Force Academy's motto, *Nulli secundus*, translates as "Second to None." (Courtesy of Special Collections, McDermott Library.)

IMAGES
of America

UNITED STATES AIR FORCE ACADEMY

Amanda K. Hess
Foreword by Alexander R. Hess

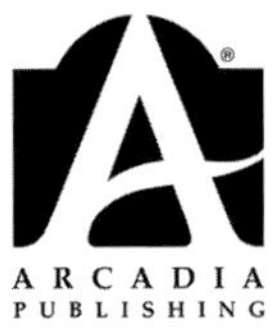
ARCADIA
PUBLISHING

ISBN 978-1-4671-6143-5

Published by Arcadia Publishing
Charleston, South Carolina

Printed in the United States of America

Library of Congress Control Number: 2024952274

For all general information, please contact Arcadia Publishing:
Telephone 843-853-2070
Fax 843-853-0044
E-mail sales@arcadiapublishing.com

Visit us on the Internet at www.arcadiapublishing.com

For my Pap, Col. Robert Charles Hess, who helped establish the Long Blue Line as an air training officer, dedicated himself to integrating women into the Air Force Academy as director of academy plans and projects, and led this family with love and strength.

Contents

Foreword

From its perch on the front range of the Rocky Mountains, the United States Air Force Academy towers above the plains of eastern Colorado. To an outside observer, the white marble buildings and the glistening spires of the Cadet Chapel give sharp contrast to the granite and green of the natural landscape. It is a mysterious, beautiful, and imposing place to behold.

For those who have passed its doors, endured its hardships, and come out on the other side, it is so much more than a place. It is a school that demands every ounce of your attention. It is a proving ground where your leadership ability is honed by trial after trial. It is a machine purposely designed to push you to your limit and beyond.

More than anything, the Air Force Academy is an institution that provides an unshakable foundation for your character. No one leaves the same person as when they entered. You are forever changed.

–Alexander R. Hess
Class of 2011

ACKNOWLEDGMENTS

I would like to express my heartfelt gratitude to everyone who contributed to the completion of this book. First and foremost, I want to thank my family, especially my parents and my husband, Robert, for their unwavering support and encouragement throughout this process. Thank you for being my first peer reviewers and editors; your feedback and insights are truly invaluable.

A special acknowledgment goes to Marianne LaRivee, Kathy Wilson, Steve Simon, Christopher Miller, and Stephen and Donna Randolph for their expertise and guidance, which greatly enriched the content of this work. I would like to recognize the contribution of Jack Anthony, who shared his wealth of knowledge on the history of the Air Force Academy and the pioneer history of the region; our correspondence played a crucial role in shaping this book.

I extend my heartfelt thanks to Ruth Kindreich and Joel Hebert from Clark Special Collections of the McDermott Library for their invaluable assistance in digitizing these historic photographs, for securing permissions, and for their dedicated stewardship of Air Force Academy history. I also want to thank Erinn Barnes for providing photographs from the Regional History & Genealogy collections at the Pikes Peak Library District. Finally, thank you to the Friends of the Air Force Academy Library for their support of this project.

Unless otherwise noted, all images appear courtesy of the Clark Special Collections Branch of the United States Air Force Academy McDermott Library.

Introduction

The United States Air Force Academy's mission is "to educate, train and inspire men and women to become officers of character motivated to lead the U.S. Air Force and U.S. Space Force in service to our nation." The academy celebrated its 70th anniversary in 2024 and has graduated 65 classes of leaders that personify its core values of "integrity first, service before self, excellence in all we do." This book is intended to provide a snapshot of the significance and richness of the United States Air Force Academy, its history and heritage, its mission, and its people.

The Air Force Academy was established in 1954, becoming the nation's fifth service academy dedicated to the education and commissioning of officers to serve in the US armed forces. The establishment of an air academy was a dream that began in the early days of manned flight. Just four years after the Wright brothers' first successful flight at Kitty Hawk, North Carolina, on December 17, 1903, there was a growing interest in the military application of aircraft and the training of young officers to lead a new aeronautical service. By the end of the First World War, the newly established Air Service held strong convictions about airpower's capabilities to accomplish the nation's military objectives and began advocating for a service of equal standing to that of the Army and Navy. It also began to push for an aeronautical academy to provide the specialized training required of pilots, modeled after the United States Military Academy at West Point and the United States Naval Academy at Annapolis (hereafter referred to as West Point and Annapolis). Gen. William "Billy" Mitchell, an outspoken advocate for airpower and an independent service, stated to members of the House of Representatives in January 1925 that it was vital "to have an air academy to form the basis for the permanent backbone of your air service . . . very much in the same way that West Point does for the Army, or the Naval Academy for the Navy." Lt. Col. A.J. Hanlon said very much the same in 1918, declaring that "no service can flourish without some such institution to inculcate into its embryonic officers love of country, proper conception of duty and highest regard for honor." Between the world wars, there was an ongoing and fervent dialogue about an aeronautical academy, but little was accomplished in establishing one.

World War II demonstrated the effectiveness of airpower and intensified the desires of air-minded individuals to establish an academy aimed at producing the highly qualified cadre of officers needed to meet the challenges of the atomic age, advancements in aviation technology, and the impending space age. At that time, the Army Air Forces were still under the Department of the Army, and while independent-minded air thinkers were pushing for a separate air arm of equal status and a service academy of their own, the Army and the Navy were concerned about competition for limited federal funding and jurisdiction.

The establishment of the US Air Force as a separate service under the National Security Act of 1947 finally gave proponents of an Air Force academy a solid foundation on which to make their case, though the path forward remained difficult and would take an additional seven years. Debates continued over where an academy would be located, the faculty, the curriculum, and whether flying training should be part of its program. There were some who questioned if another service academy was even necessary. Gen. Dwight D. Eisenhower, then president of Columbia University, supported the idea of a unified service academy. He argued that separate academies contributed to parochialism and division, but a unified academy would foster a greater sense of jointness between the services. Eisenhower favored combining the existing academies into the United Service Academy with branches at West Point and Annapolis. It was this opinion that he carried into his position as vice chairman on the Service Academy Board, also known as the Stearns-Eisenhower Board, in 1949. The board was tasked to evaluate the educational programs of the armed forces, including the existing service academies and the creation of a new air academy. Through his service on the board, Eisenhower reconsidered his earlier position and voted in favor of a separate academy. Six years later, he played a very significant role in its founding. The final report of the Stearns-Eisenhower Board was released in January 1950 and strongly recommended the creation of an Air Force academy.

In 1949, the chief of staff of the Air Force, Gen. Hoyt S. Vandenberg, created the Office of Special Assistant for Air Force Academy Matters and appointed Lt. Gen. Hubert R. Harmon to manage the Air Force's planning and legislative efforts. Harmon retired on February 28, 1953, when he reached the mandatory retirement age but was recalled to active status the following day to continue to serve as the special assistant, expecting that academy legislation would soon be given congressional approval. Between 1919 and 1953, dozens of bills had been introduced in Congress to establish an air academy, but all were rejected until HR 5337 was introduced to the House of Representatives on May 21, 1953. When the bill was not approved by June of that year, Harmon decided to retire once more, this time moving from Washington, DC, to San Antonio, Texas. With the help from his friend and West Point classmate General Eisenhower, now president of the United States, HR 5337 was slated to be the subject of congressional hearings in early 1954. As a result, Harmon was once again recalled to active duty to support the final legislative push and serve as the first superintendent of the new United States Air Force Academy. Final congressional approval came on March 29, 1954. On April 1, 1954, President Eisenhower, surrounded by a handful of the men who had brought the dream of the Air Force Academy into reality, signed Public Law 325, "The Air Force Academy Act." This day is celebrated annually at the academy as "Founders Day."

One

The Academy at Lowry Air Force Base

On August 14, 1954, Lt. Gen. Hubert R. Harmon signed General Order No. 1, activating a portion of Lowry Air Force Base near Denver, Colorado, as the temporary home of the new Air Force Academy. Activated on February 26, 1938, Lowry was one of the oldest facilities in Air Training Command at the time. Named for Lt. Francis B. Lowry, Denver's first pilot casualty of World War I, the facility served as a training base for the Army Air Forces during World War II and as President Eisenhower's "Summer White House" between 1953 and 1955. It continued training operations until its closure in 1994.

Under the joint-tenancy agreement of 1955 and the supervision of Maj. Arthur Witters, a section of the existing buildings and facilities were refurbished to serve the Air Force Academy's mission. The renovations included administrative and academic buildings, dormitories, a dining hall, a chapel, athletic facilities, a cadet store, and a parade ground. The meager academy staff had just under 11 months from the signing of General Order No. 1 to the arrival of the first cadets. During this short time, the academy staff had to overcome logistical and financial problems, including base renovations and procuring uniforms, supplies, and equipment. Further, they needed to design an academic curriculum and a military training program and to define procedures for cadet selection and recruitment.

The development of the cadet training programs at the new academy was heavily influenced by the Fourth-Class System at West Point, where upperclassmen were responsible for the military indoctrination and training of the younger classes. This system was based on the notion that one must first learn to follow before one can lead. However, as the first class at the academy would not have an upper class to follow, a group of lieutenants were selected to act as the Air Force Academy's upperclassmen. They were called air training officers (ATOs). While tough on the new cadets, their influence deeply impacted the success of the first three classes of cadets at the fledgling academy, and the class of 1959 adopted them as honorary members of their class.

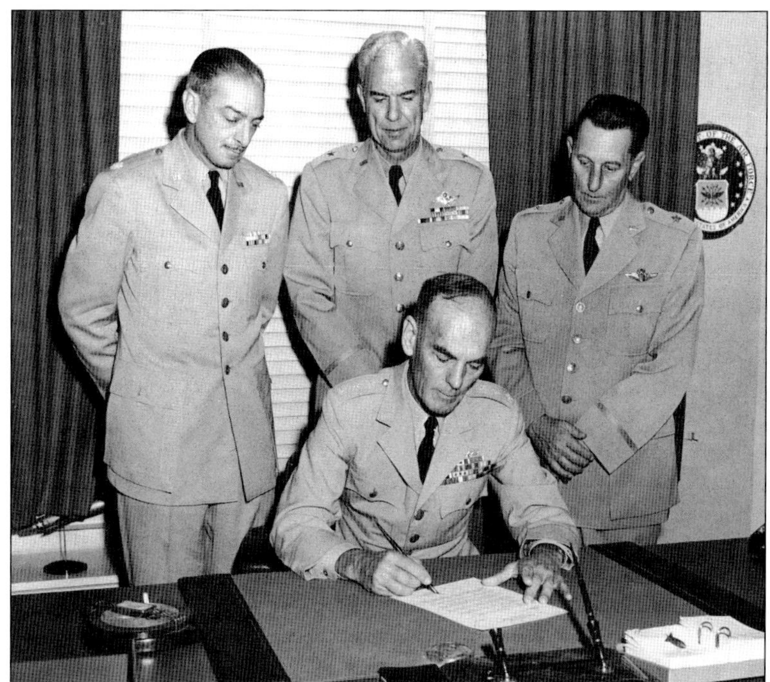

Lieutenant General Harmon signed General Order No. 1, activating the Air Force Academy Command, and assumed command as superintendent on August 14, 1954, at the desk of Lowry Air Force Base commander Brig. Gen. John T. Sprague. Standing behind Lieutenant General Harmon are, from left to right, Lt. Col. Gilbert C. Cook, Brig. Gen. Don Z. Zimmerman, and Brig. Gen. John T. Sprague.

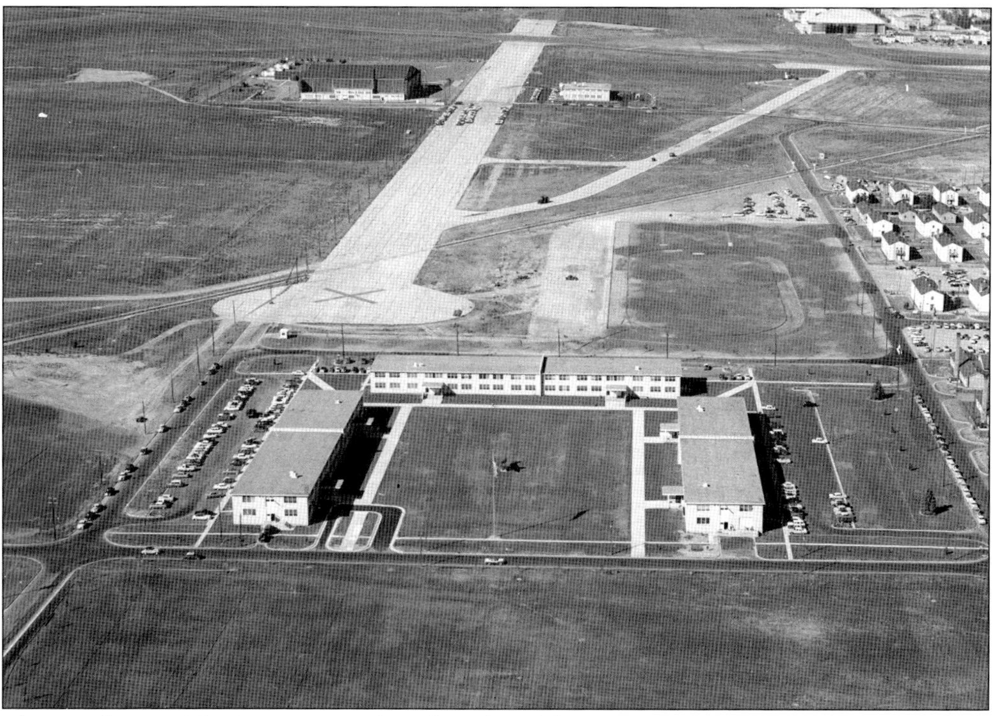

This aerial view of the Air Force Academy "quadrangle" at Lowry Air Force Base in Denver shows the academic campus of the Air Force Academy in 1955. The Headquarters building is on the left, the Library and English Department is housed in the center building, and the Sciences building is to the right. The cadet dormitories, wooden barracks built during World War II, can be seen to the right of the main campus.

Secretary of the Air Force Harold Talbott and Lieutenant General Harmon admire a sign identifying the academy area of Lowry Air Force Base. In his 1955 dedication address, Secretary Talbott spoke of the expected greatness of the Air Force Academy, stating "with feet planted firmly in the solid center of the United States and with eyes on the stars, the Air Force Academy will move onward to a rendezvous with destiny."

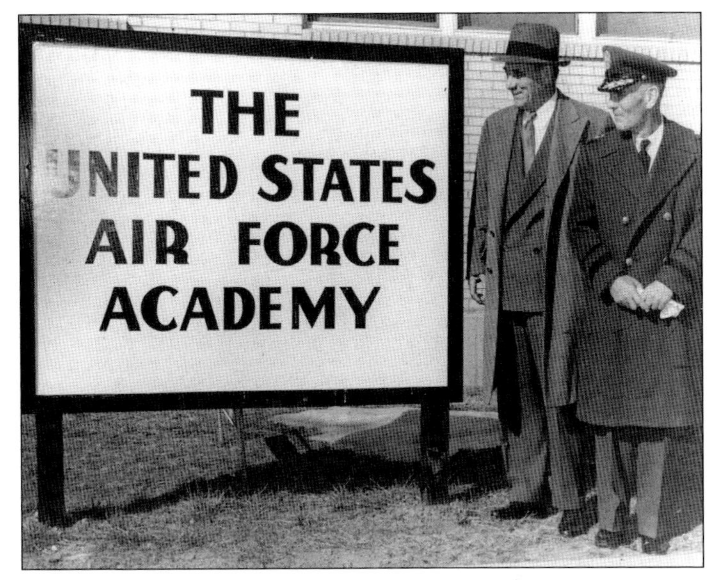

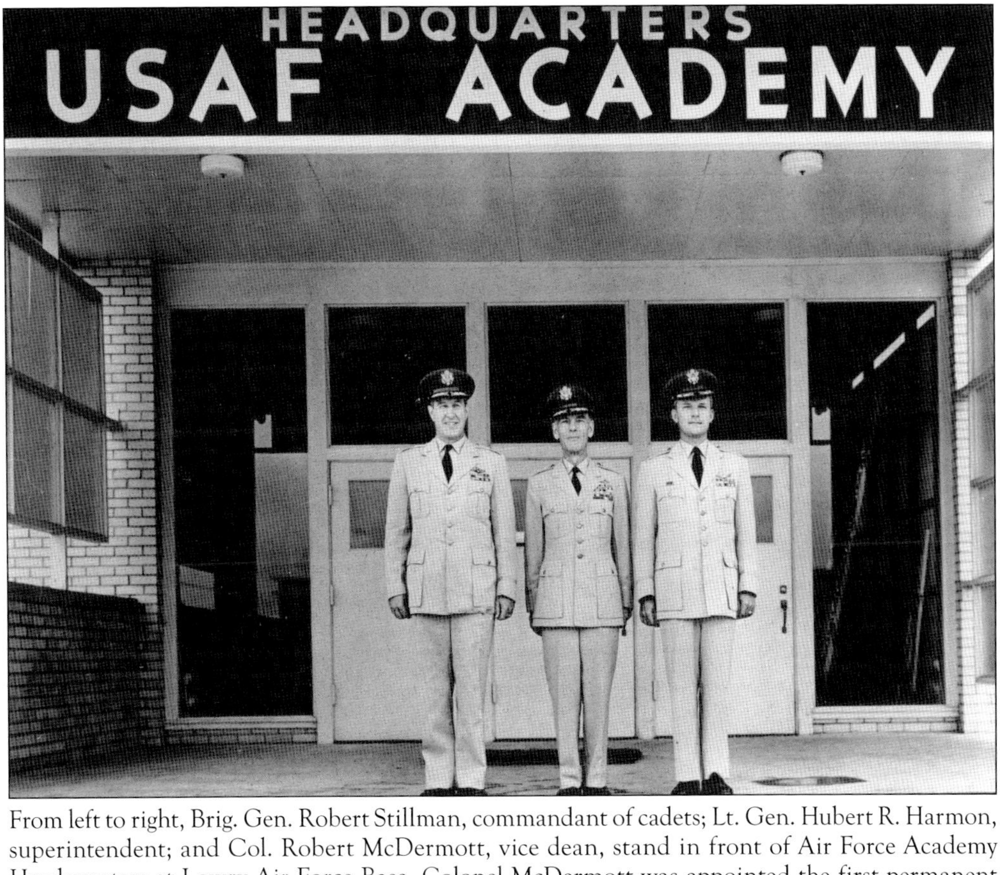

From left to right, Brig. Gen. Robert Stillman, commandant of cadets; Lt. Gen. Hubert R. Harmon, superintendent; and Col. Robert McDermott, vice dean, stand in front of Air Force Academy Headquarters at Lowry Air Force Base. Colonel McDermott was appointed the first permanent dean of the faculty in 1959. Upon his appointment, McDermott was promoted to brigadier general, becoming the youngest general officer on active duty at that time.

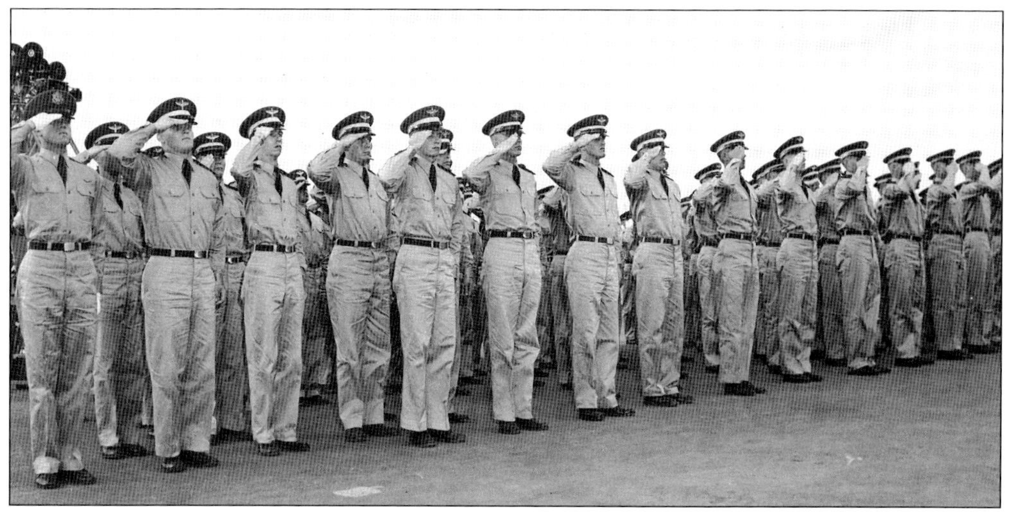

On July 11, 1955, three hundred six young men arrived to form the class of 1959. Sixty-six rated Air Force officers were selected to act as the class of 1959's upperclassmen. Of these, 24 were graduates from ROTC programs, 11 graduated from Annapolis, and 8 graduated from West Point. The different commissioning sources would affect the training methods they would employ during their time at the Air Force Academy.

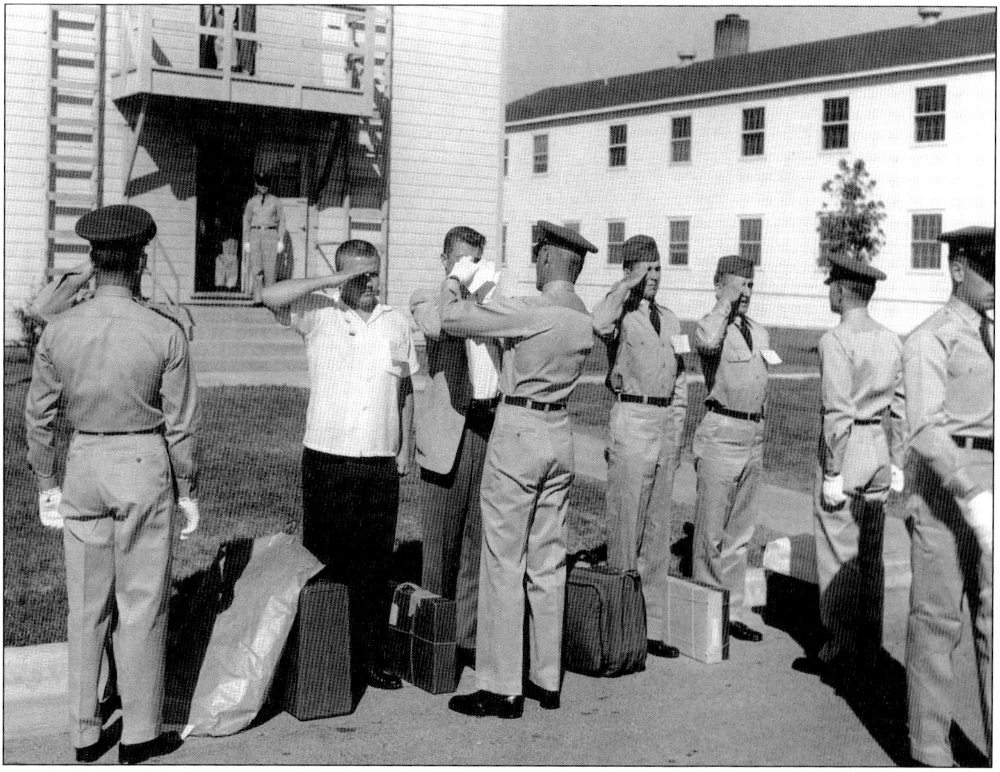

After routine medical examinations and registration processing were complete, new cadets were handed over to the ATOs and their military training began. Here, ATOs teach a group of new cadets in the class of 1960 the proper way to salute, a skill that will be used daily throughout their time at the academy and upon their graduation as second lieutenants.

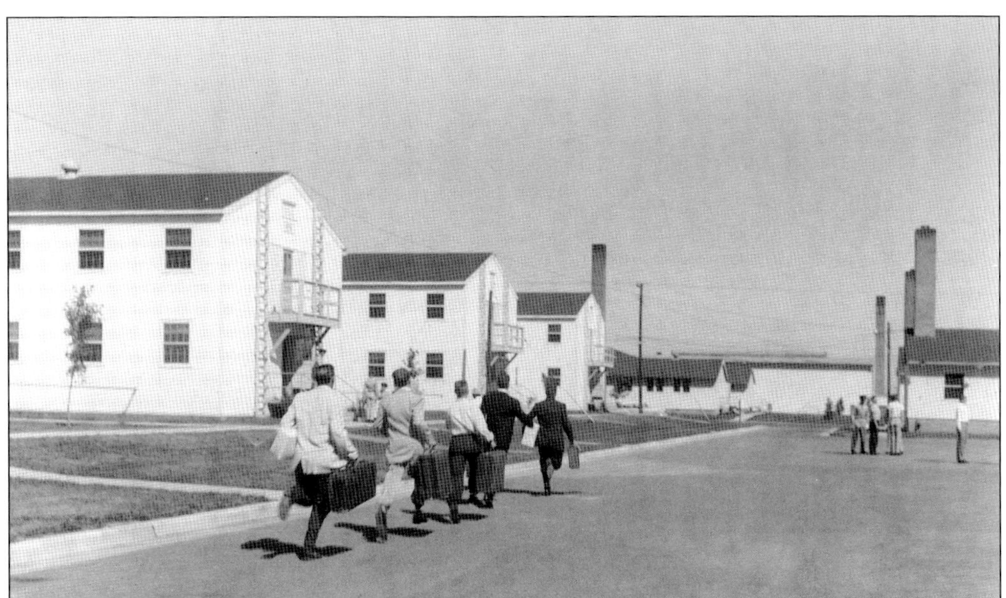

Leaving the Headquarters building, newly in-processed cadets learned that they would have to run at "double-time" to their destinations, making square corners on all turns. First-year cadets were permitted to walk only to and from the chapel and when returning from meals. Additionally, they were required to carry their backpacks in their left hands and slow only to render salutes to officers. This custom is still observed today.

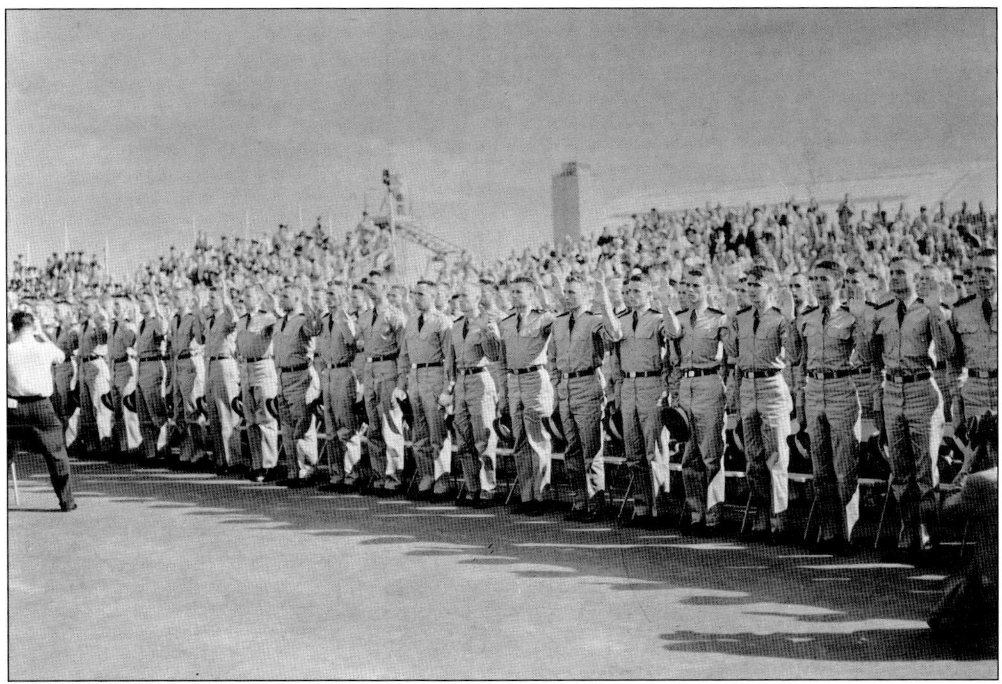

The dedication of the United States Air Force Academy at Lowry Air Force Base was held in the afternoon on July 11, 1955. Cadets raised their right hands to take the oath of allegiance during the swearing-in ceremony. Note that it appears the cadets are using their left hands to take the oath; the original photograph was printed in reverse.

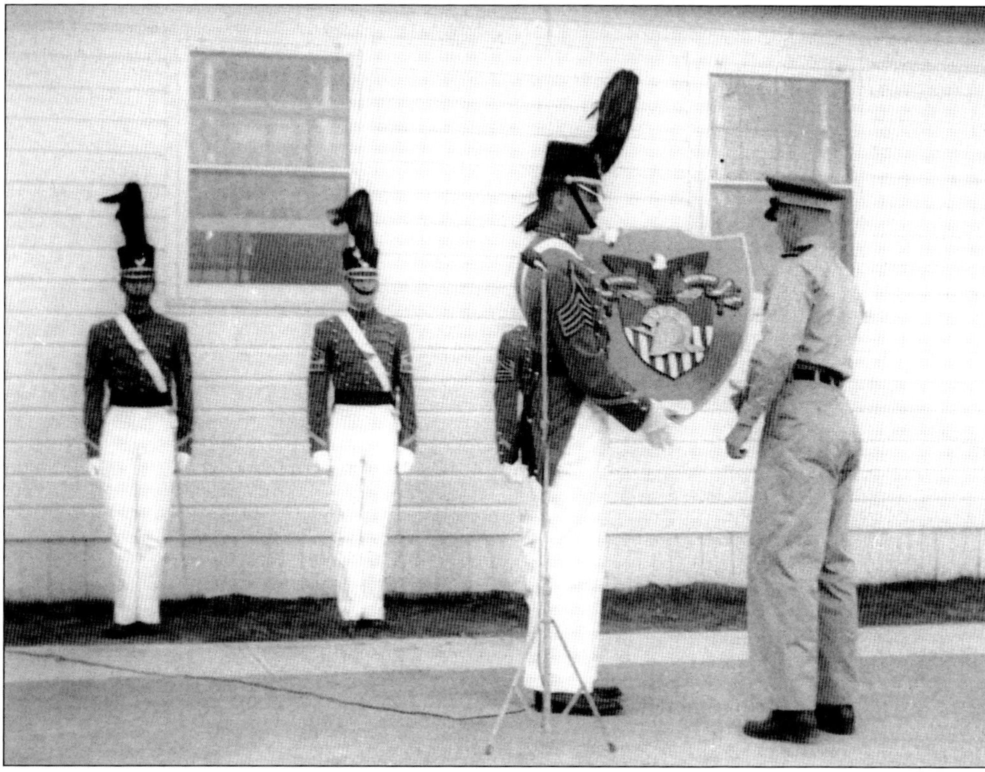

A member of the class of 1959 accepts a plaque from the visiting West Point contingent during the dedication ceremonies. Sixty-five West Point cadets and 45 midshipmen from Annapolis, along with representatives from six foreign Air Force academies, were present at the dedication.

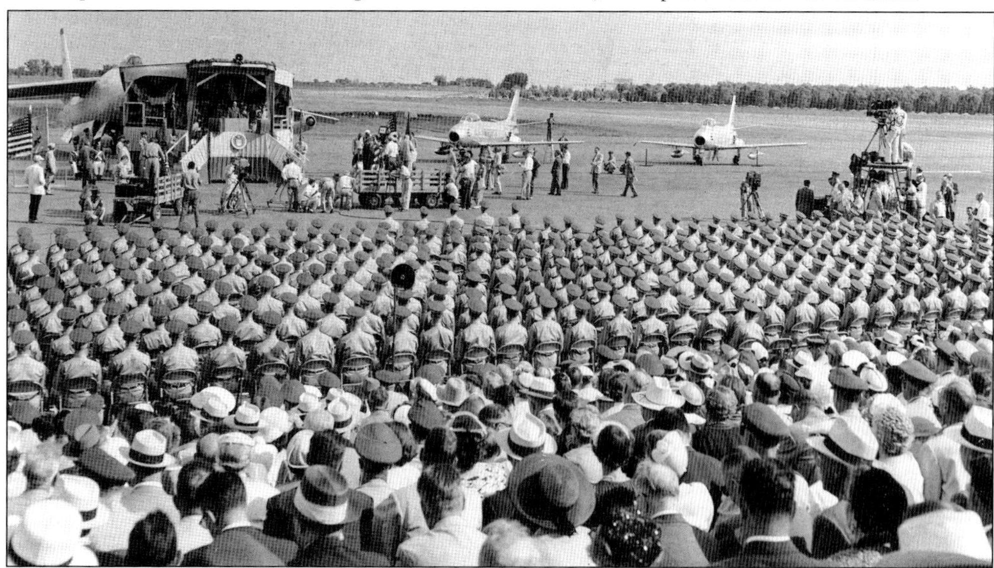

Air Force Academy cadets and distinguished guests watch a group of television, newsreel, and motion picture cameramen in operation during the dedication ceremonies on July 11, 1955. Columbia Broadcasting System broadcast the ceremony nationwide, and the Air Photographic and Charting Service from Orlando Air Force Base took photographs and videos of the event.

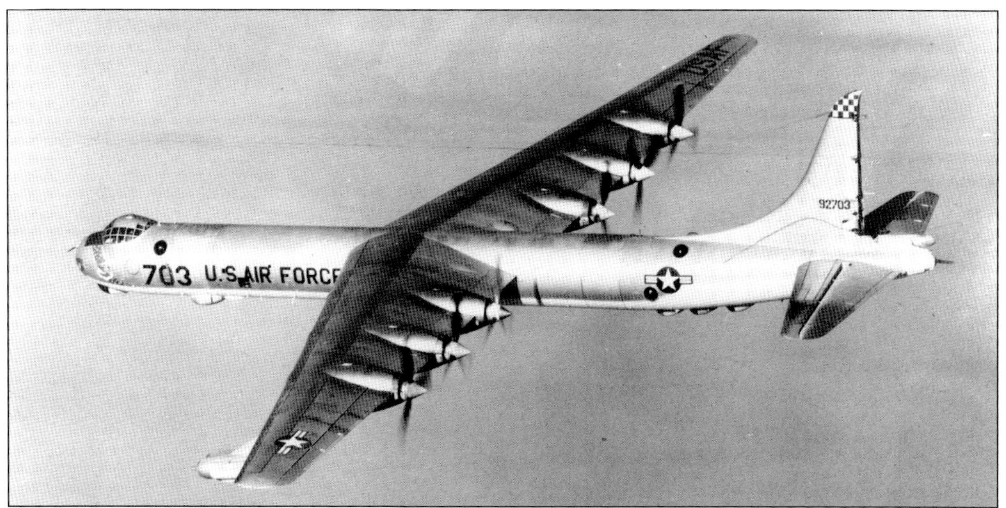

Spectators at the dedication ceremonies enjoyed flyovers by several heavy and medium bombers as well as fighter aircraft. This plane, a Convair RB-36 Peacemaker commanded by Maj. William W. Deyerle from Fairchild Air Force Base, Washington, lost a rudder while approaching the ceremony. The rudder landed in a farmer's field approximately 30 miles from Denver. The disabled 150-ton aircraft successfully landed at Ellsworth Air Force Base, South Dakota.

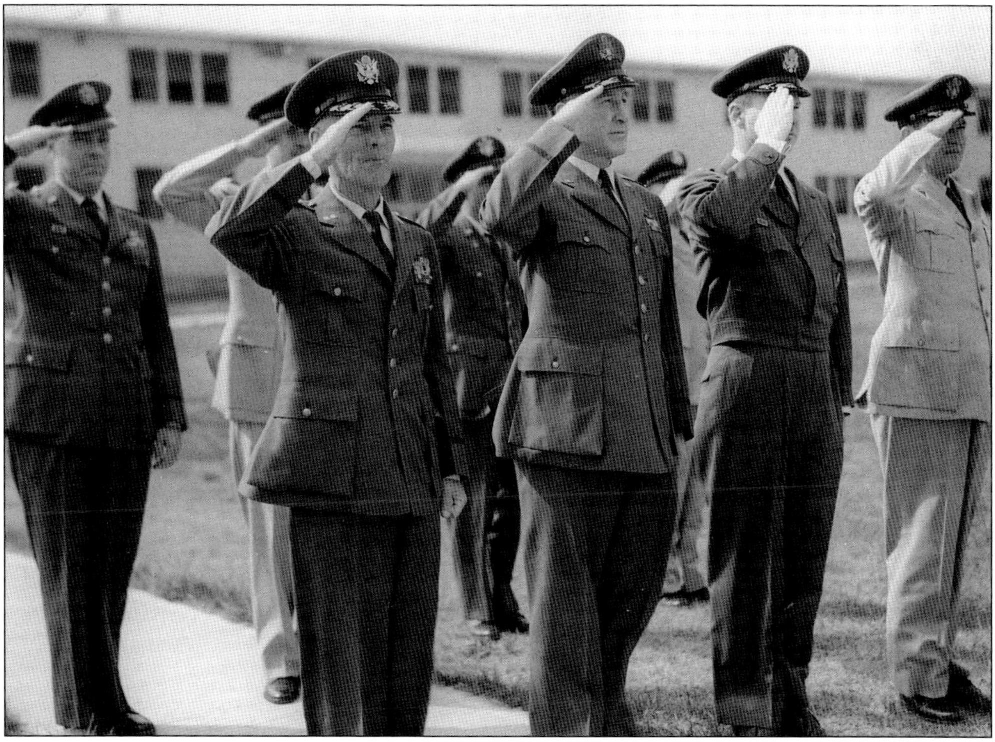

Superintendent Harmon and his staff salute the colors as the flag is being raised on the first day of classes in September 1955. At the Air Force Academy's commencement, academy staff held differing opinions on the educational and training philosophy. Lieutenant General Harmon wanted to introduce a broader array of liberal arts classes to the curriculum, in contrast to the other service academies, which at the time focused heavily on science, engineering, and technology.

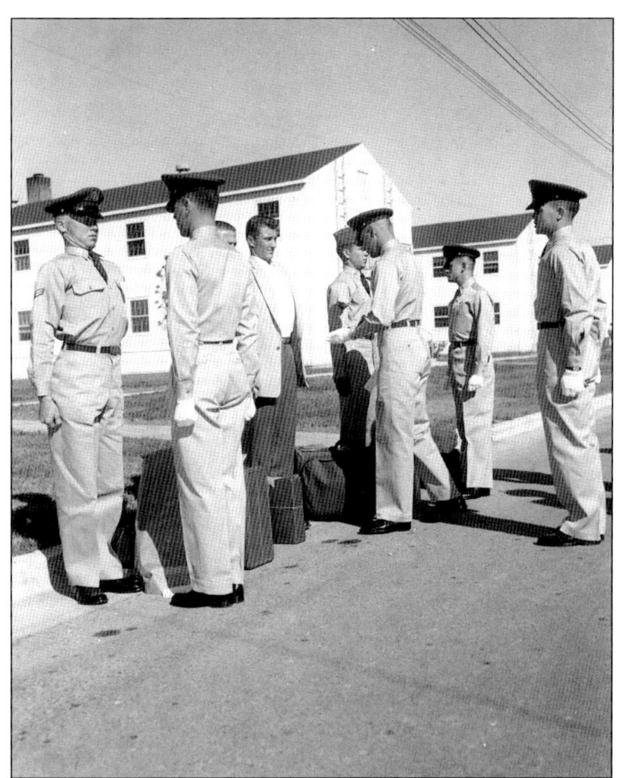

ATOs drill cadets in a position known as a "brace." This modified form of standing at attention requires cadets to force their chin down while keeping their shoulders pulled back, heels together, and arms fixed at the side. ATOs could be heard to scream out "more wrinkles!" if they deemed that the cadet's chin was not tucked in enough.

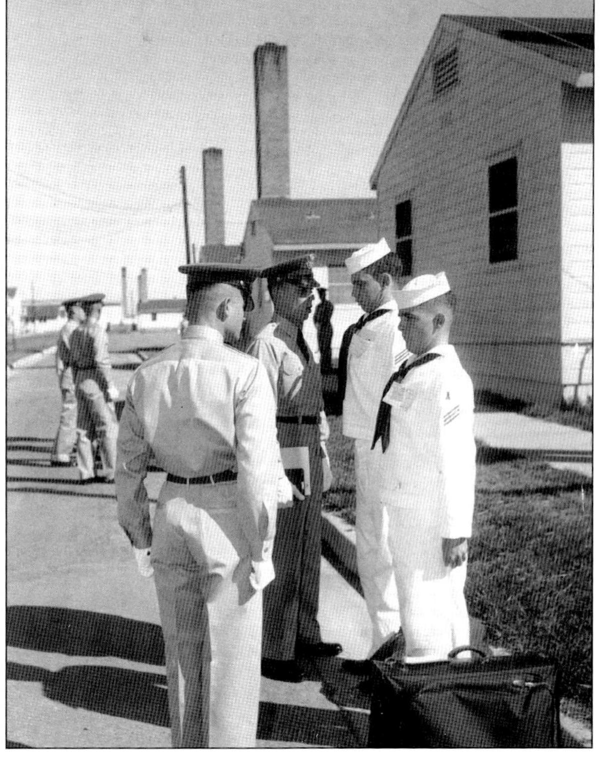

When the Air Force Academy opened, it attracted cadets from all parts of the country and other branches of the military. Here, two former members of the US Navy receive an introduction to cadet life from ATOs. Cadets learned quickly that the only acceptable responses were, "Yes, Sir!", "No Sir!", "Sir, I do not know," and "No excuse, Sir!"

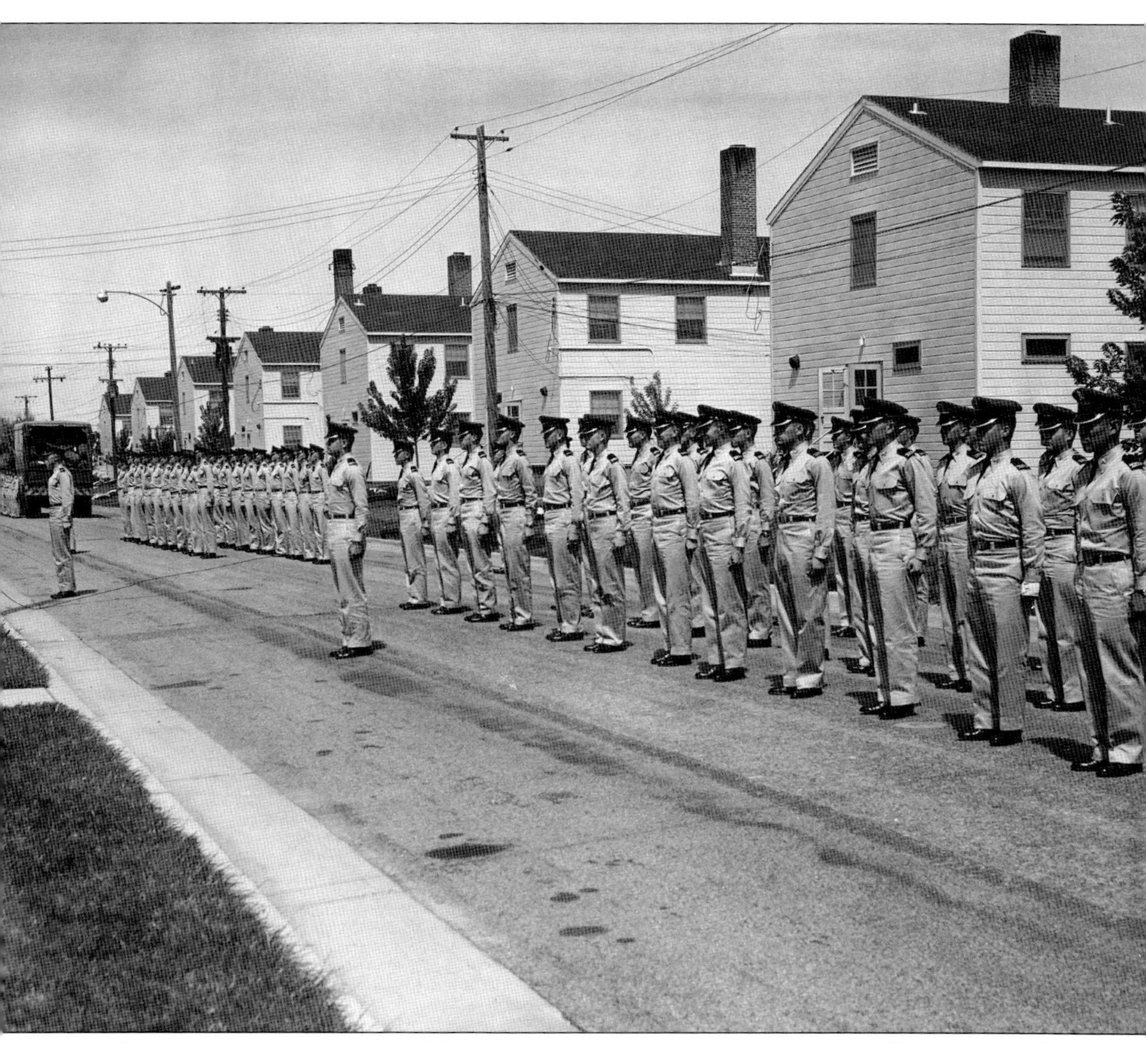

Cadets form up in front of their living quarters as the ATOs inspect the ranks. Thirty-six open-bay barracks were reconfigured to house cadets in two-person rooms. Cadets were assigned a single bed, desk, chair, floor lamp, closet, and rifle rack. Roommates would share bookshelves, a shoeshine kit, and a portable typewriter. Each cadet was responsible for his side of the room, but one cadet was tasked with the overall cleanliness of the room on any given day. There was a latrine on each floor, but showers were only available on the first floor. A single two-person room with an attached bathroom, for use by the ATOs, was located on every floor. Each dormitory stationed a "minute-caller" at the bottom of the stairway five minutes prior to any impending event. At one-minute intervals, the caller would inform the cadets of pertinent details, such as the required uniform, and would order them to fall out for formation when one minute remained.

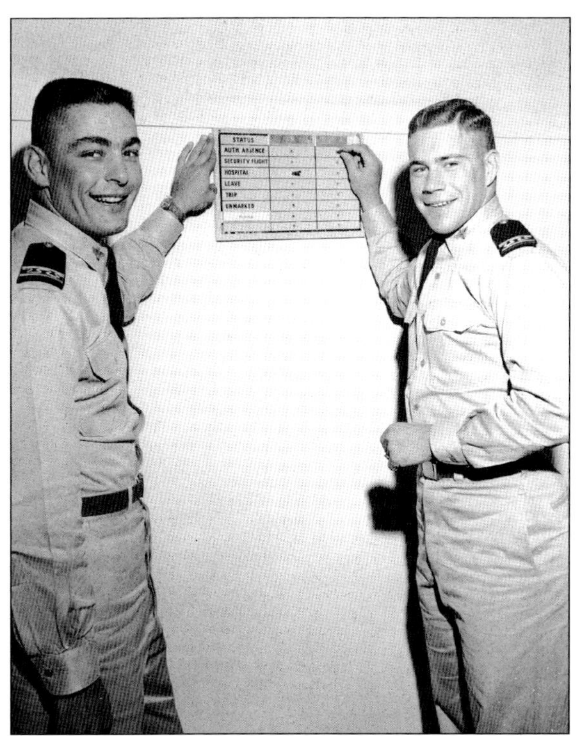

Cadets in the class of 1959 show off their wooden sign-out board. Located in each room, the pegboard had a side for each cadet to indicate their location when officers came to inspect. Statuses included authorized absence, security flight, hospital, leave, trip, and flying. A final check was made by the ATOs after "lights-out" at 10:00 p.m.

"A place for everything and everything in its place" is the foundational proverb for the cadet's living quarters. The Cadet Regulations book outlined the proper storage of all items in the cadet dormitory, including the dimensions for folded clothing items, as can be seen in this photograph. While cadets could expect a room inspection at any time, they were guaranteed a Saturday A.M. Inspection, otherwise known as a "SAMI."

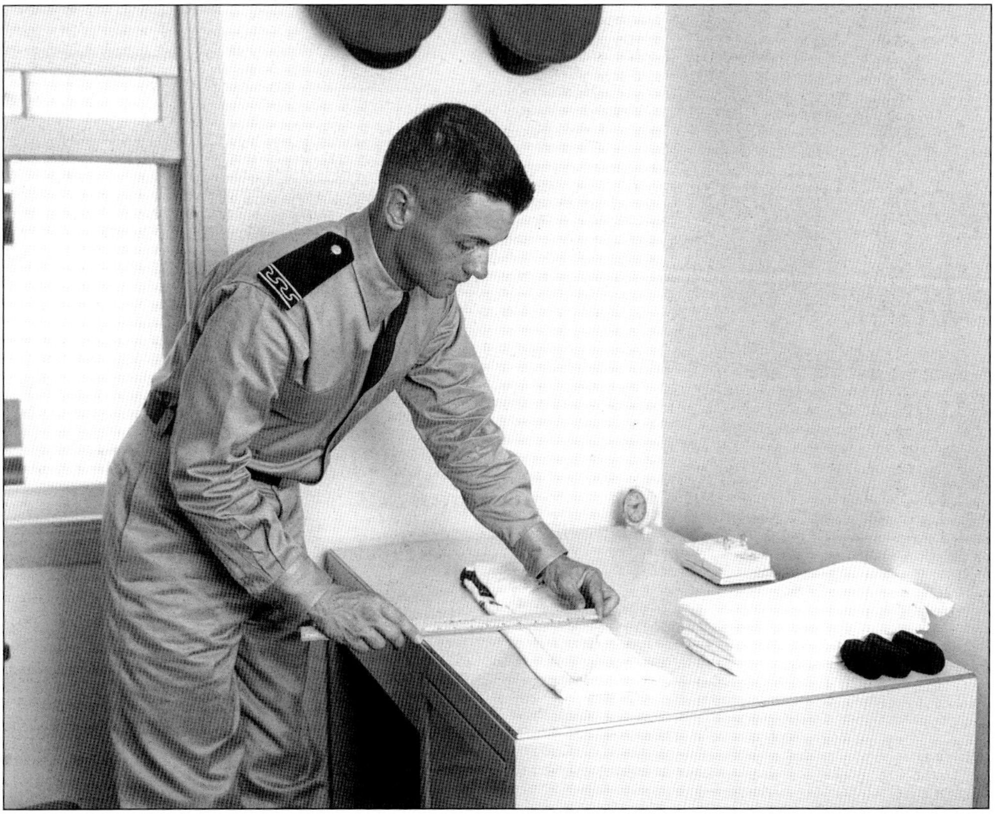

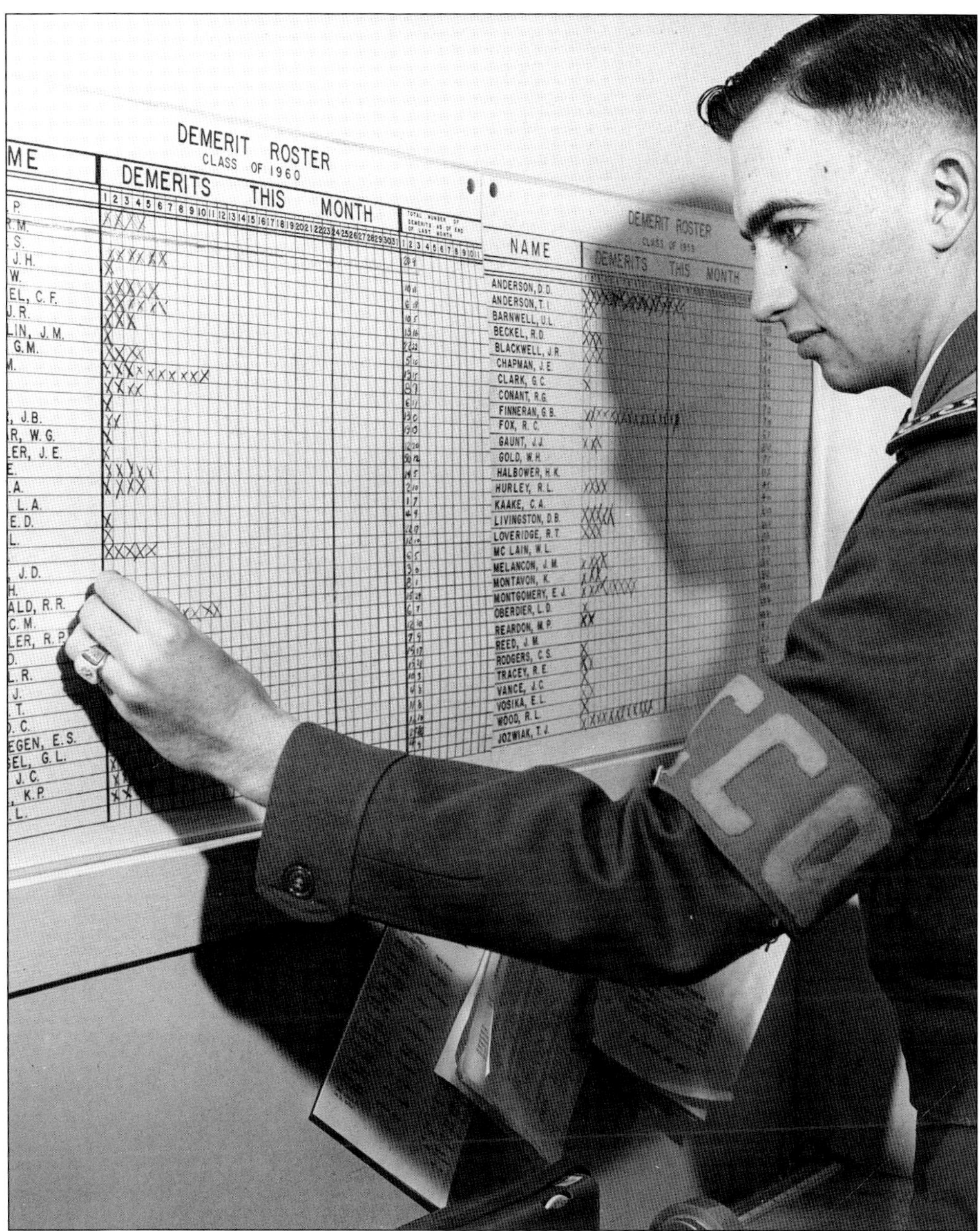

In this 1956 photograph, the cadet in charge of quarters is shown charting the monthly demerits incurred by the classes of 1959 and 1960. Infractions of cadet rules and regulations result in demerits, punishment tours, or confinement to the dormitory. A punishment tour involved walking at attention, with an M-1 rifle, in the West Quadrangle for a one-hour period. Freshmen cadets were permitted one demerit per day and required to walk punishment tours for every demerit over 23 within a 30-day period. If any cadet exceeded the maximum allowance of demerits over a six-month period, he was considered "deficient in conduct" and met with a board to decide whether he should remain at the academy. Visiting heads of state could "forgive" punishment tours incurred prior to their visit; however, this did not affect the cadet's demerits. During President Eisenhower's brief visit in September 1955, he exercised this power to grant amnesty from all punishments.

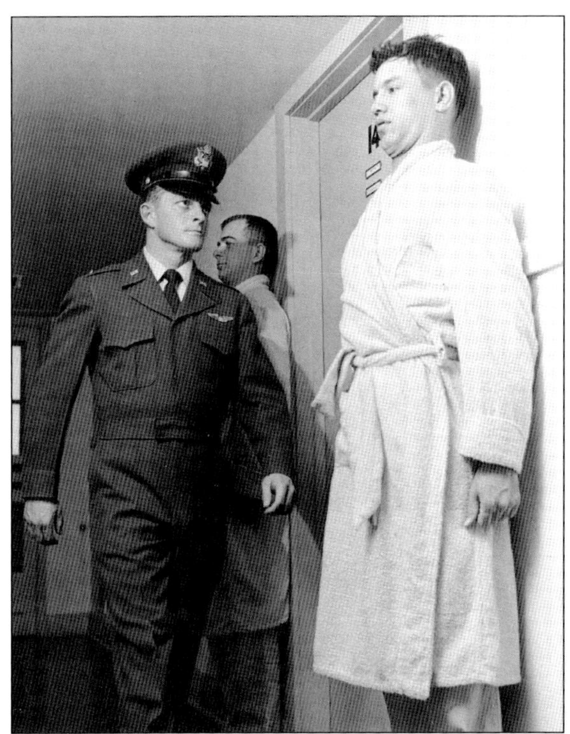

An ATO inspects cadets outside their dorm room. Any occasion was an opportunity for ATOs to harass new cadets with questions on "Fourth Class Knowledge," the information found in the pocket-sized cadet handbook, *Contrails*, which cadets were required to memorize. Incorrect answers were met with chastisement and punishment, usually in the form of push-ups. (Courtesy of Special Collections, Pikes Peak Library District, 001-1952.)

The ATOs often got creative with their punishments. As penance for accidentally deploying his parachute inside the T-29 "Flying Classroom," this cadet was required to carry the D-ring to a parachute with him everywhere he went for an entire week. Here, he holds the D-ring during the evening meal.

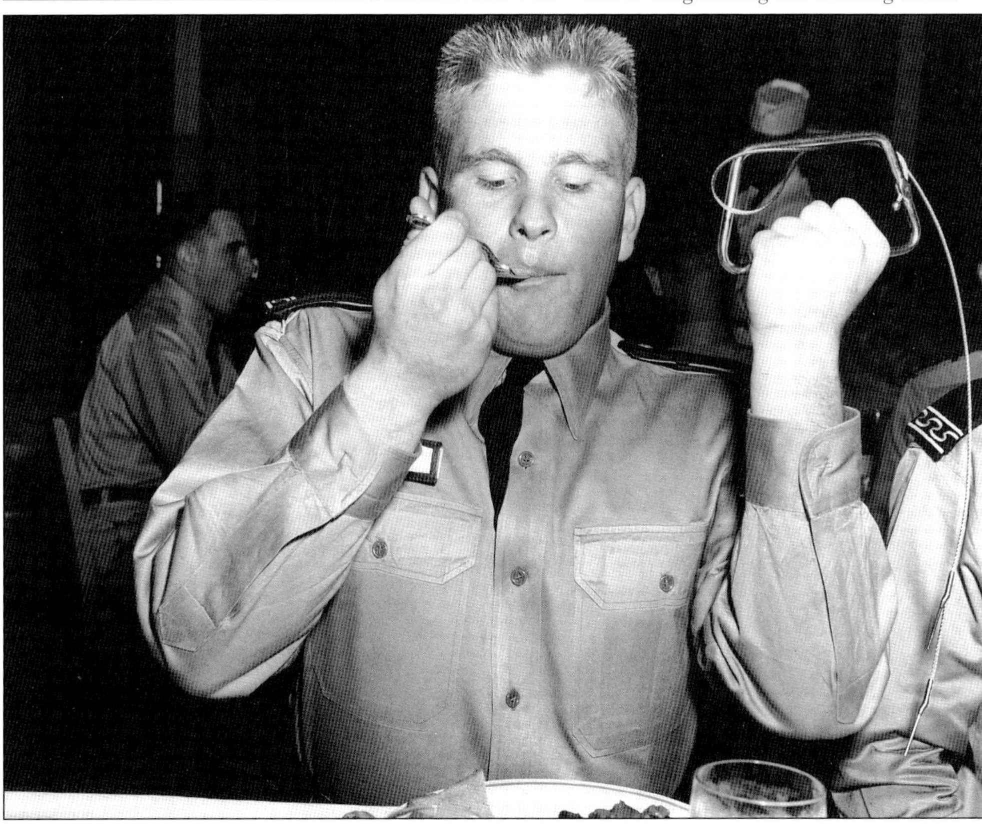

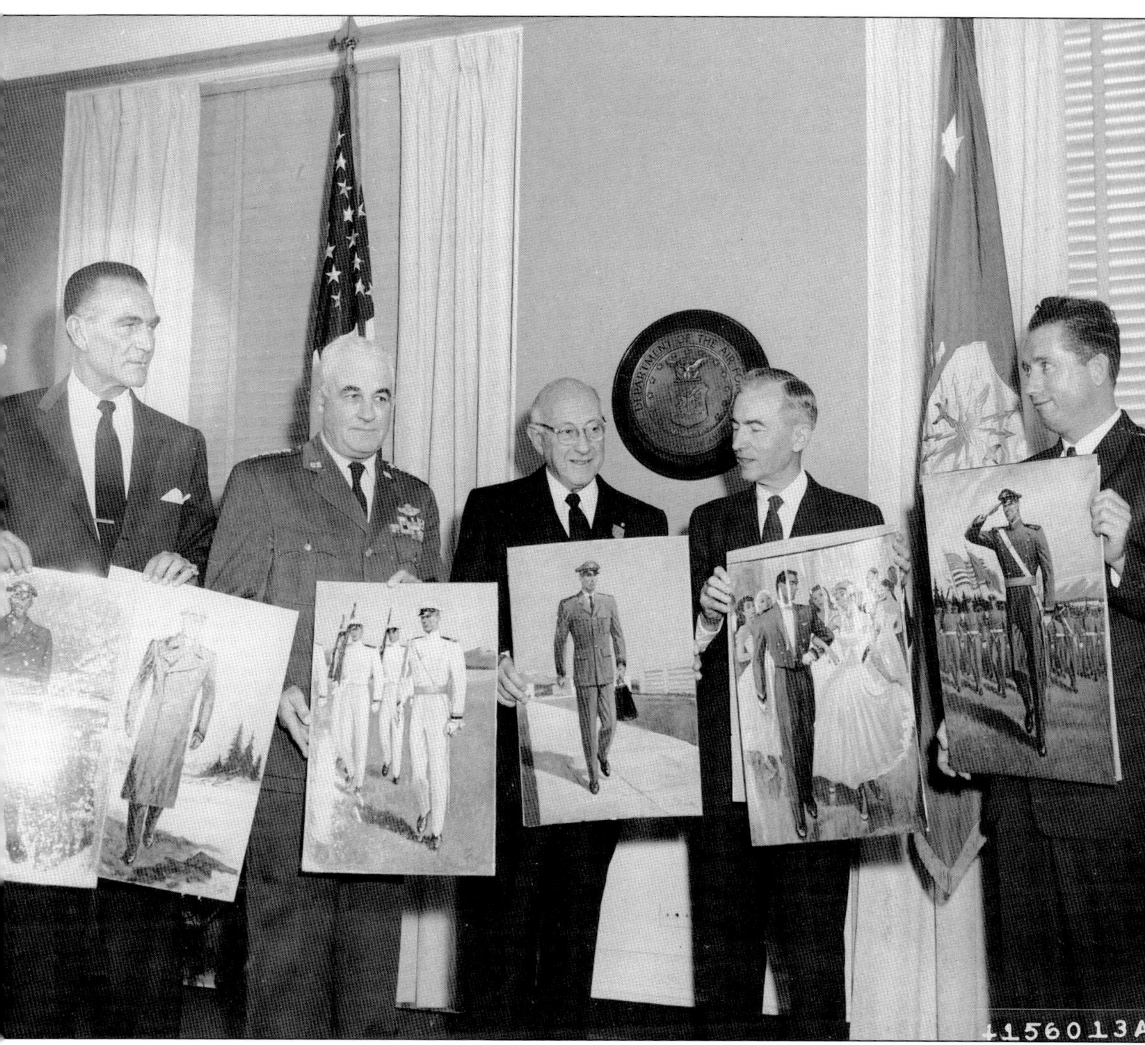

Lieutenant General Harmon's staff desired a distinctive set of Air Force Academy uniforms. Having been disappointed by the many designs submitted by military tailors, including a garish lightning bolt and cloud patterned uniform, Secretary of the Air Force Harold Talbott reached out to his friend Hollywood legend Cecil B. DeMille for an exclusive design. As a director and producer at Paramount Pictures, DeMille was known for his creativity and vast knowledge of historical military uniforms. DeMille, along with members of his staff A.B. Hinton, John Jensen, and Henry Wilcoxon, produced designs for five new cadet uniforms. DeMille's vision for the cadet uniform was one that was "attractive, but thoroughly masculine." He quipped, "If the man in the uniforms is happy with them, that is the main thing; if his girl admires them, that is even more important." Proudly displaying artists' sketches of the DeMille uniforms and overcoat are, from left to right, Henry Wilcoxon, Gen. Nathan F. Twining, Cecil B. DeMille, Secretary of the Air Force Donald Quarles, and John Jensen.

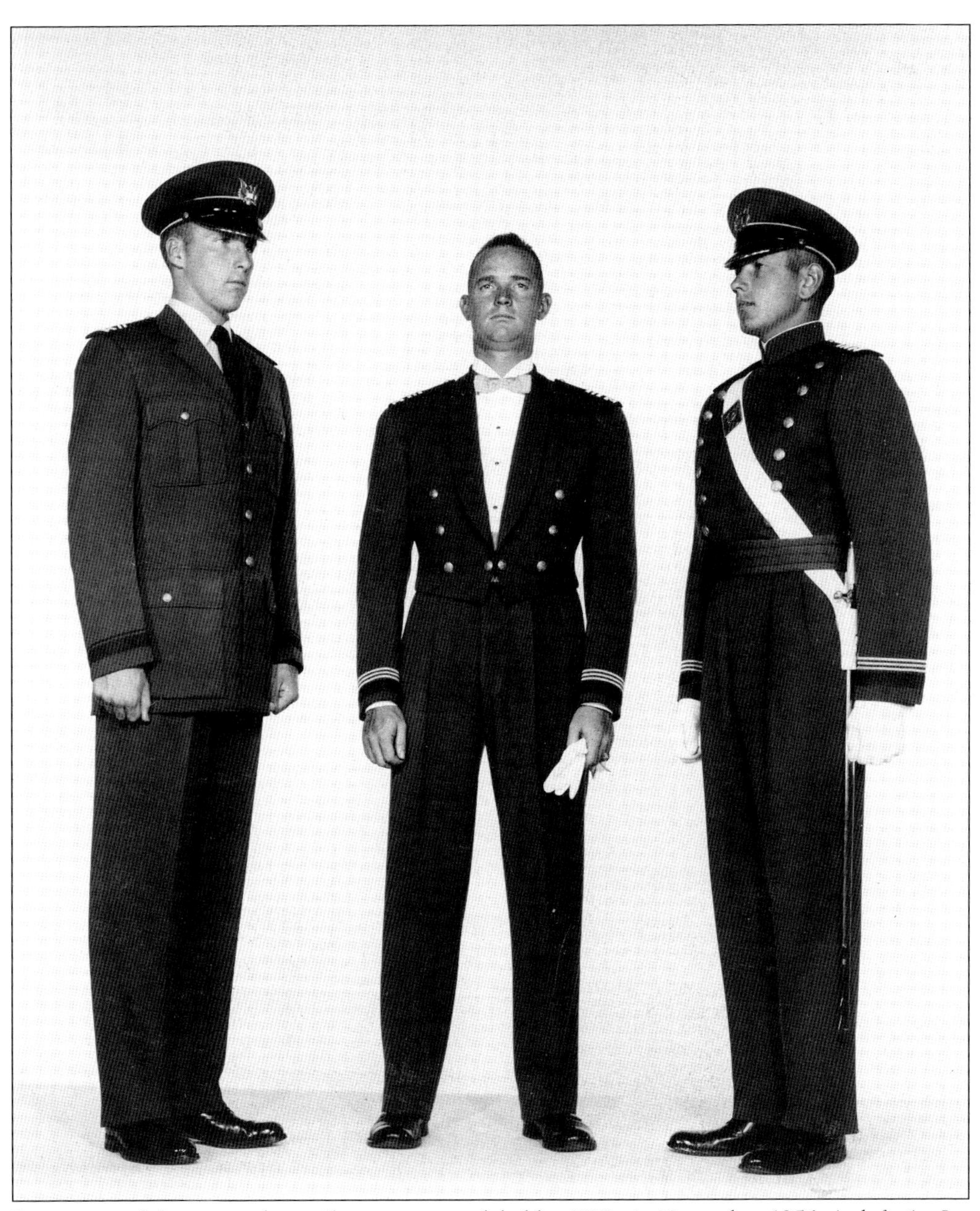

Prototypes of the new cadet uniforms were modeled by ATOs in November 1956. At left, 1st Lt. Jerald Till wears the winter dress uniform, intended to be worn to classes, meals, athletic events, and during travel. In the center, 1st Lt. James Clendenen is wearing the evening dress uniform, designed for wear at formal social functions. At right, 1st Lt. Frank Drew showcases the winter parade dress uniform with the sash, sword, and white leather and silver-buckled sword belt of a cadet officer. The winter parade dress uniform is worn at parades, ceremonies, and chapel services. The distinctive cap, worn with most uniforms, is indigo blue with darker blue braid around the crown. Its black visor has a silver-colored, metal-edged brim. The insignia shown on the prototypes was temporary, as decisions on permanent insignia were not made until later. Cadets were required to purchase these new uniforms from their cadet pay of $111.15 per month. When the new uniform designs were shown, cadets overwhelmingly and enthusiastically supported them.

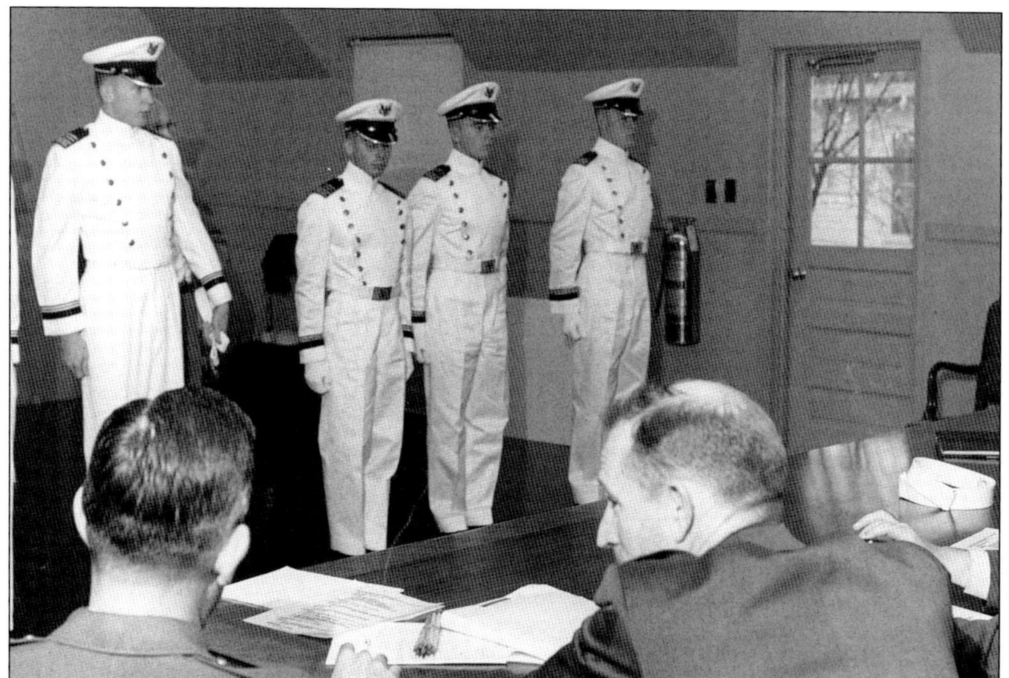

On April 26, 1957, the Uniform Board met to review fabric choices for the proposed summer parade dress uniform. The Globe Tailoring Company of Cincinnati, Ohio, was awarded the contract to manufacture the new uniforms and began delivering them in the fall of 1957.

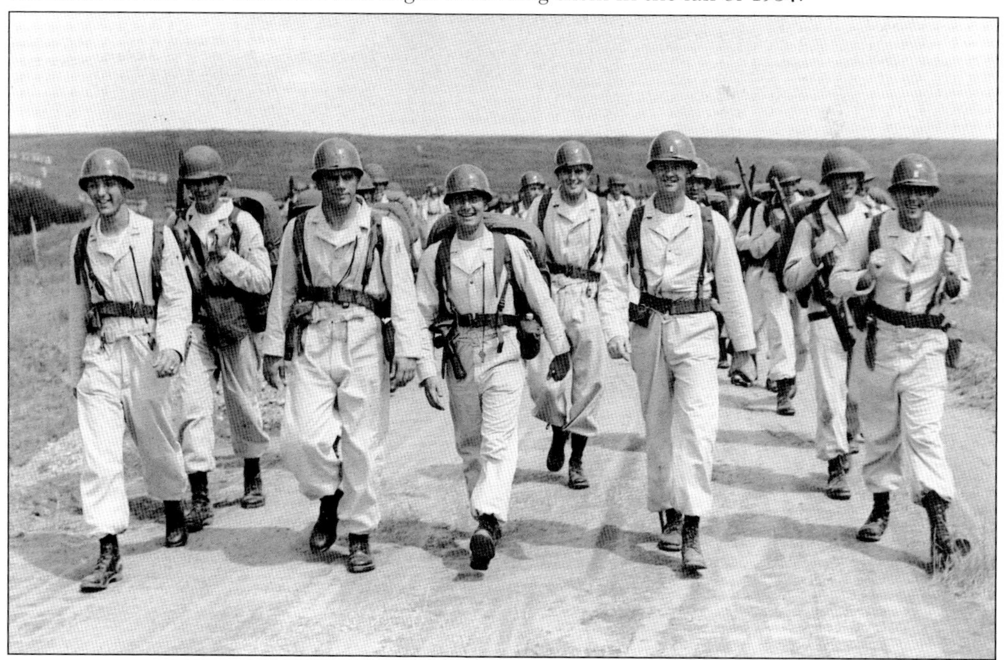

In 1955, ATOs led the class of 1959, clad in sky-blue "bunny suits," on a 15-mile hike to Buckley Naval Air Station for summer bivouac. The first class at the Air Force Academy had three summer squadrons. During the march, an ATO in an F-86 Sabre jet simulated a low-level attack, prompting the marching cadets to take cover.

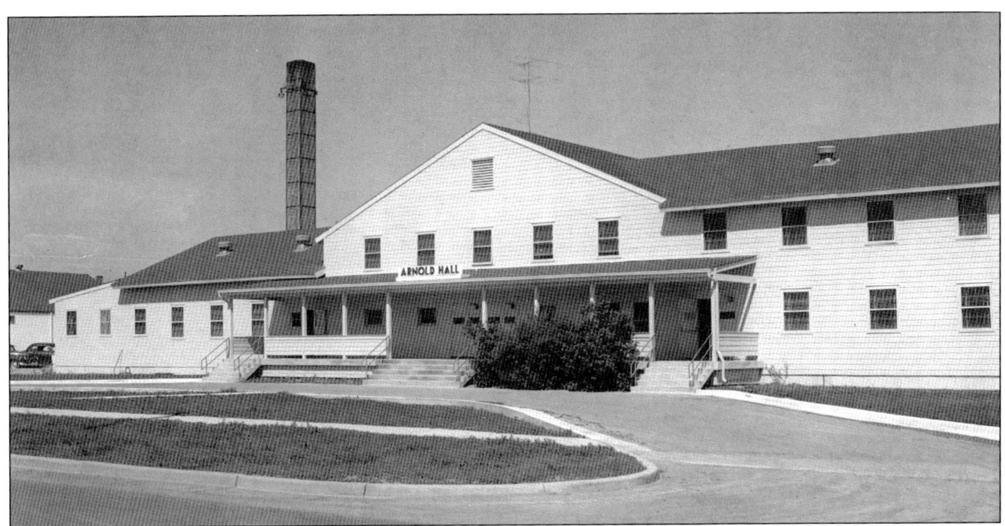

Arnold Hall, the cadet social center, was a popular spot for academy cadets. Named after Gen. Henry "Hap" Arnold, the facility included a snack bar; a large, well-furnished lounge; a ballroom featuring a gallery of paintings of famous Air Force generals; a pool and table tennis room; and a game room. Cadets were generally restricted from leaving Lowry but could receive guests at Arnold Hall when it did not conflict with classes, study periods, or the military training schedule. Although the first few classes of cadets had to remain at the Air Force Academy for the holidays, social activities were organized for them, and they were granted new privileges, including the use of a radio and phonograph.

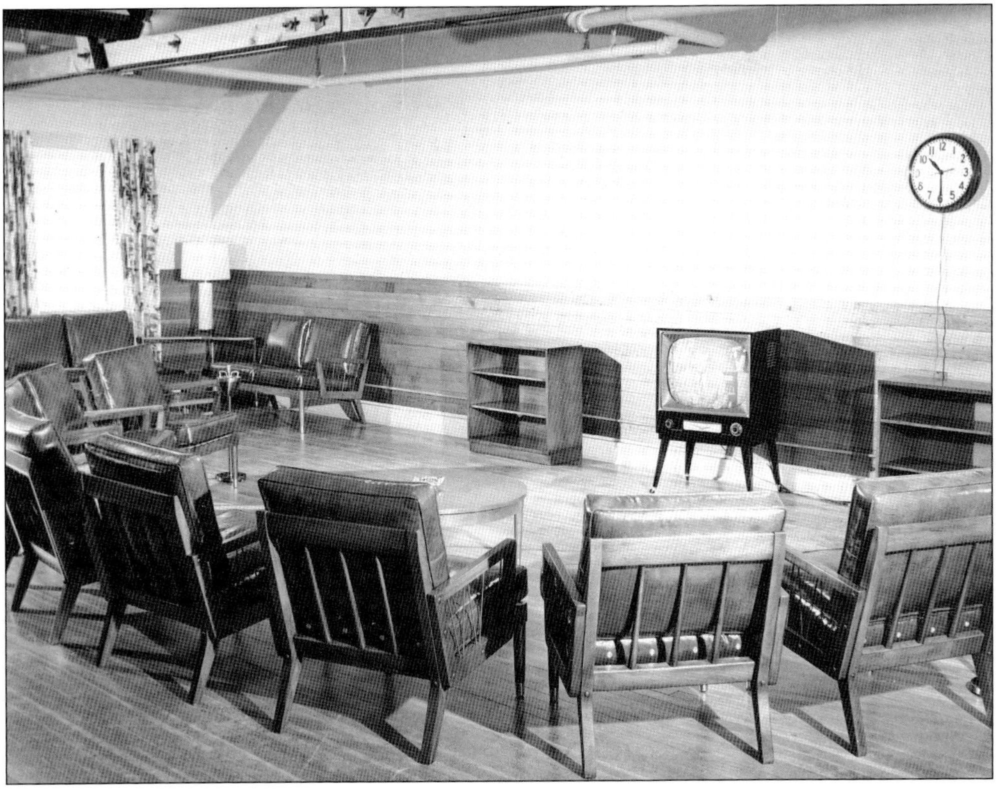

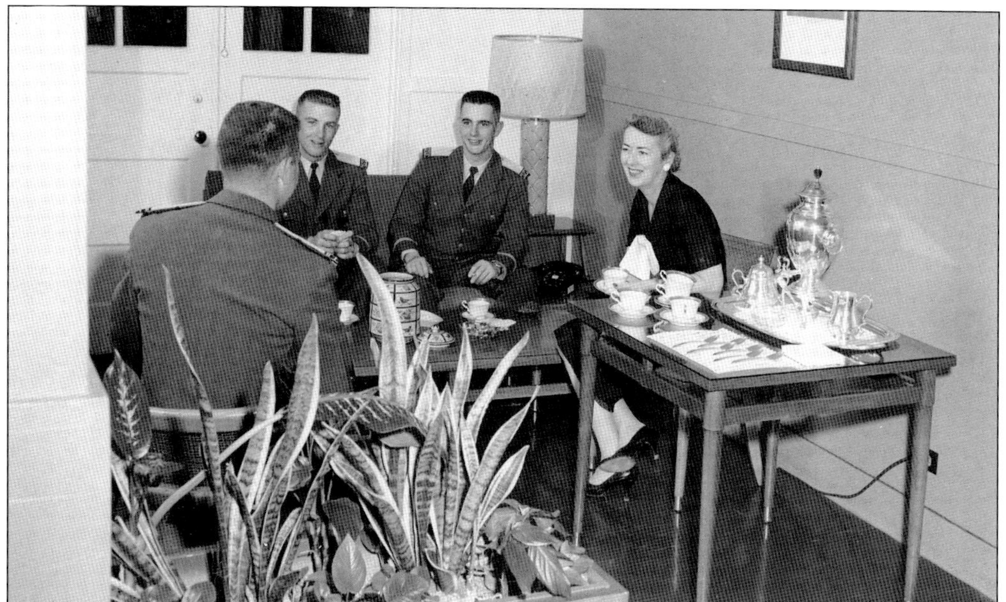

Taught by the cadet wing hostess, Gail McComas, cadets received lessons on decorum and social courtesy to ensure the graduates of the Air Force Academy behaved like cultured gentlemen. Formal dances and receptions were held in Arnold Hall starting in December 1955 with women from local colleges in attendance. The cadet wing hostess position has been removed from the staff.

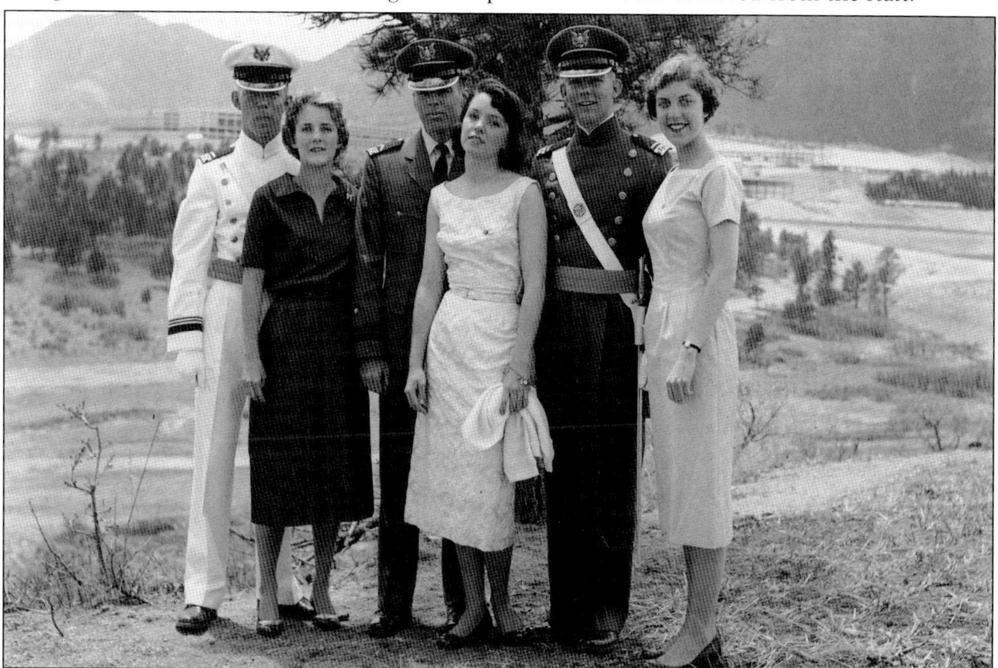

In 1958, promotional photographs of cadets and female students from nearby Colorado College were taken at the permanent site. After the photographs were taken, the cadets hurried back to Denver for a Saturday parade, and the coeds returned to school with the academy's thanks. From left to right are Cadet Brian Parker, Sara Ward, Cadet Bradley Hosmer, Dottie Emmerson, Cadet James Rhodes, and Judith Frame.

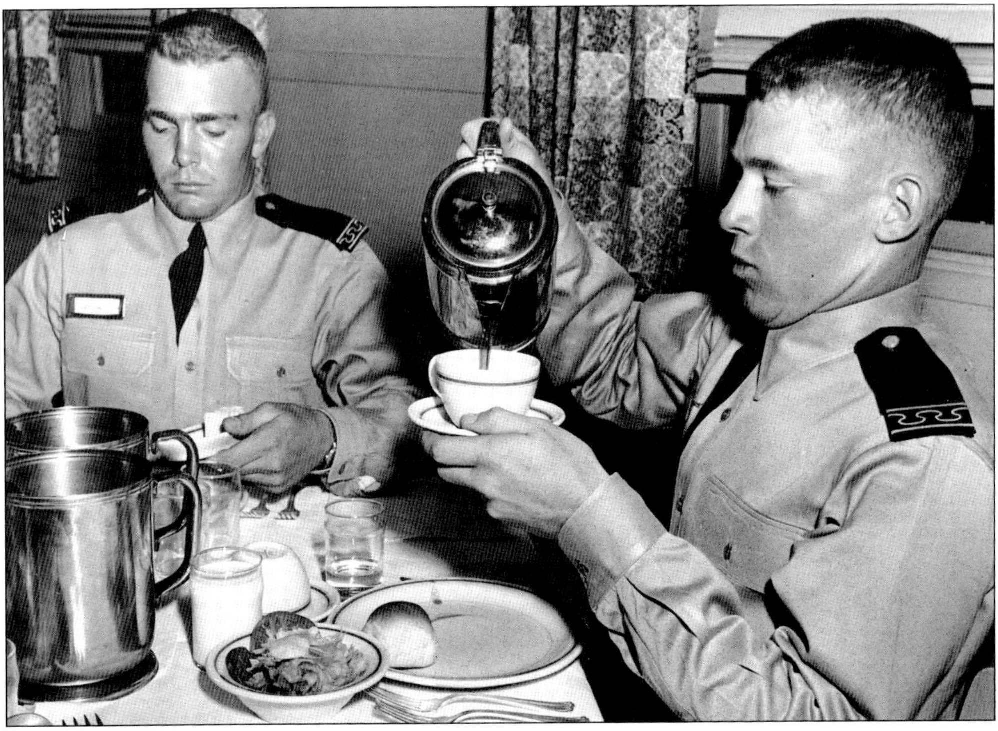

Mealtimes at Lowry were rigid affairs, as fourth-class cadets were required to eat "square," sitting at attention, touching only the first six inches of their seats, and following a strict set of rules. During the meal, cadets were bombarded with questions on "Fourth Class Knowledge." Language at mealtimes was thoroughly aeronautical: the table was called "the ramp," the kitchen "the hangar," and the supervising ATO "the tower." Cadets were assigned roles for serving their tablemates during the family-style meal. The "forward air controller" announced the arrival of the meal, the "hot pilot" and "cold pilot" were responsible for pouring hot or cold beverages, and the crew chief was responsible for stacking used dishes. Thanks to the small class size, cake was served frequently, as each cadet received a cake for his birthday.

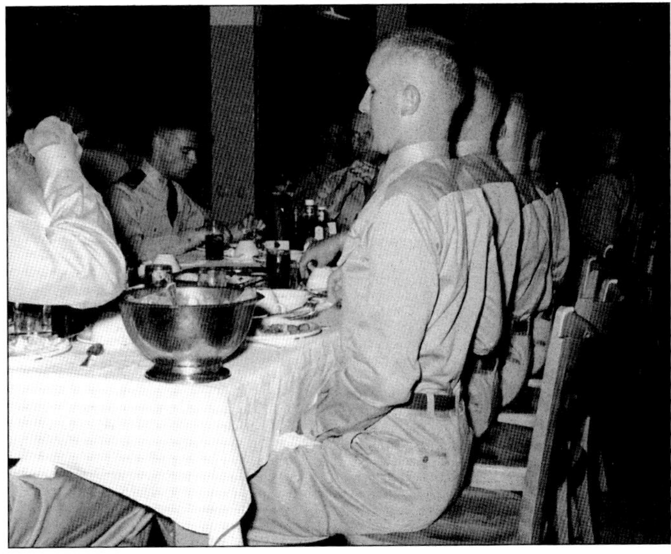

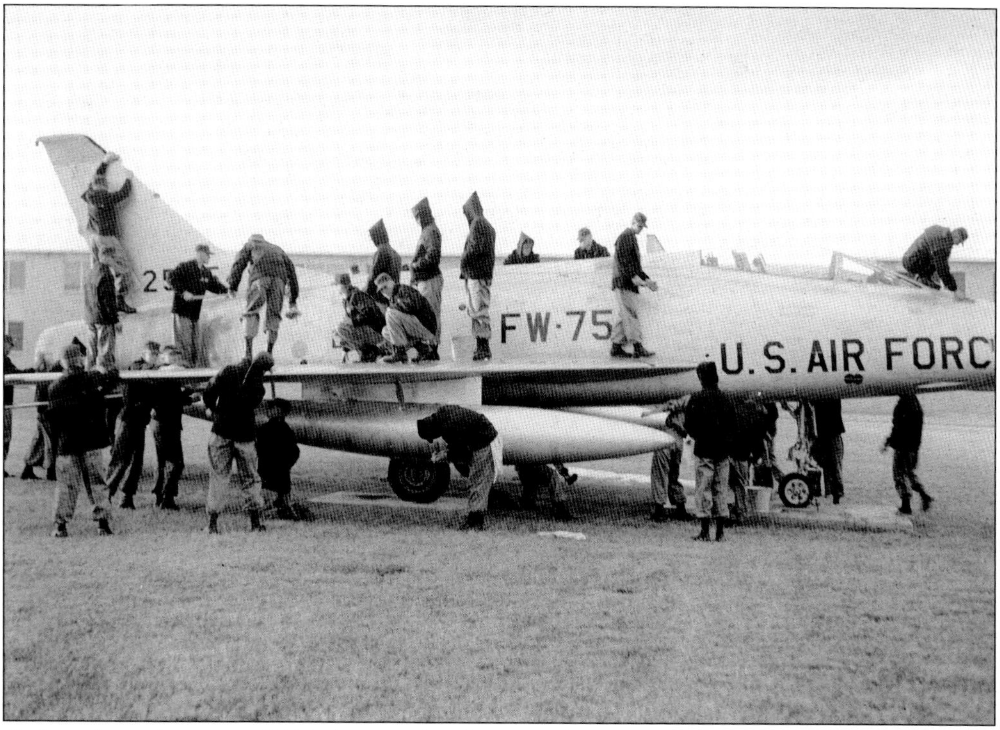

Cadets clean their new YF-100A aircraft. The aircraft was gifted to the Cadet Wing upon its retirement and replaced the bright red Matador missile on static display in the academic quadrangle.

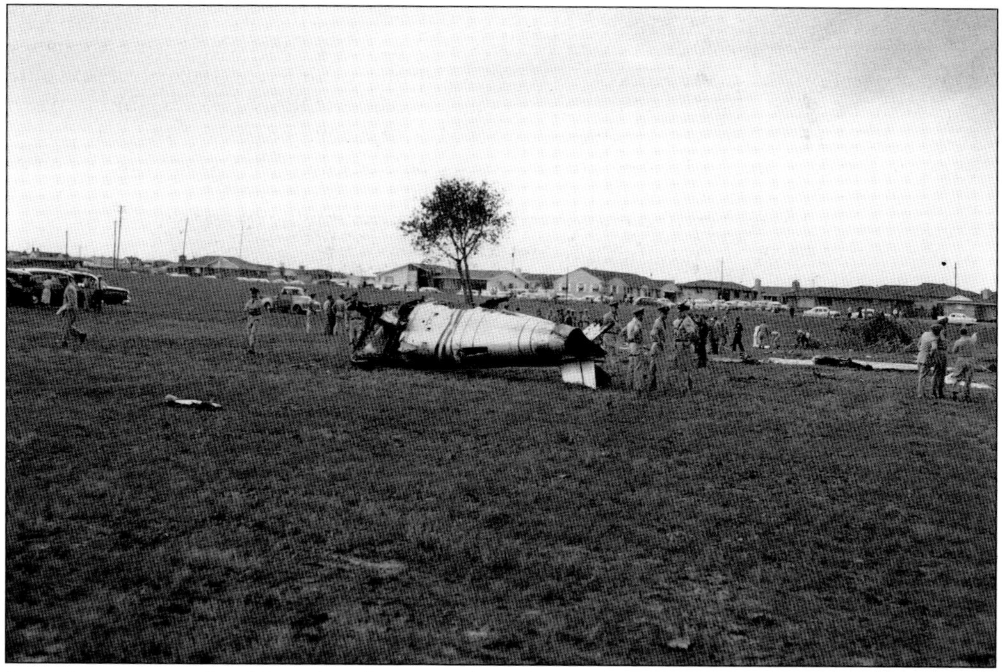

In a sobering example of the risks inherent in the military profession, ATO 1st Lt. George Frederick was killed on August 7, 1956, when the F-86D aircraft he was flying struck a tree while he was attempting a dead stick landing. His was the first active-duty military death at the Air Force Academy.

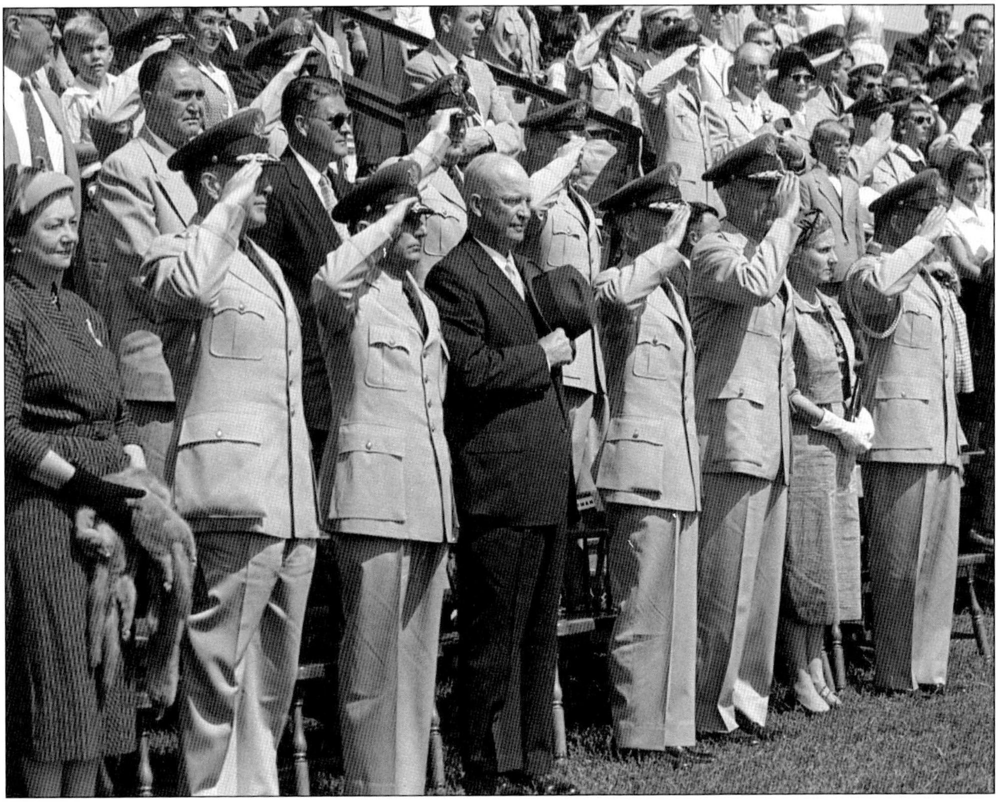

President Eisenhower lowers his hat as the uniformed officers render a salute during an early Cadet Wing parade. From left to right are Elizabeth Sprague; Brigadier General Stillman; Brigadier General Sprague; President Eisenhower; Lieutenant General Harmon; Brigadier General Zimmerman, first dean of the faculty; Rose-Maye Harmon, and unidentified. Cadet parades were highly attended events during the years at Lowry.

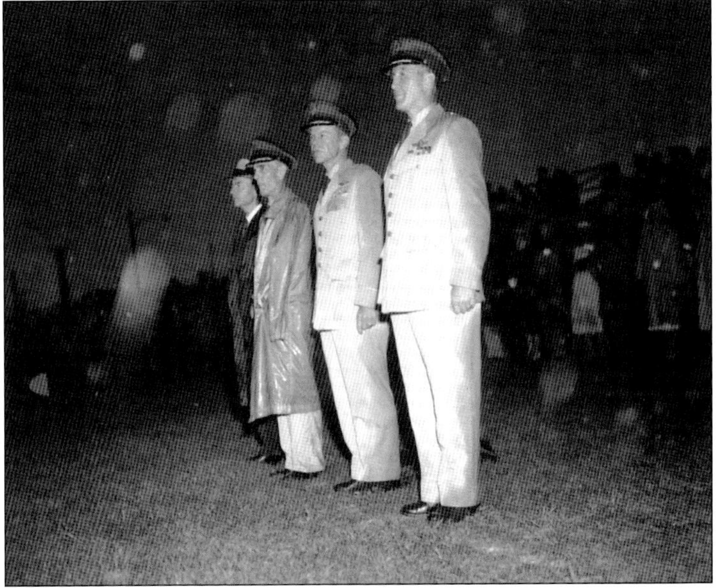

Lieutenant General Harmon handed over the Air Force Academy to Maj. Gen. James E. Briggs on July 27, 1956. Despite suffering from advanced lung cancer, Harmon stood in the rain for the duration of the ceremonies. From left to right, Secretary of the Air Force Donald A. Quarles, Lieutenant General Harmon, Major General Briggs, and Brigadier General Stillman observe the parade during the Change of Command ceremony at Lowry.

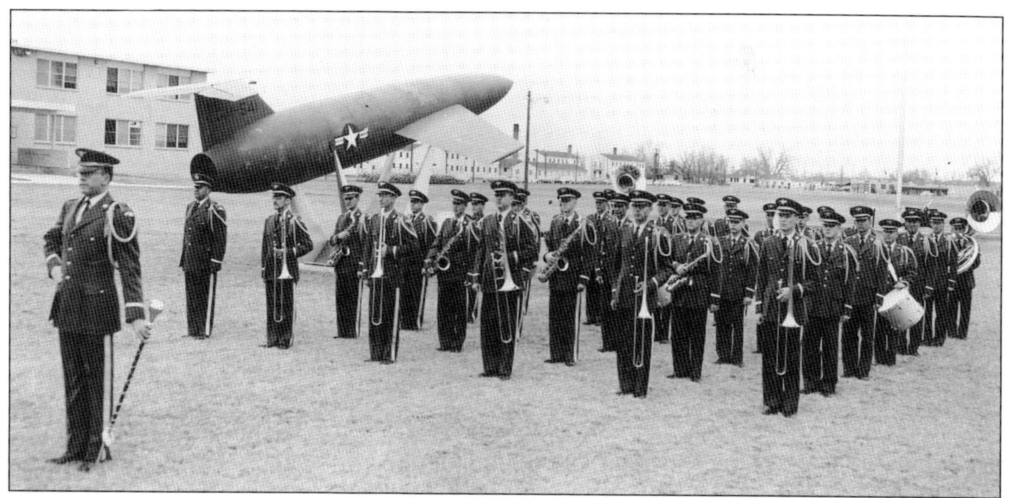

The 739th Band, recognized as one of the best bands in the European theater of operations during World War II, was reactivated in May 1955 and assigned to the Air Force Academy. It was renamed the Air Force Academy Band in 1958 before being moved to Peterson Air Force Base in 1993 and renamed the Band of the Rockies.

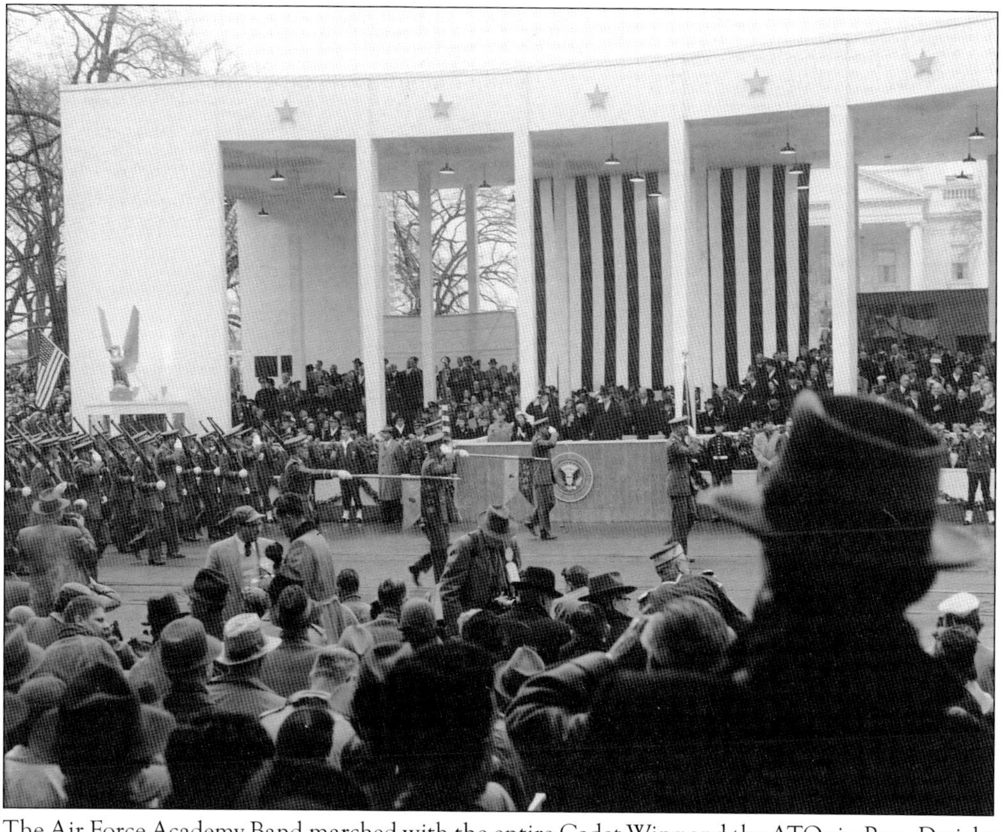

The Air Force Academy Band marched with the entire Cadet Wing and the ATOs in Pres. Dwight D. Eisenhower's second inaugural parade on January 21, 1957. It took 14 C-124 Globemaster aircraft to transport the academy contingent to the East Coast. After the official inaugural functions, the cadets were treated to a dance hosted by the Bolling Air Force Base Wives Club.

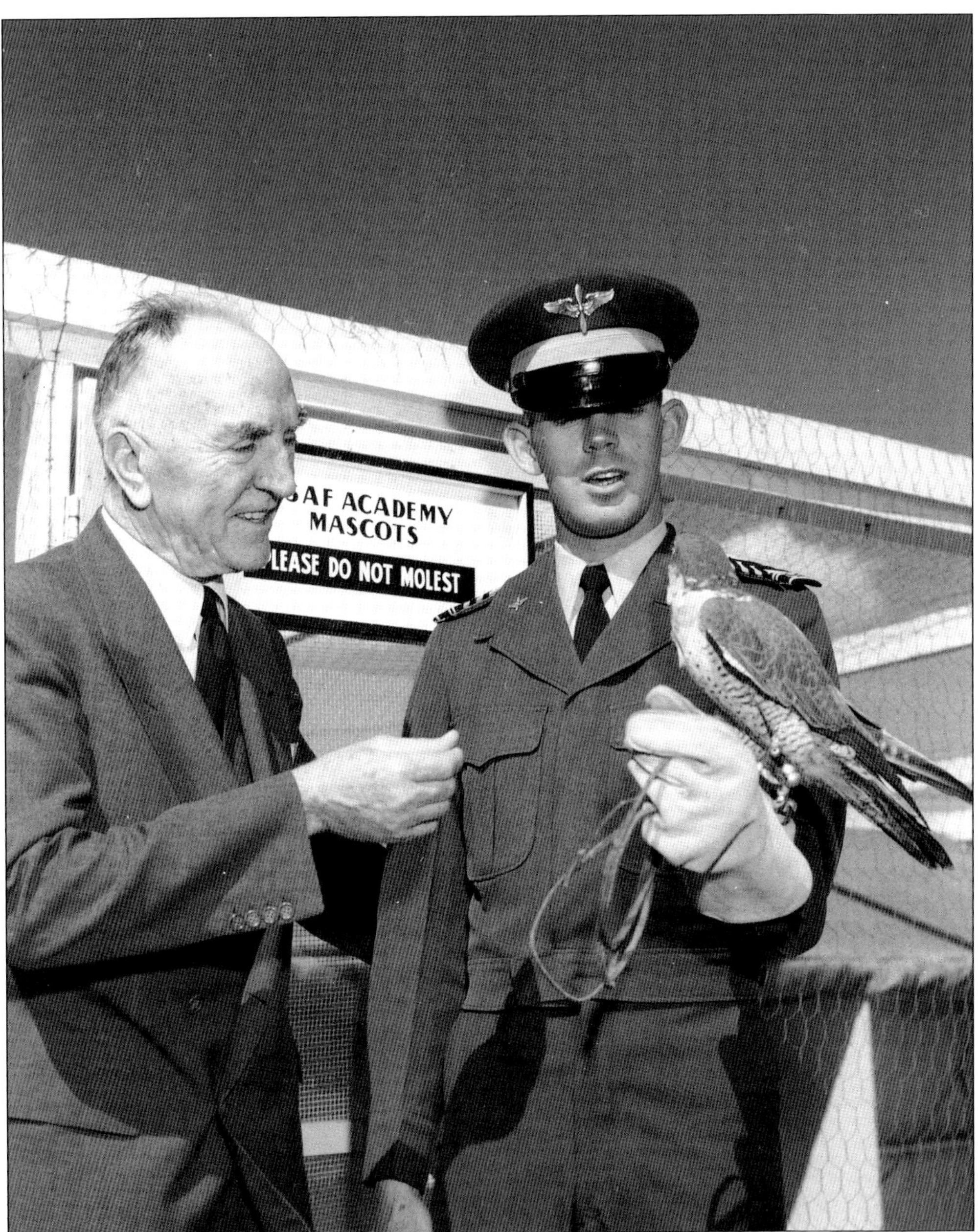

Mach 1, a peregrine falcon, meets Eddie Rickenbacker during the famed flyer's visit to the Air Force Academy in 1956. The noble bird is being held by the chief of cadet falconers. The falcon was chosen as the official academy mascot by the class of 1959, who were suitably impressed by the bird's graceful flight, speed, keen eyesight, and ferocity during a demonstration put on by local falconer Harold Webster. Other animals had been considered, and prior to the demonstration, the Cadet Wing, and even the commandant of cadets, considered selecting the tiger to represent them. Mach 1 was gifted to the Air Force Academy in 1955 and appeared at the first football game played by the academy only three days after her arrival in Denver. Cadet falconers began performing free-flying routines during halftime of football games on October 20, 1956, against the Colorado School of Mines in the Denver University Stadium.

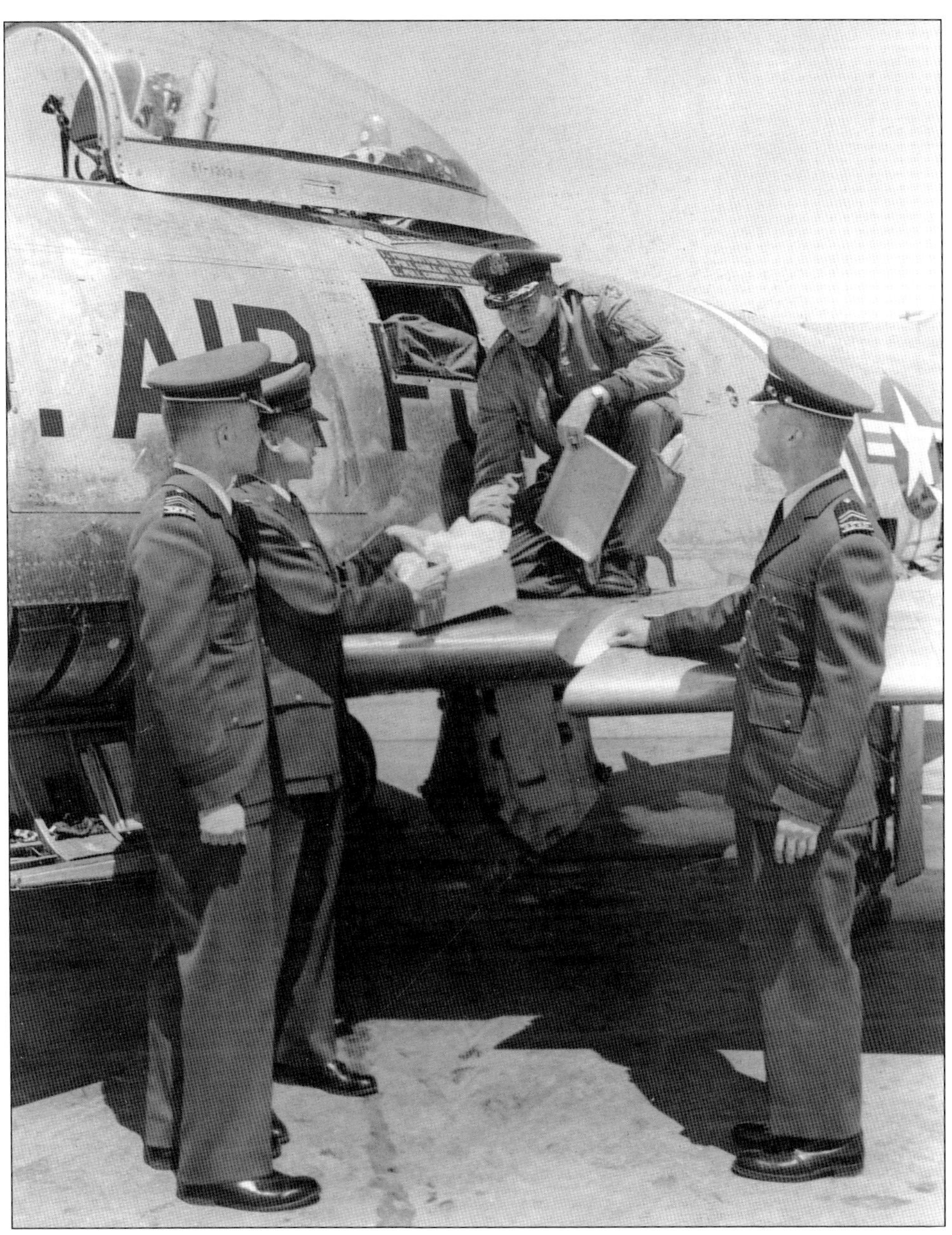

In 1958, Col. Benjamin B. Cassiday Jr., deputy commandant of cadets, flew the class of 1959's rings through the sound barrier in an F-86 Sabre jet, providing a "sonic baptism." Colonel Cassiday is seen passing the rings to the Class Ring Committee. The rings were presented to the class later that evening. This practice failed to become a tradition, as Air Force Headquarters ordered its cessation following this flight. The custom of wearing a ring to commemorate graduation in the United States began with the West Point class of 1835 and is a treasured tradition of all service academies. The Air Force Academy ring is unique among service academies for being crafted from white gold rather than yellow. The ring bears the Class Crest opposite the Air Force Academy Crest. Until graduation, the ring is worn with the academy crest facing inward. After graduation, it is turned, symbolizing an officer ready and willing to protect and defend the nation. The Air Force Academy is the only service academy to have a ring for each of its graduating classes.

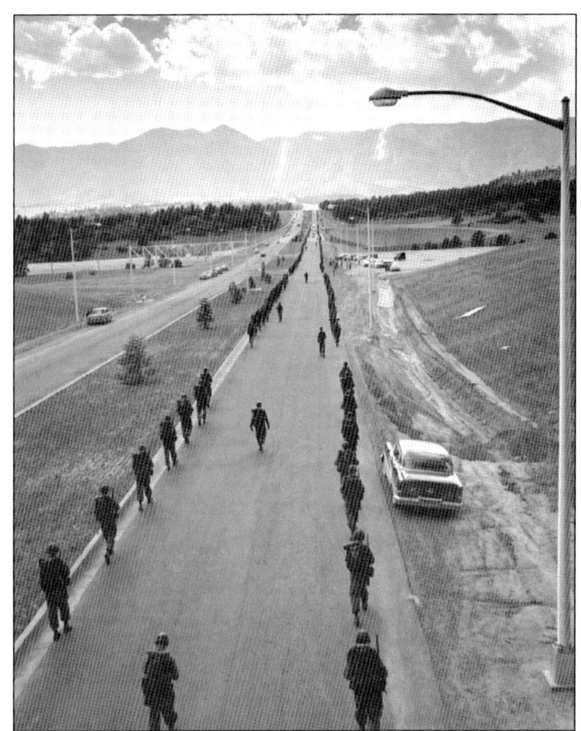

After three years of training at the interim site at Lowry Air Force Base, the cadets were moved to the permanent site near Colorado Springs. Academy lore holds that in August 1958, the cadets marched the entire way from Denver to the new facility. In reality, cadets were bused to the current site of the North Gate and then marched only five miles to the Cadet Area.

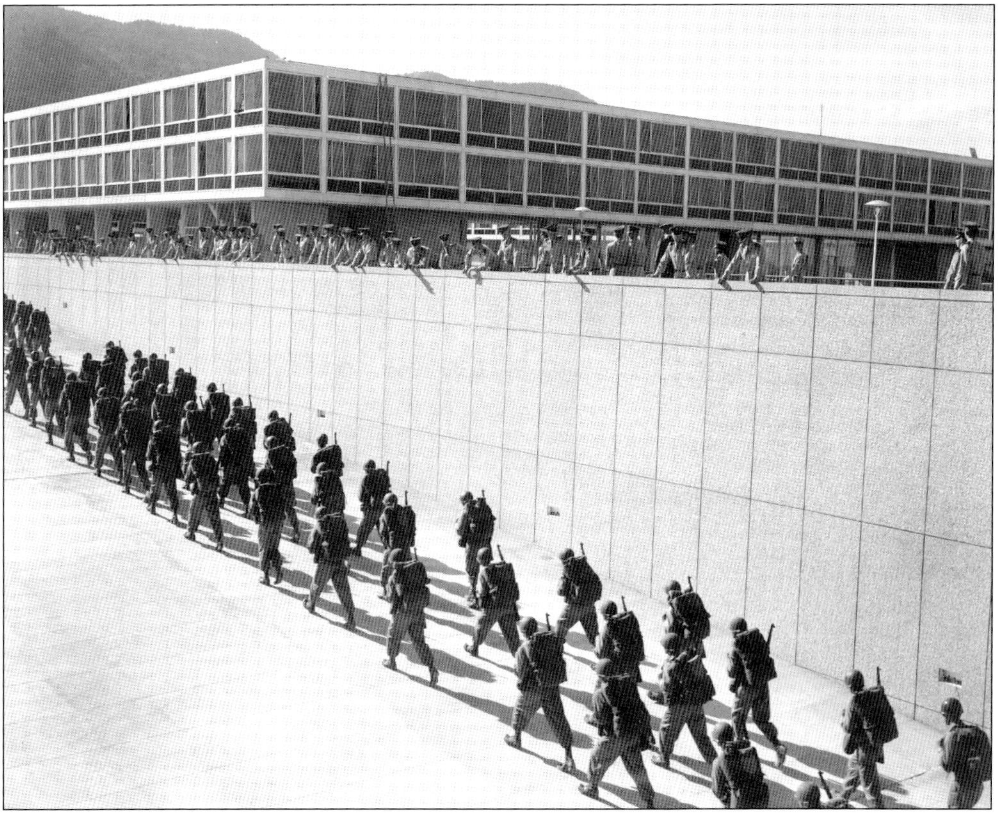

Two

A Permanent Home

The process of selecting a permanent home for the Air Force Academy began while Congress was still debating whether an air academy was needed. In 1949, the secretary of the Air Force formed the Site Selection Board to evaluate potential sites. They considered hundreds of locations, assessing their aesthetic beauty, cost, and community factors as well as conditions affecting flying training. The board recommended a site north of Colorado Springs, Colorado, near the towns of Monument and Husted. The eruption of the Korean War in the summer of 1950 stalled any further legislative efforts to establish an air academy, and the board's decision was not made public. The second attempt to secure a permanent location for the academy began immediately after the Air Force Academy Act was signed in 1954. The new Site Selection Commission, using similar criteria as the original board, examined more than 300 locations before offering three potential sites to the secretary of the Air Force: Colorado Springs, Colorado; Alton, Illinois; and Lake Geneva, Wisconsin. Secretary Talbott announced his selection of Colorado Springs, Colorado, on June 23, 1954.

The selection of Colorado Springs is due in large part to the enthusiasm shown by civic leaders in the local community. A committee of local businessmen and community boosters lobbied aggressively through the media, printed brochures, and their congressman. The state legislature, eager for the Air Force Academy to be located in Colorado and hoping to avoid skyrocketing land costs due to speculation, formed the Colorado Land Acquisition Commission. The commission was allocated $1 million of state funds to begin acquiring the land around the proposed site to then be deeded to the federal government at cost. Initially, the site proposal included 15,000 acres, but it expanded to 18,500 acres with the addition of the affluent neighborhood of Pine Valley.

The natural beauty of the land that transfixed the Site Selection Board has been captivating individuals for centuries, providing a rich and layered history. Before the Air Force Academy, the land was home to Native Americans, pioneers, entrepreneurs, and ranchers. The mountains called to adventurers and those seeking a quiet Western lifestyle alike.

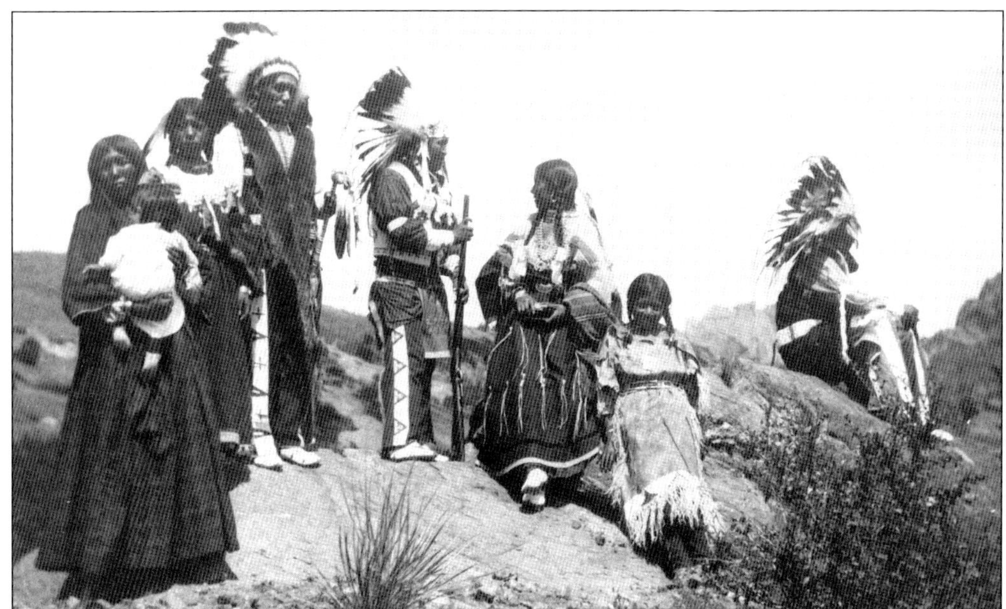

For thousands of years before Euro-American settlement, the region was home to tribes of Ute, Arapaho, Cheyenne, Comanche, Kiowa, and Pawnee. The Ute, pictured here in 1913, are the oldest residents of Colorado. In the latter half of the 19th century, the Ute were forcibly removed from their ancestral homelands to three reservations in Colorado and Utah. (Photograph by Stewarts Commercial Photographers, © Pikes Peak Library District, 013-5862.)

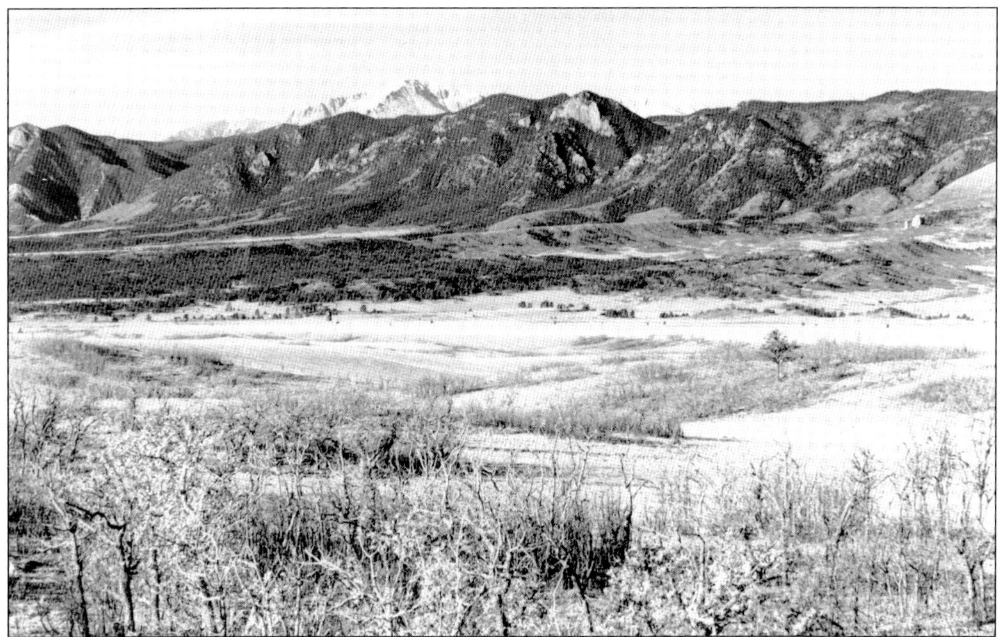

The summit of Pikes Peak, viewed from the northern Air Force Academy grounds, towers over Rampart Range. The 14,000-foot mountain was named after Zebulon Pike, who led the 1806 expeditionary force sent to map the land acquired by the United States in the 1803 Louisiana Purchase. Although commonly known as Pikes Peak, the indigenous Ute peoples had already named it Tavá Kaa-vi, or Sun Mountain.

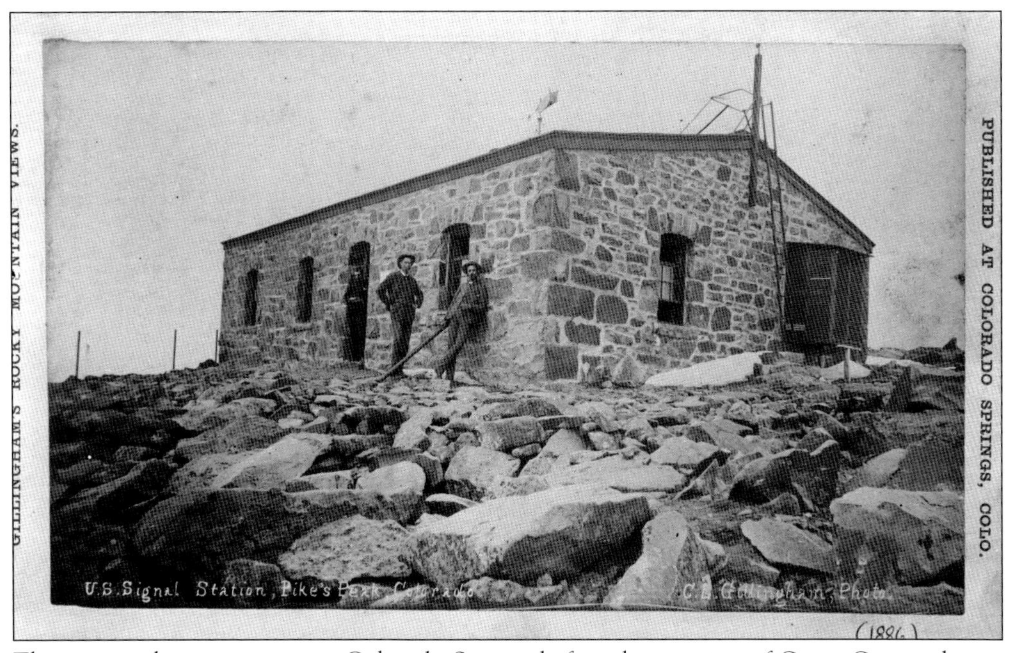

The main military presence in Colorado Springs before the opening of Camp Carson during World War II was the US Signal Corps Weather Station, established in 1873 on the summit of Pikes Peak. Here, two weather observers stand outside the station that served as both their living quarters and duty station. (Photograph by Stewarts Commercial Photographers, © Pikes Peak Library District, 013-7341.)

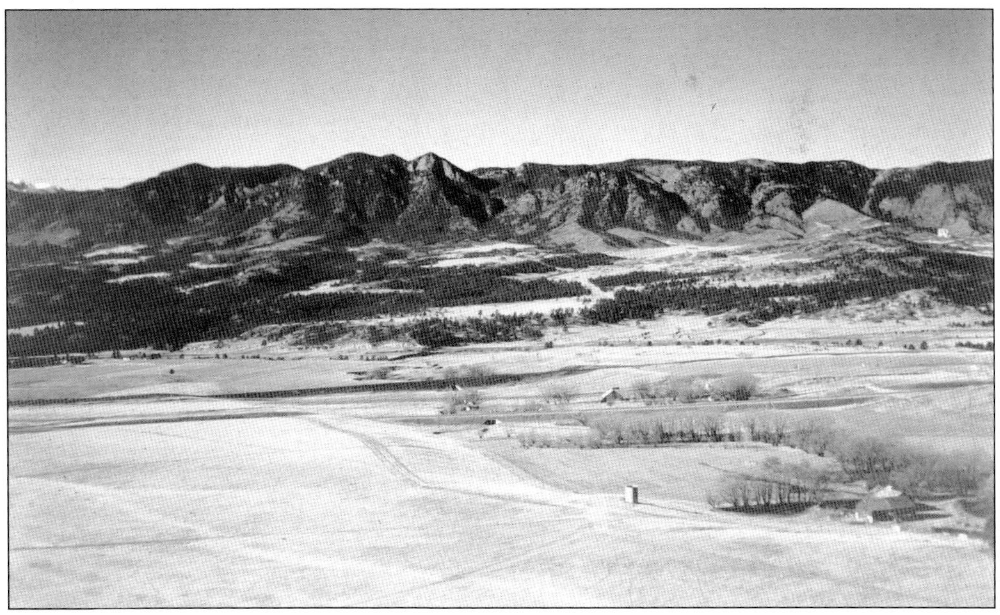

Pioneer settlers flocked to the area, shown here in 1954, after the 1862 Homestead Act encouraged westward migration by promising homesteaders 160-acre tracts of land after five years of settlement and improvement. This resulted in the relocation of many of the area's indigenous tribes. One of the early pioneer families to settle the land was the McAlroy family, whose descendent David McAlroy graduated from the Air Force Academy in 2003.

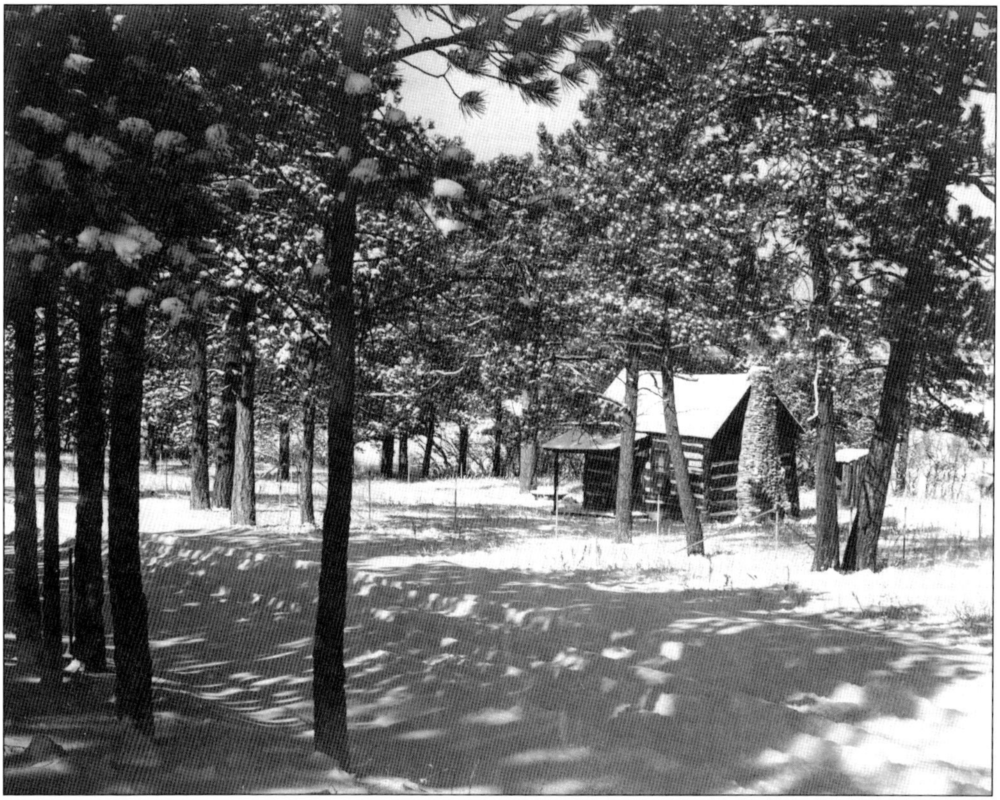

The oldest extant building on the academy grounds, and one of the oldest in the region, is the Pioneer Cabin, also known as the Burgess Cabin. According to Doris Burgess, the 1955 purchase of the one-room cabin, built between 1871 and 1877 by William Alexander Burgess, was contingent on the federal government's commitment to its preservation. The cabin was placed in the National Register of Historic Places in 1975.

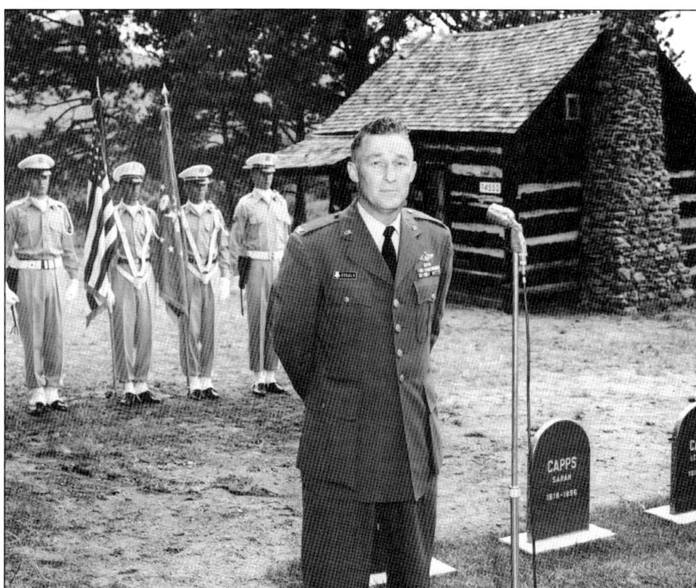

Prior to the excavation of the football stadium and Douglass Valley housing complex, the Air Force Academy learned of five graves in the area. Leonard and Mary Ann Capps's graves were relocated from the future Falcon Stadium's 50-yard line to the Burgess Cabin, along with three of their children's graves from the housing complex. In 1961, Col. Edward Stealy, deputy base commander, and the Palmer Lake Historical Society dedicated the Pioneer Cemetery.

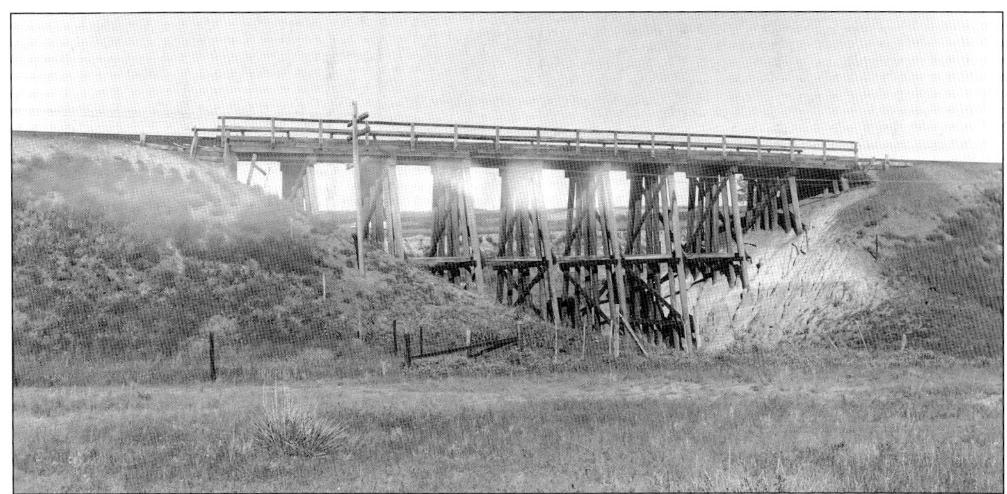

The Denver & Rio Grande Railroad was completed in 1872 to link Denver with Pueblo, laying tracks through what would later become the Air Force Academy's land, including this trestle crossing Monument Creek. In 1887, the Sante Fe Railroad was built along what would serve as the eastern boundary of the site. Railroad towns such as Husted and Edgerton emerged with depots, accommodations for travelers, and shipping services for local industries.

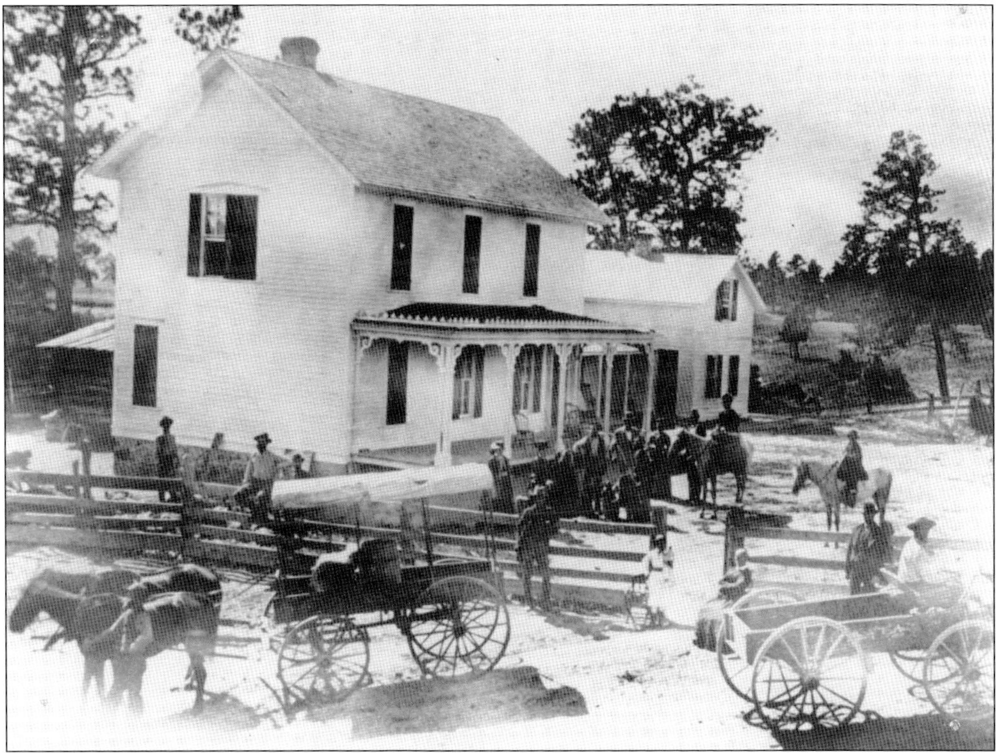

Edgerton was located near the Air Force Academy's southern border, close to the present-day Service and Supply Area. Pictured here is the Teachout Hotel, built around 1868 by Harlow Teachout and run by his mother, Leafy. The hotel was located near the stagecoach road, which was used by the weekly mail service between Pueblo and Denver. In winter months, Edgerton was home to a thriving ice-cutting industry.

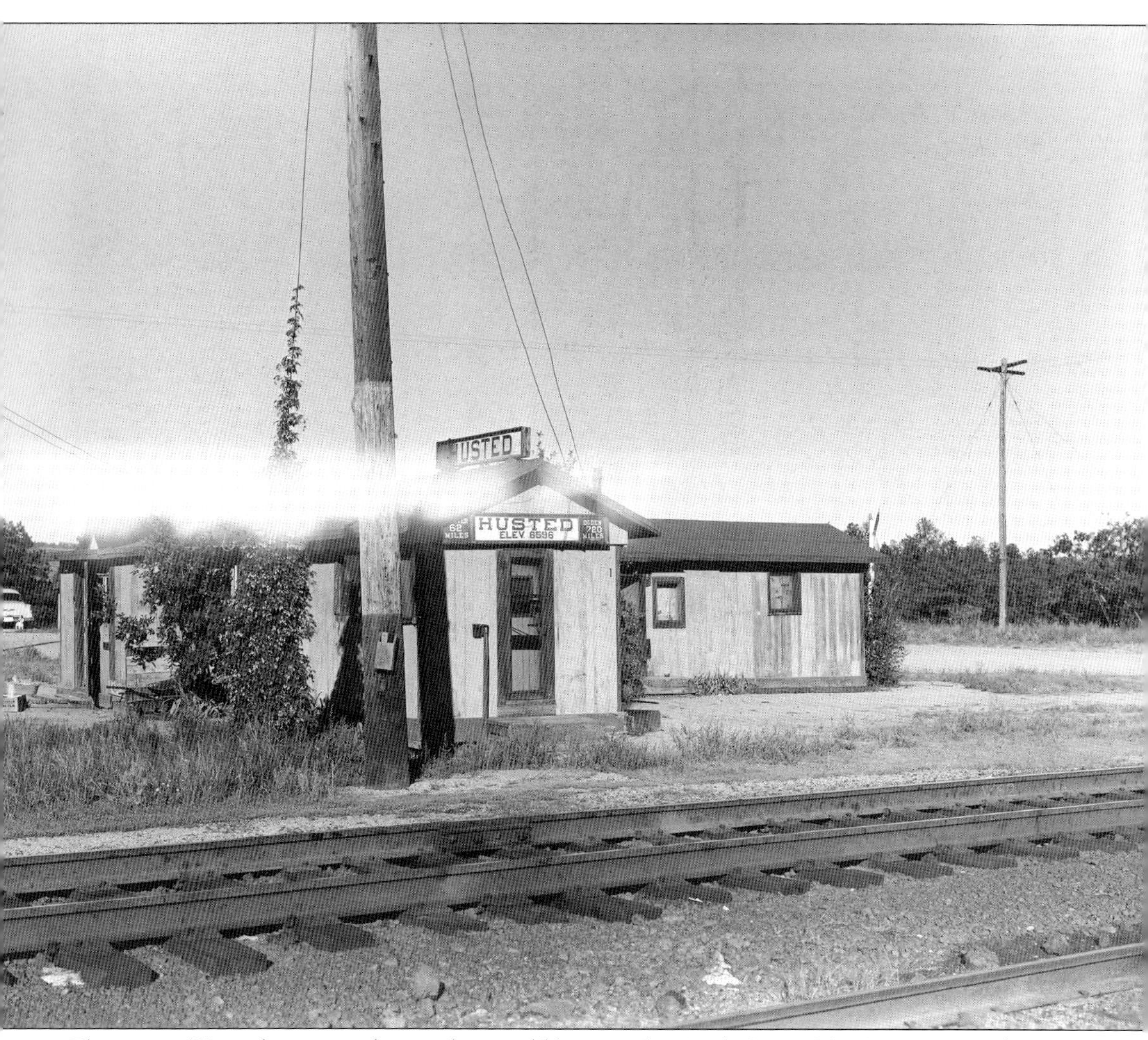

The town of Husted once stood near what would become the North Gate of the Air Force Academy. It was named for Calvin J. Husted, who established a homestead and sawmill on the western edge of Black Forest around 1865 that grew into a thriving lumber business. The Denver & Rio Grande Railroad passed through Husted's land, and he provided lumber for ties and trestles. In the 1870s, a small community developed built on shipping lumber and cattle and supporting the railroad. The railroad station, built from old boxcars, is pictured here. By the mid-20th century, the town of Husted had severely declined. In February 1955, an Air Force photographer came down from Lowry to capture historic places around the site. Unfortunately, his photographs were damaged by a leak in his camera, causing the white streak seen here. When he returned two days later, he found the railroad station and the remaining buildings in the town of Husted had been demolished. An article dated July 13, 1956, in the *Colorado Springs Gazette* reported that the Air Force had acquired the ghost town for $551.25.

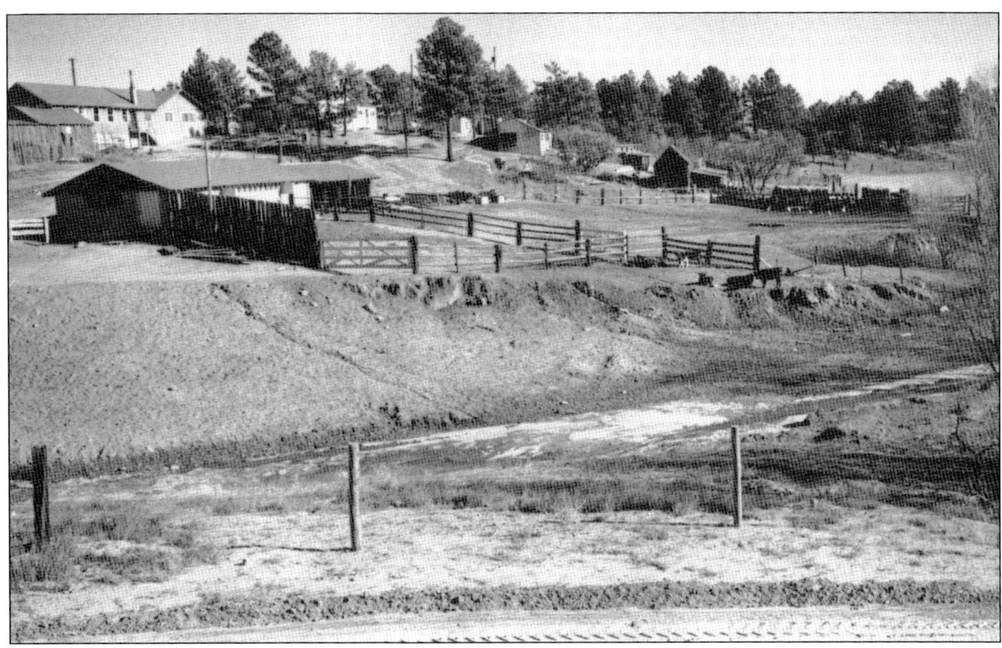

Mohl Hill, a ranch and dairy farm near Husted, belonged to Leo Mohl. Originally from Austria, Mohl bought the ranch in 1946 after immigrating to the United States. A bookseller and political activist against the Nazis, he was interned in the Buchenwald concentration camp until 1939. The barn stored inventory for Mohl's bookshop, the Book Home, in downtown Colorado Springs. (Courtesy of Special Collections, Pikes Peak Library District, 415-58.)

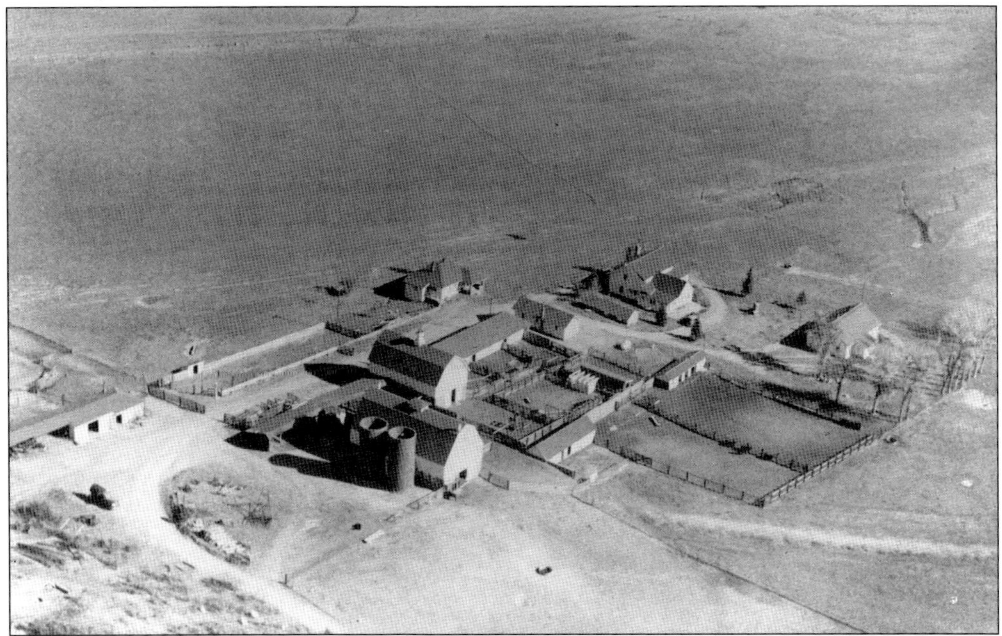

Lehman Ranch, also known as Cathedral Rock Ranch due to its monumental geologic formation, was the first land purchased by the Colorado Land Acquisition Commission. The sprawling 4,500-acre ranch was once home to herds of Aberdeen-Angus cattle. The buildings seen here remained on the site until they were torn down in 1960 to create the Cadet Athletic Fields.

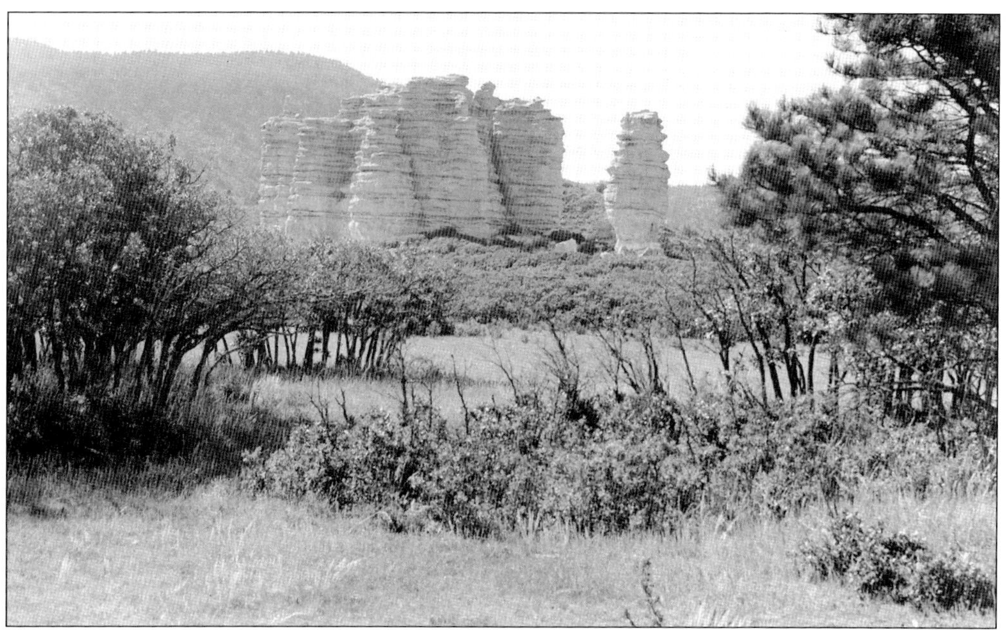

Cathedral Rock, located towards the northern end of the Air Force Academy property, was a significant gathering place for indigenous people of the region. The striking sandstone and clay formation stands 120 feet high and was formed when the underlying Dawson Arkose, the area's bedrock, eroded, leaving behind the distinct spires. The rock formation is now a protected national historic site.

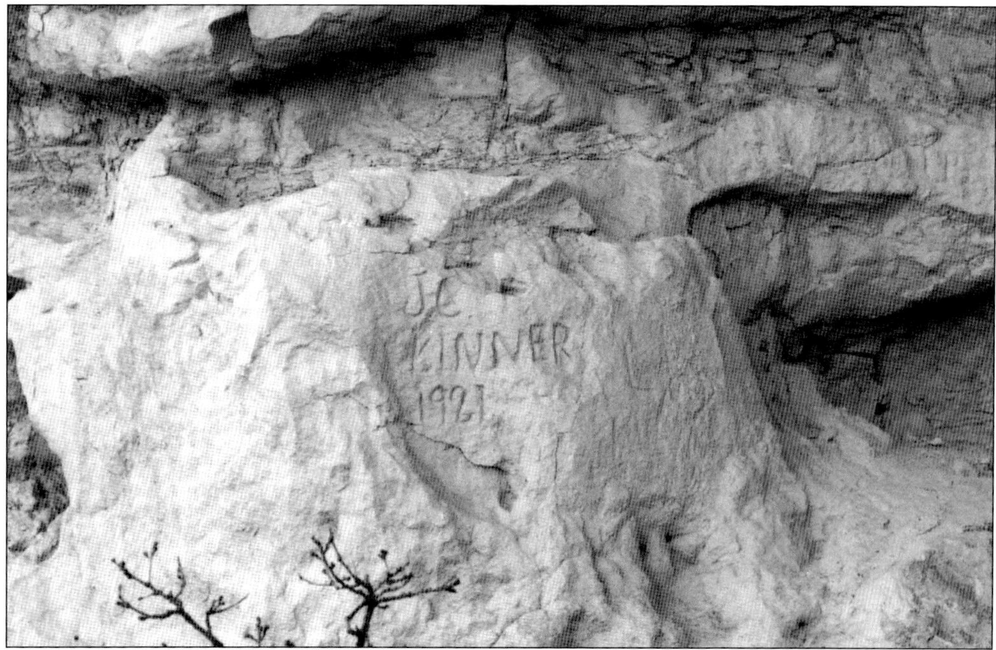

Cathedral Rock was a popular picnic spot for early settlers of the area, and they left their mark. There are numerous names and dates carved into the base of the outcrop dating back to 1870. Among these inscriptions is a signature dated 1921 belonging to J.C. Kinner, who operated the general store in the nearby town of Husted. (Photograph by Martin Oetting; courtesy of Jack Anthony.)

Most roads in the area were unpaved, except for one leading into the Pine Valley community. In this photograph, paved Highway 85-87 runs along the bottom. The Denver & Rio Grande Railroad is visible along Monument Creek, while the Atchison, Topeka & Santa Fe tracks are seen close to the highway. Husted Road, a dirt road, leads from the highway toward the mountains. (Photograph by Stewarts Commercial Photographers, © Pikes Peak Library District.)

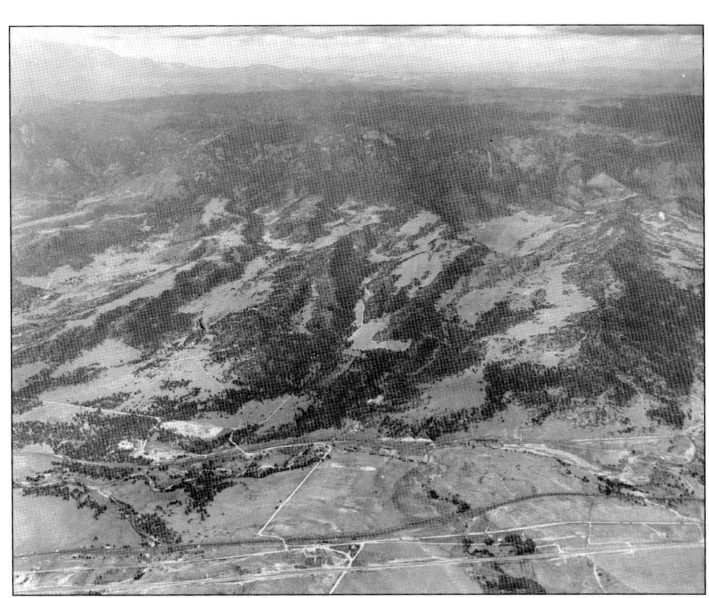

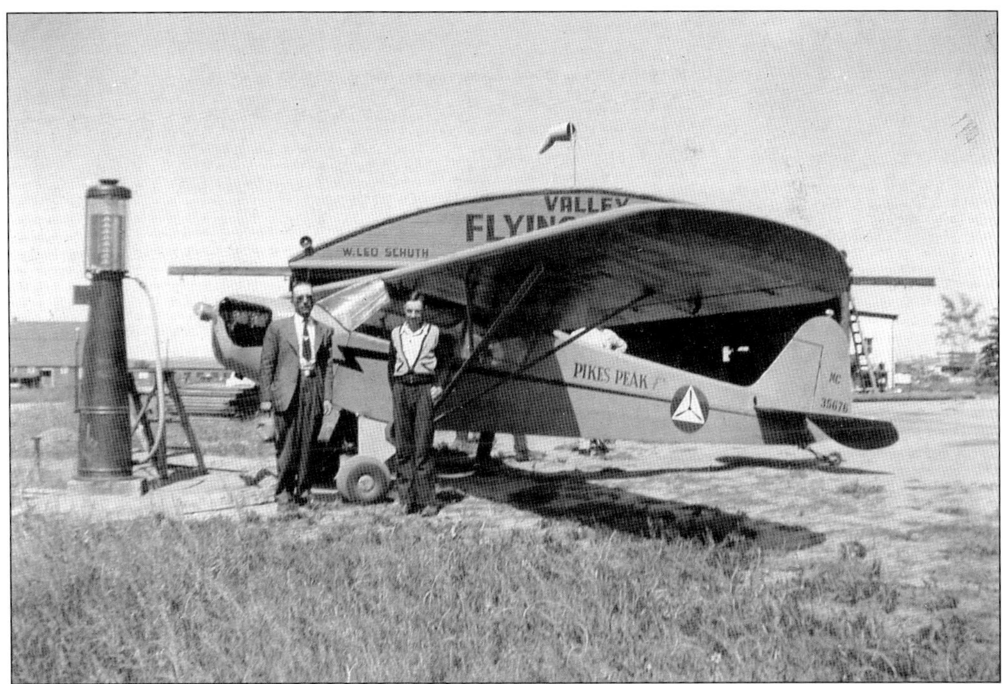

W. Leo Schuth (left) opened the Valley Flying Service in 1939 to provide aviation services to the community. He sold it in 1942 to Robert Donner, who expanded the facility and renamed it Pine Valley Airport. The airport was leased in 1951 and operated as Pikes Peak Air Services until 1955, when it became part of the Air Force Academy. (Courtesy of Special Collections, Pikes Peak Library District, 216-5512.)

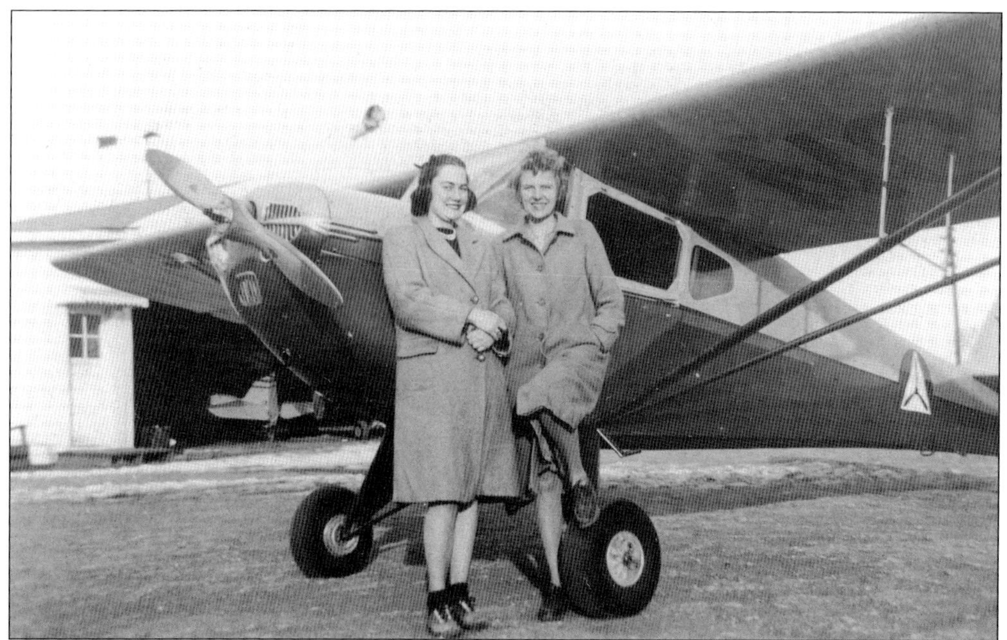

Pictured here, local aviators Rosemary Regan (left) and Dorothy "Dottie" Jones (right) stand beside a Taylorcraft BC-12 aircraft in front of the original wooden hangar of Pine Valley Airport. In 1943, Dottie Jones served as an instructor pilot, while Regan was the airport clearance clerk as well as a student pilot, earning her pilot license in 1945. Regan returned here for the 1974 dedication of the new Air Force Academy airfield facility.

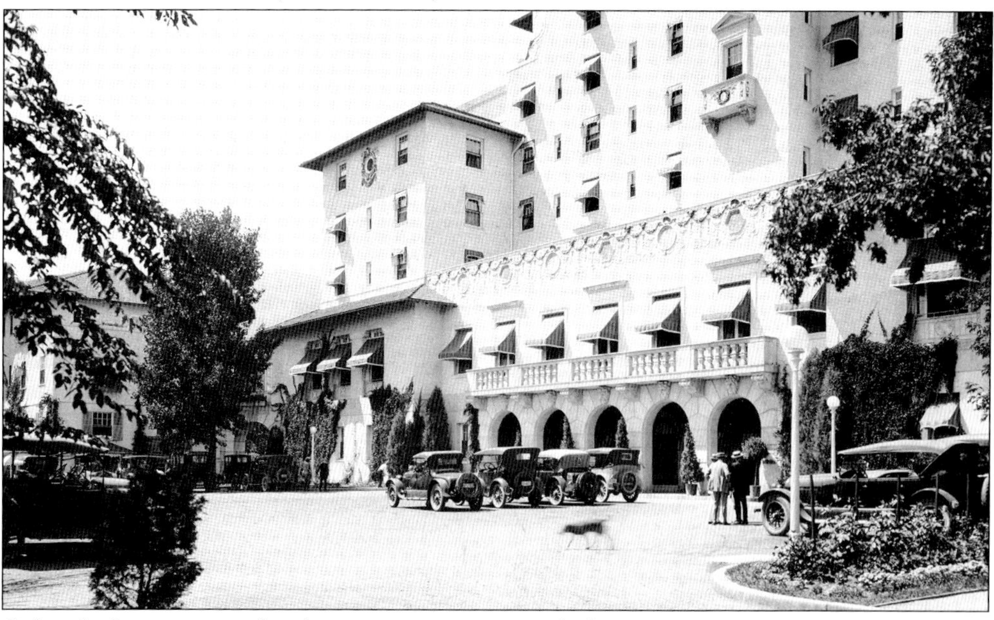

Colorado Springs was a bustling tourist community before experiencing a postwar economic downturn in the 1940s. Travelers were drawn by the breathtaking landscapes and an annual average of 300 days of sunshine. While most came for leisure, the area was also known for its health tourism. This photograph of the prominent Broadmoor Hotel was taken in 1922. (Photograph by Stewarts Commercial Photographers, © Pikes Peak Library District, 013-8426.)

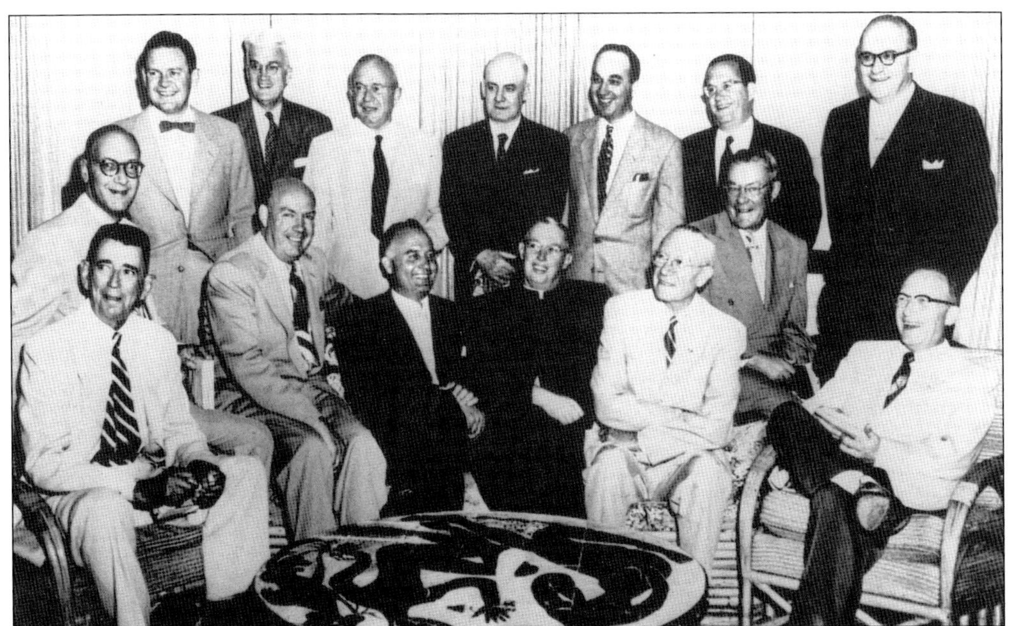

The Citizens Committee of the chamber of commerce worked tirelessly to attract the Site Selection Commission. They sought the economic benefits and prestige the Air Force Academy would bring to their community. In 1954, they celebrated their efforts at the Broadmoor Hotel. Joseph A. Reich, standing far right, initiated the campaign to bring the academy to Colorado Springs and was honored with a Cadet Wing parade in 1984. (Photograph by Robert McIntyre; courtesy of Special Collections, McDermott Library.)

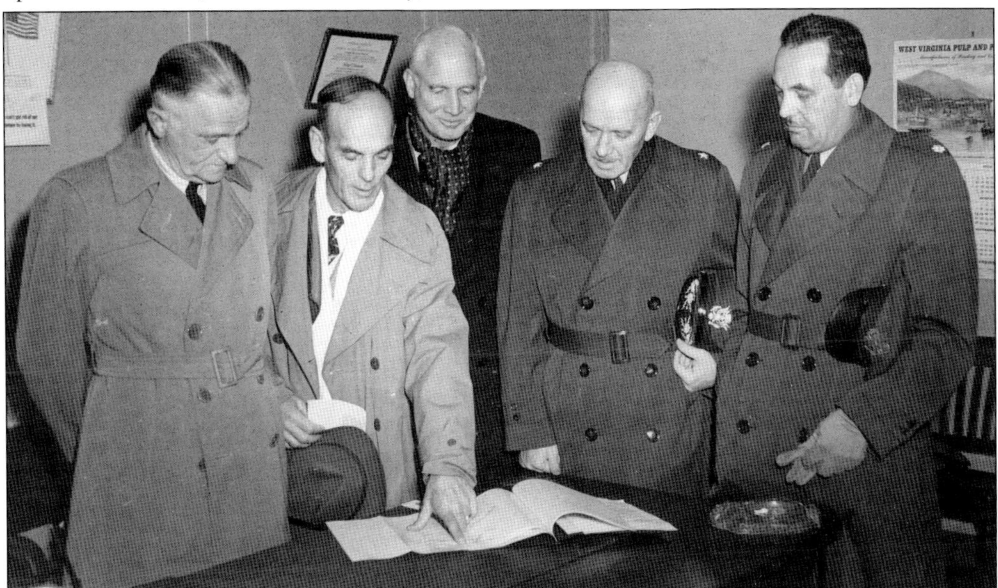

Members of the 1949 Site Selection Board are seen here during a site visit near St. Louis, Missouri, one of several locations for the proposed academy offered by the state. From left to right, Gen. Carl Spaatz, Lt. Gen. Hubert Harmon, Dr. Bruce Hopper, Brig. Gen. Harold Clark, and Lt. Col Arthur Boudreau, recorder for the board, are shown during their visit to the proposed site near Alton, Illinois.

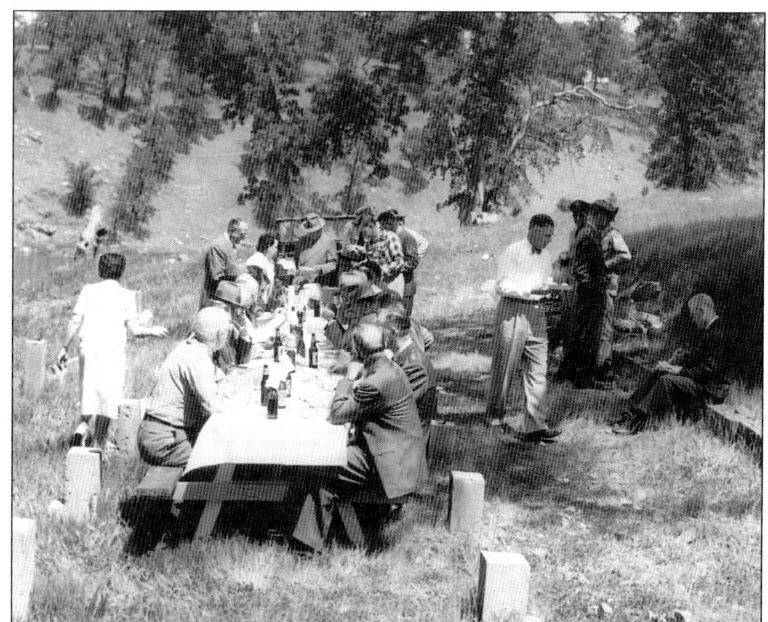

Between April and June 1954, the Site Selection Commission traveled across the country to assess potential locations. Only four of the existing 48 states did not compete to host the Air Force Academy. Pictured here, the "old mules," as General Spaatz jokingly called the group, are taking a break during their site survey for a picnic lunch.

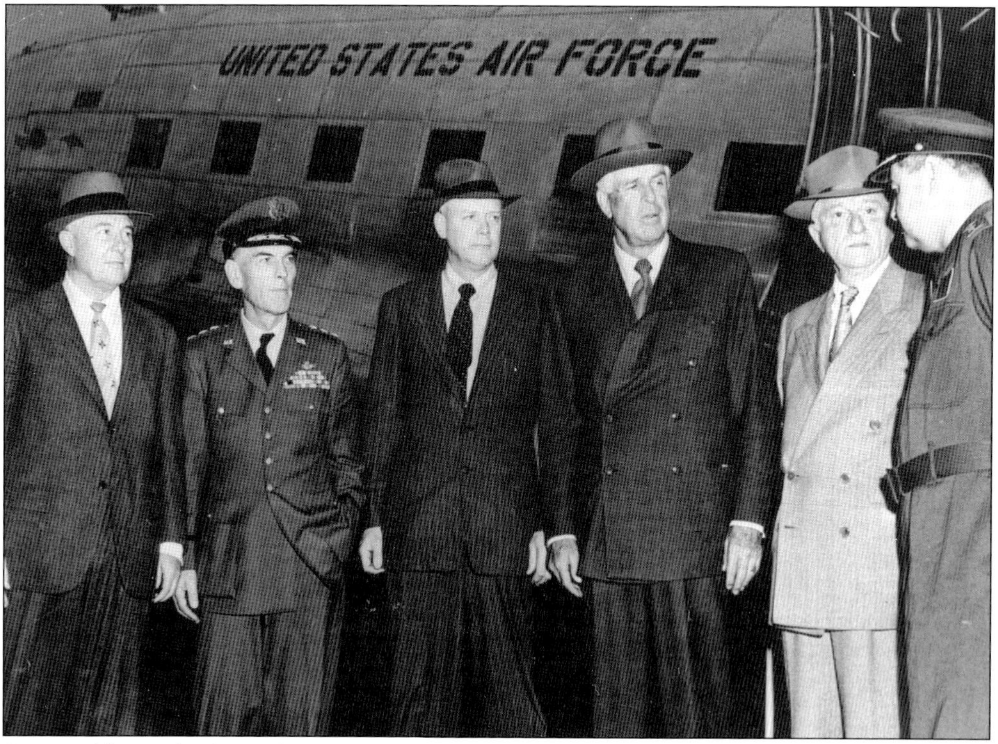

Captured here, the Site Selection Commission, from left to right, Dr. Virgil Hancher, Lt. Gen. Hubert Harmon, Brig. Gen. Charles Lindbergh, Merrill Meigs, and Gen. Carl Spaatz, speaks with Gen. Curtis LeMay (far right) after arriving at Peterson Field in Colorado Springs for a final site inspection in May 1954. The commissioners rented a small plane from the Pine Valley Airport, and in a frequently told anecdote, the airport manager was stunned to discover that the pilot requesting the aircraft was Charles Lindbergh, not having recognized the renowned aviator.

Three

Constructing the Academy

Shortly after the Air Force Academy Act was signed into law, the Air Force announced a national competition to hire an architect, soliciting applications through the American Institute of Architects and the American Institute of Consulting Engineers. More than 300 applications were reviewed. On July 23, 1954, the Chicago-based firm of Skidmore, Owings, and Merrill (SOM) was selected as the architect-engineer responsible for the master planning, site design, and construction supervision of the academy project. SOM had the required experience with government projects, having built the Manhattan Project town of Oak Ridge, Tennessee, and the Naval Postgraduate School in Monterey, California. Most importantly, SOM was concerned about getting the cadets into the facility by the time the first class graduated in 1959. Walter Netsch, a young SOM partner and graduate of the Massachusetts Institute of Technology, was chosen as the director of design. SOM knew from the outset that it would be constructing a national monument but also that the building industry was looking for new ideas, innovative methods, novel materials, and modern technologies. Intended to reflect a national, modern style as opposed to a regional architectural style, SOM selected aluminum, stainless steel, and glass as the primary architectural materials. SOM viewed its design of the Air Force Academy as timeless.

Equally timeless is the controversy caused by Congress appropriating large sums of money for government works. The public, although supportive of the Air Force Academy, balked at the price tag, partly due to a lack of understanding of the project's scope. A 1955 fact sheet issued by the Air Force Academy Office of Information Services defended the $126 million authorized by Congress as necessary to build "a complete city of 8,000 to 10,000 inhabitants, with a college, an Air Force base, a military training and maneuver area, business offices of a major command and all the facilities to support these activities and normal living necessities of the population." Details on the construction of the academy found in the following two chapters were partially drawn from the books *Modernism at Mid-Century, Skidmore, Owings, and Merrill: The Experiment since 1936* and *Walter A. Netsch, FAIA: A Critical Appreciation and Sourcebook.*

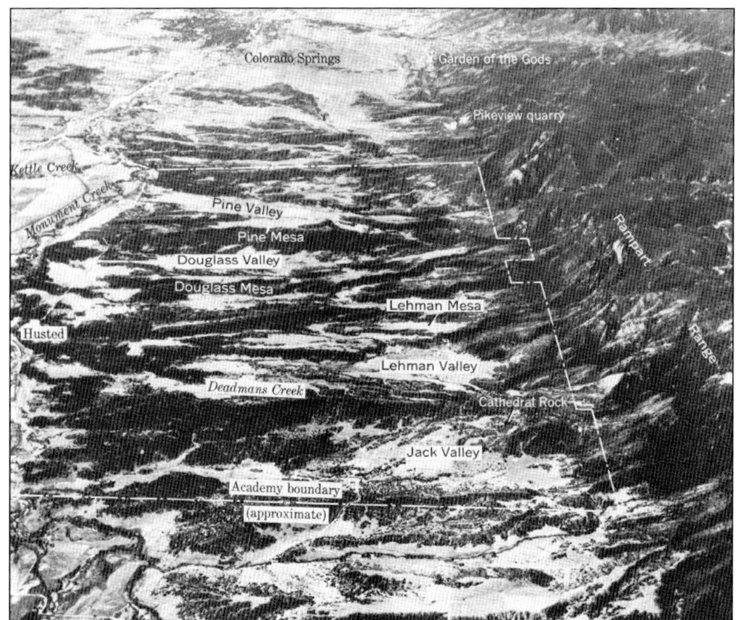

The series of ridges, mesas, and valleys that make up the Air Force Academy's land offered five separate areas for consideration for the Cadet Area. Some favored a site in the relatively flat Douglass Valley; however, SOM preferred a dynamic location as close to the mountains as possible. The lower valley locations were disregarded, and a site on the Lehman Mesa, 7,258 feet above sea level, was chosen for the "acropolis."

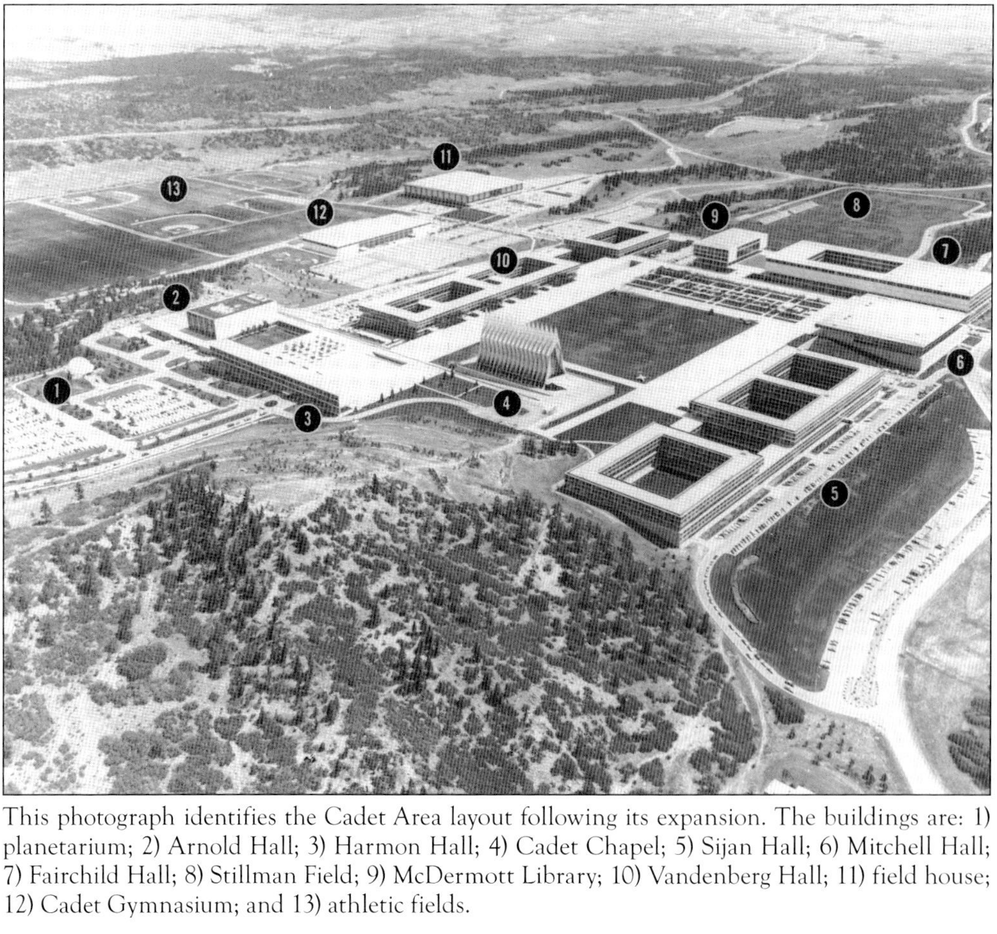

This photograph identifies the Cadet Area layout following its expansion. The buildings are: 1) planetarium; 2) Arnold Hall; 3) Harmon Hall; 4) Cadet Chapel; 5) Sijan Hall; 6) Mitchell Hall; 7) Fairchild Hall; 8) Stillman Field; 9) McDermott Library; 10) Vandenberg Hall; 11) field house; 12) Cadet Gymnasium; and 13) athletic fields.

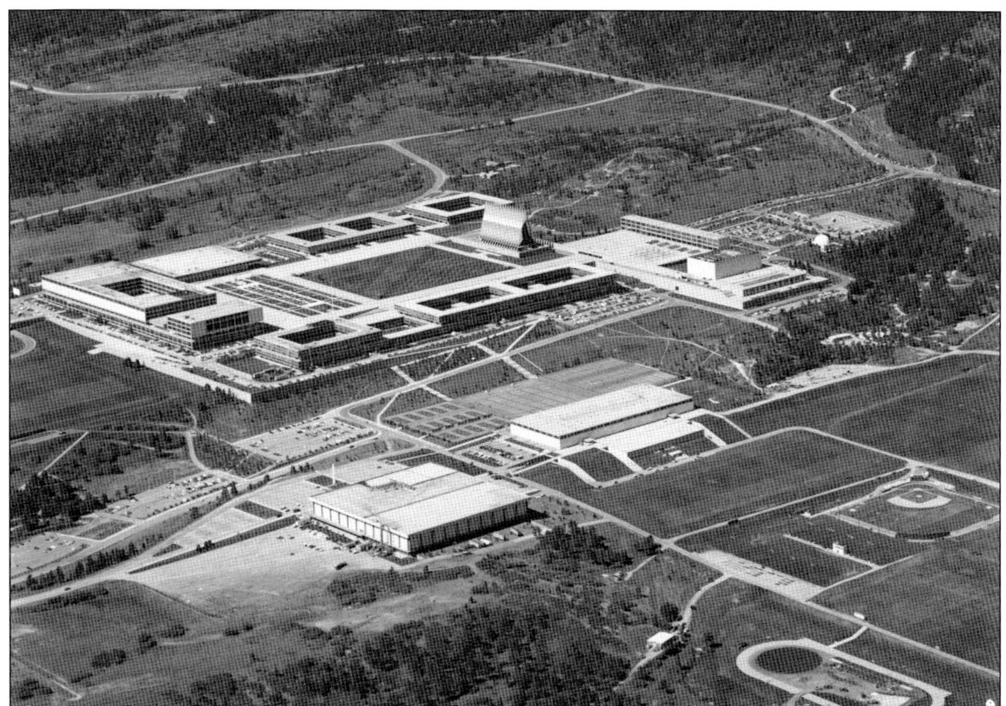

Built on four levels, the Cadet Area ascends from the athletic fields at the lowest point to the parade field and gymnasium level, which is approximately 75 feet below the Honor Court level, the highest point. Thirteen feet below the Honor Court level lies the Terrazzo, the central courtyard of the Cadet Area. The grid pattern is formed by strips of marble framing sections of terrazzo pavement.

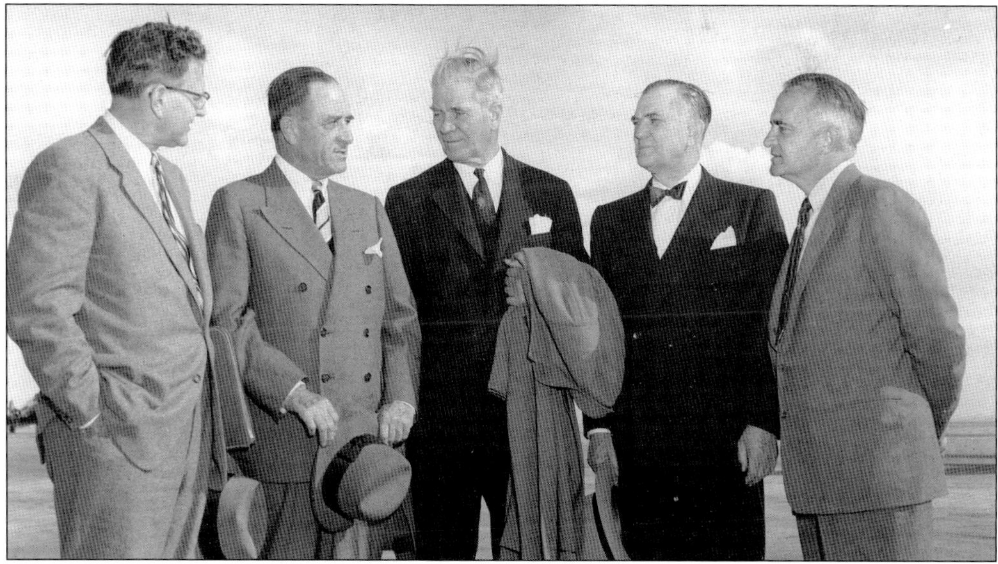

Captured here, Secretary of the Air Force Harold E. Talbott (second from left) arrives at Peterson Field with a senatorial delegation to attend the first public showing of Air Force Academy architectural concepts in May 1955. The modern style faced heavy criticism from senators, the public, and even architect Frank Lloyd Wright, who allegedly wrote to Nathaniel Owings stating that, since SOM lacked the talent, he would happily take over the project.

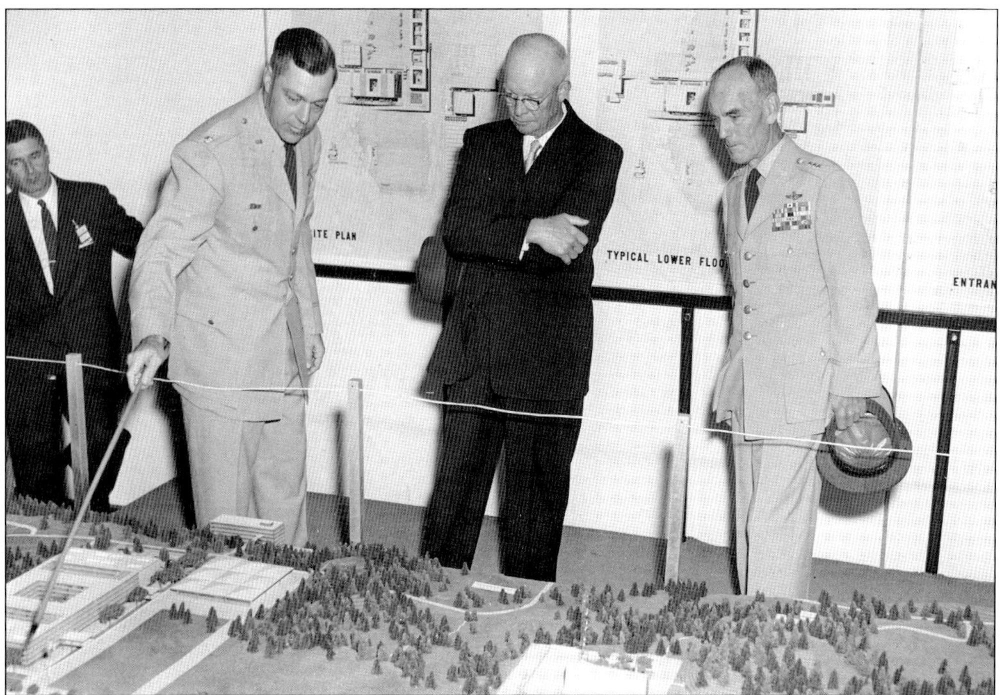

Maj. Arthur Witters, the Air Force Academy's director of installations and the first civil engineer at the academy, presents a model of the permanent academy design to President Eisenhower and Lieutenant General Harmon during the president's visit to Lowry in September 1955. Witters, who retired as a colonel and was instrumental in the development of the academy, was honored in October 2021 when the Air Force Academy's civil engineering building was renamed after him.

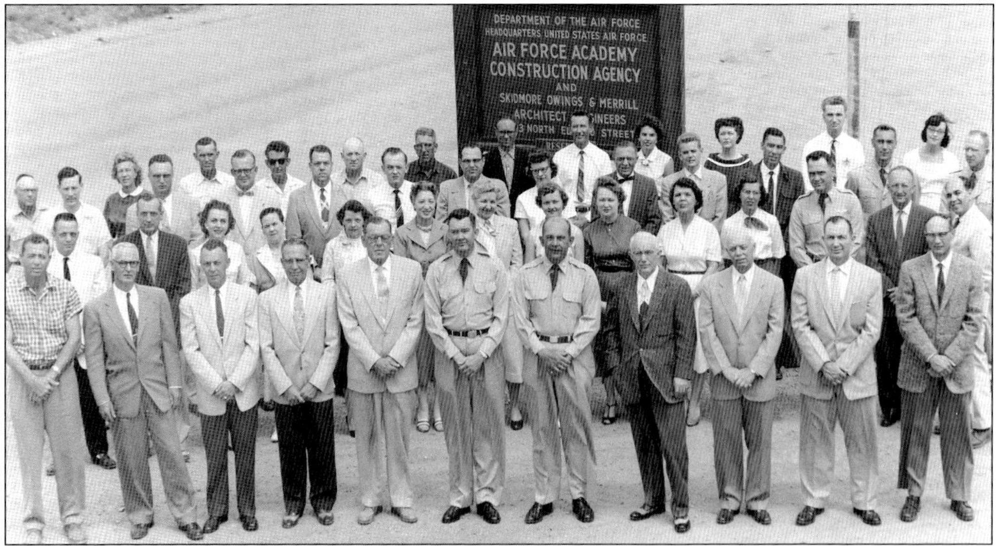

To manage the project, the Air Force Academy Construction Agency, led by Col. Albert E. Stoltz, was formed with the mission "to direct the planning, designing and construction of an Air Force Academy and simultaneously assist in the provision of facilities for the interim Academy." Pictured here, the staff of the construction agency stand in front of their headquarters at 3333 North El Paso Street in Colorado Springs.

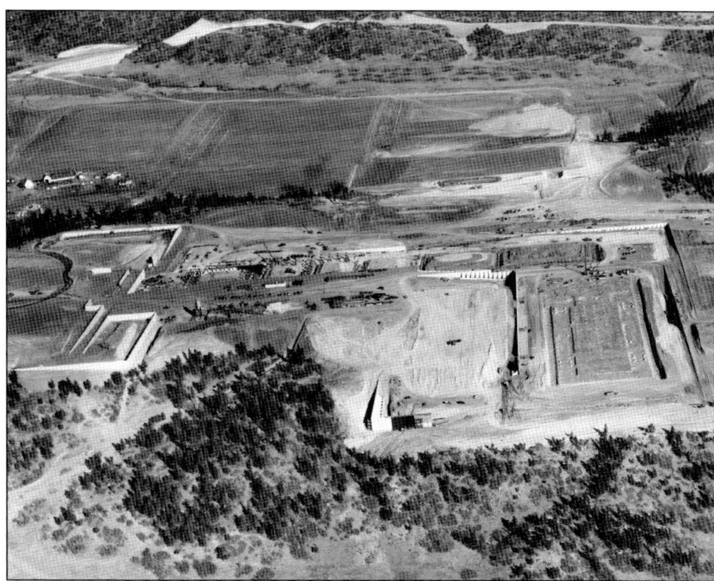

In this 1956 photograph, basic foundations of the buildings have been constructed. The ramp leading to the Cadet Chapel on the Honor Court level is visible on the left. The pilings on the far right outline the basement of Fairchild Hall. Directly to Fairchild's left is the start of the foundation for Mitchell Hall. The athletic fields in the upper right are being graded.

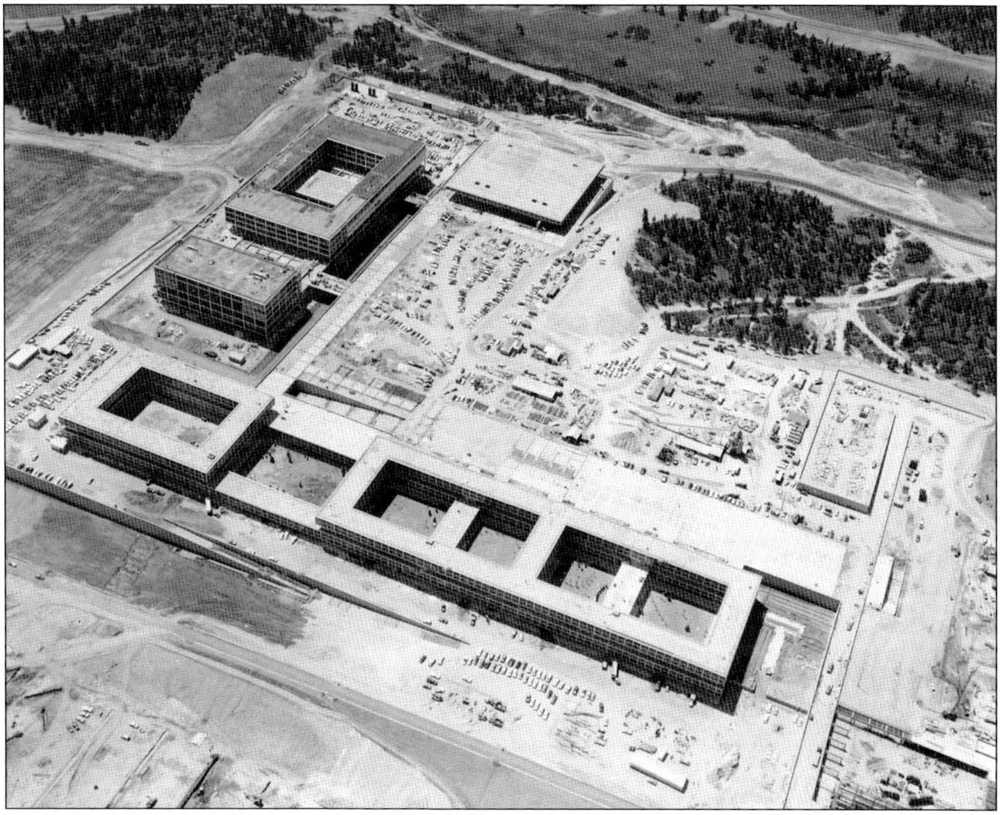

This aerial view of the Cadet Area highlights the open spaces between the upper floors of Fairchild Hall and Vandenberg Hall. Fairchild Hall (upper left) appears to be separated from the McDermott Library section. Similarly, the gap between the upper floors of Vandenberg Hall creates the impression of two distinct buildings when viewed from the Terrazzo. This design is meant to create a feeling of openness in the Cadet Area.

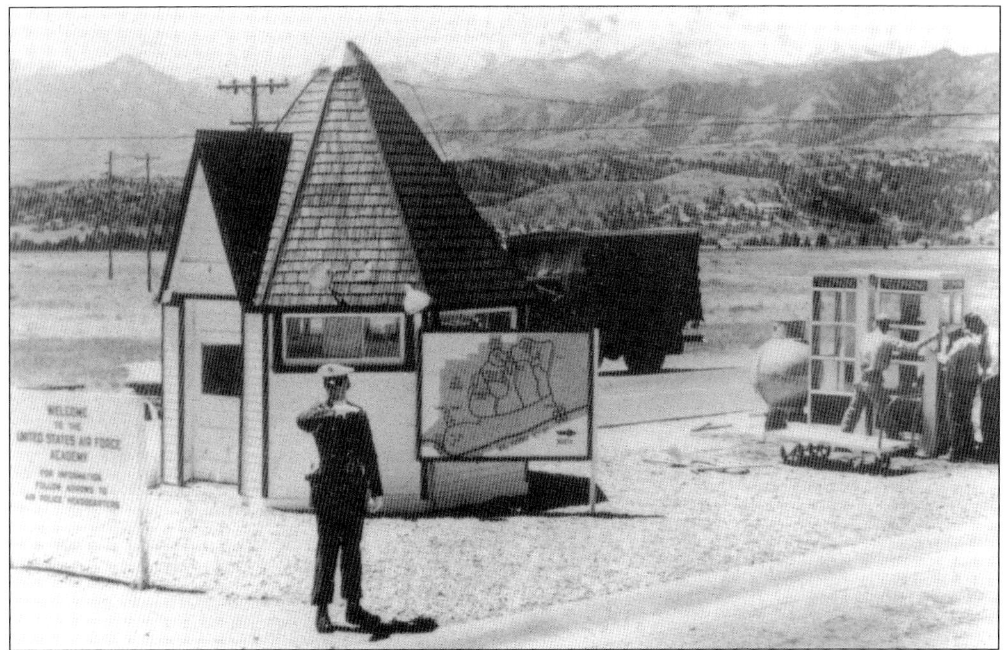

There are two entrances to the Air Force Academy from Colorado Highway 85-87, now Interstate 25: the North Gate where the town of Husted once existed and the South Gate seven miles to the south. A Gardiner Sanitary Tent was used as the South Gatehouse until a larger structure was built. The octagonal hut was originally utilized by the Woodmen Sanitorium as individual living quarters for patients recovering from tuberculosis.

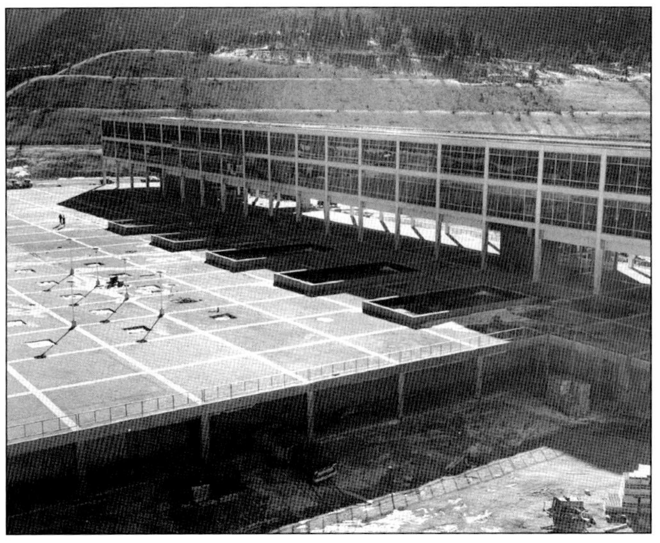

Erected on pillars at the Honor Court level, the narrow, rectilinear Harmon Hall serves as the administrative building and houses the superintendent's office. The third floor features a cantilevered balcony from which the superintendent can review cadet formations. The entrances to Harmon Hall are surrounded by red glass tiles representing the facility's administrative functions. Throughout the Cadet Area, blue tiles represent the academic buildings, and yellow tiles adorn the dormitories.

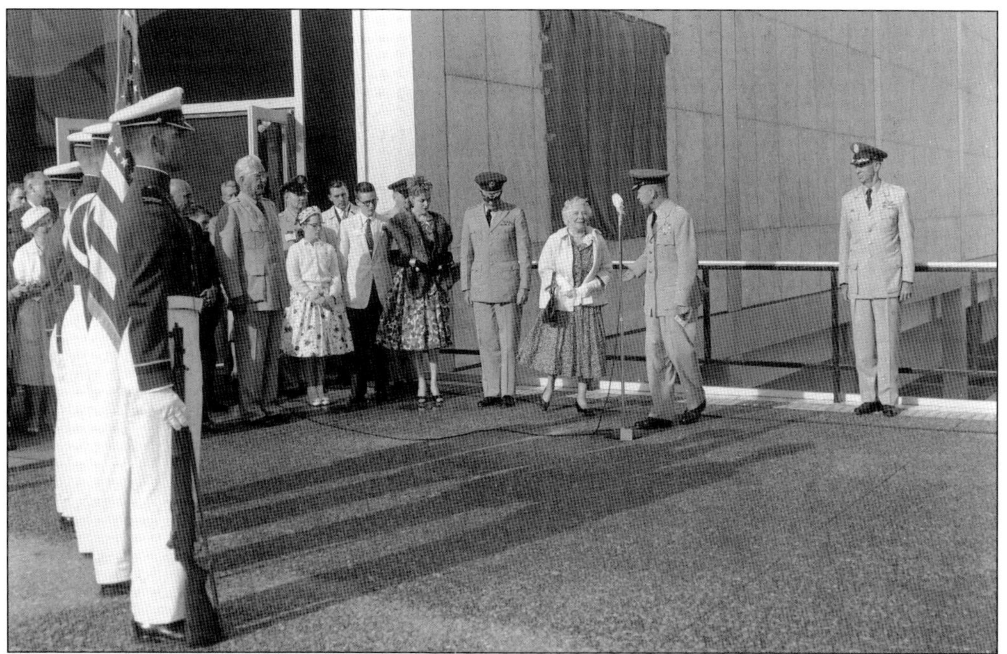

Eleanor Arnold (center), widow of General of the Air Force Henry "Hap" Arnold, attended the dedication of Arnold Hall in May 1959. The building's name carried over from the cadet social center at Lowry. Arnold Hall originally had an open-air courtyard, which was later enclosed and converted into a cafeteria during the 1966 expansion of the building. The Cadet Area was dedicated during the graduation week festivities.

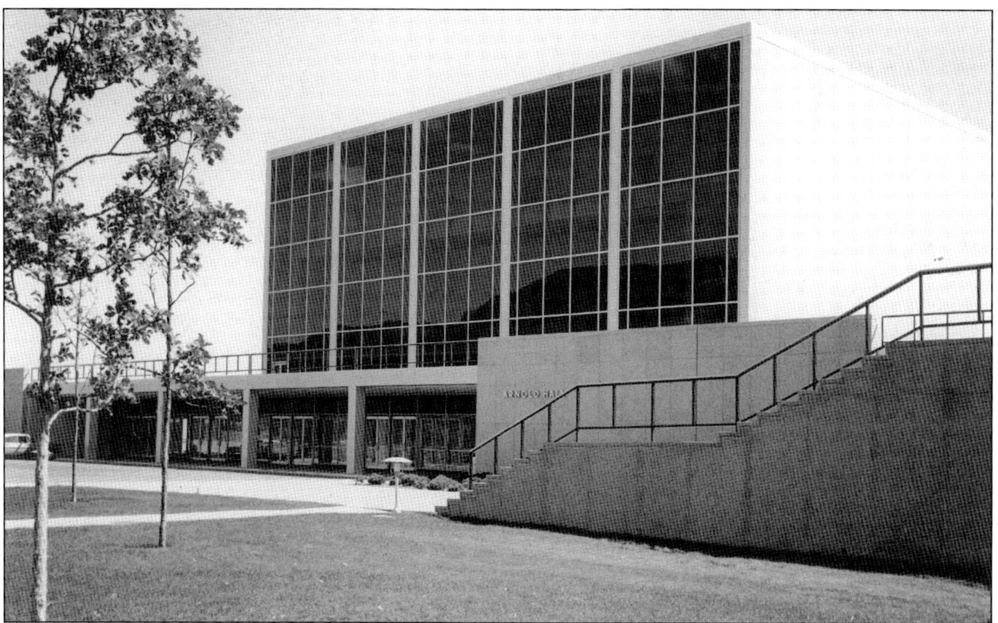

The original Arnold Hall design, shown to the public at the 1955 exhibit, depicted a three-story glass cube set on piers. This is perhaps the image that motivated famed architect Frank Lloyd Wright's reproach that the academy was a "glassified box on stilts." In response to criticism, the design was altered to incorporate warm-white marble masonry walls.

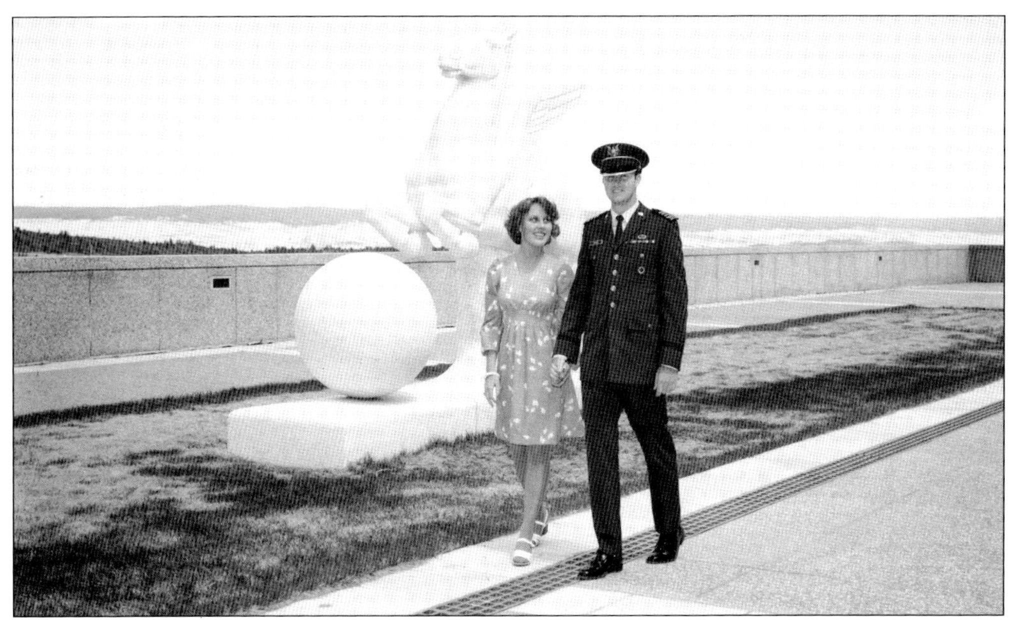

The Pegasus statue was originally located on the outdoor terrace of Arnold Hall. A gift from the Italian government, the 8.5-ton statue was presented to the Air Force Academy in May 1959. Cadets joked that if a date kissed the statue and was of the utmost virtue, the statue would fly away. To prevent people from climbing on the statue during social events, Pegasus was moved to the alumni center, Doolittle Hall, in 1994.

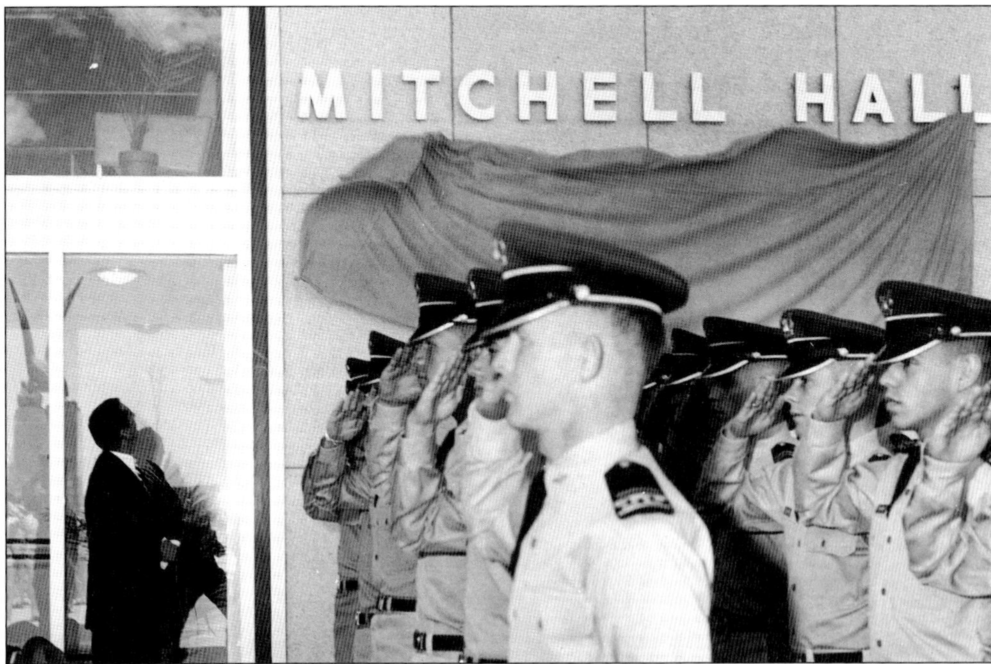

In this 1959 photograph, William Mitchell Jr. stands in front of the Cadet Wing formation admiring the lettering on the new cadet dining facility that bears his father's name. Named for Maj. Gen. William "Billy" Mitchell, a pioneer aviator and early advocate for an air academy, the facility is an architectural marvel designed by Gertrude Peterhaus.

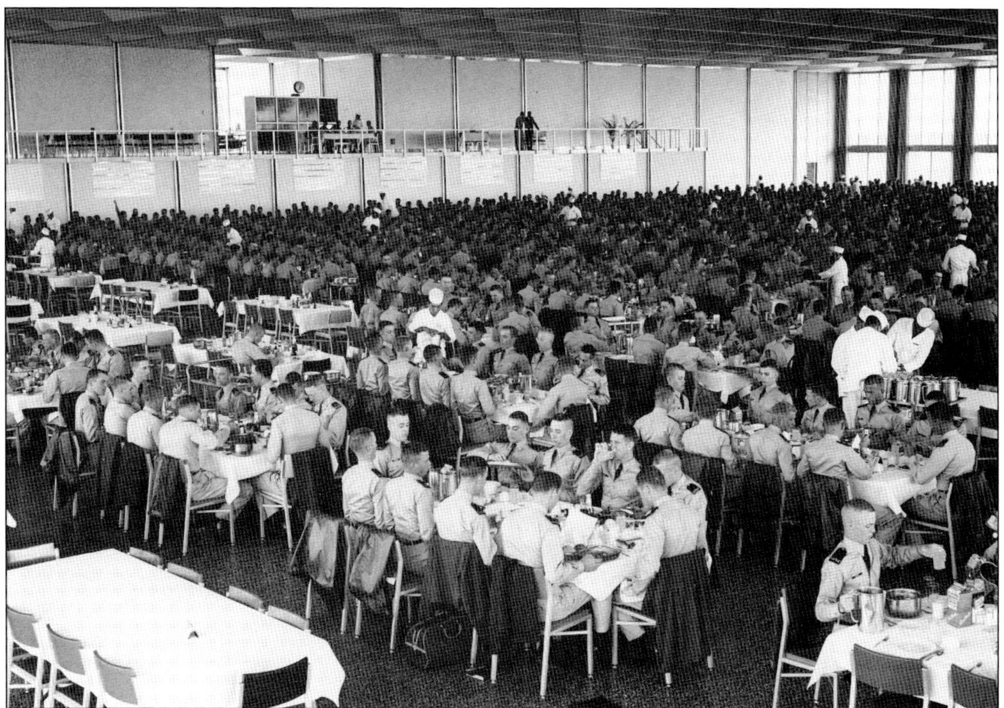

The academy program called for a facility to provide "two sunny-side-up eggs at the same temperature to all cadets," which conflicted with Peterhaus's desire to locate kitchens and service areas under the main dining area, with glass walls enclosing the dining space. Worried that power outages could disrupt elevator service, the redesign included masonry walls on one end, concealing kitchen facilities on the main level.

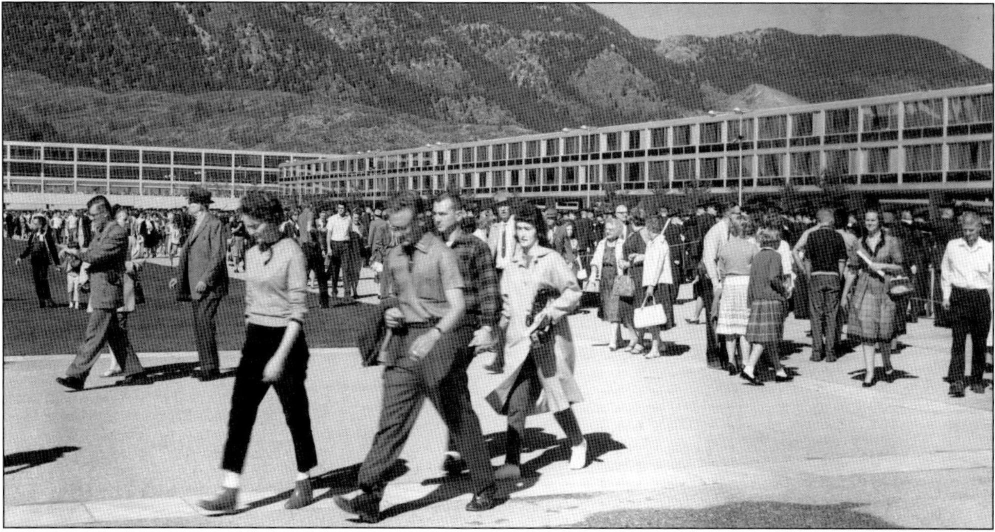

On September 22, 1962, the Air Force Academy hosted an open house to showcase the nearly completed school. An estimated 85,000 visitors toured the grounds and facilities. A presentation on "America's Future in Space" was held in Arnold Hall, demonstrations took place in Fairchild's classrooms and laboratories, and programs were offered at the planetarium every 30 minutes. Visitors could purchase a barbecue lunch near Falcon Stadium for $1.

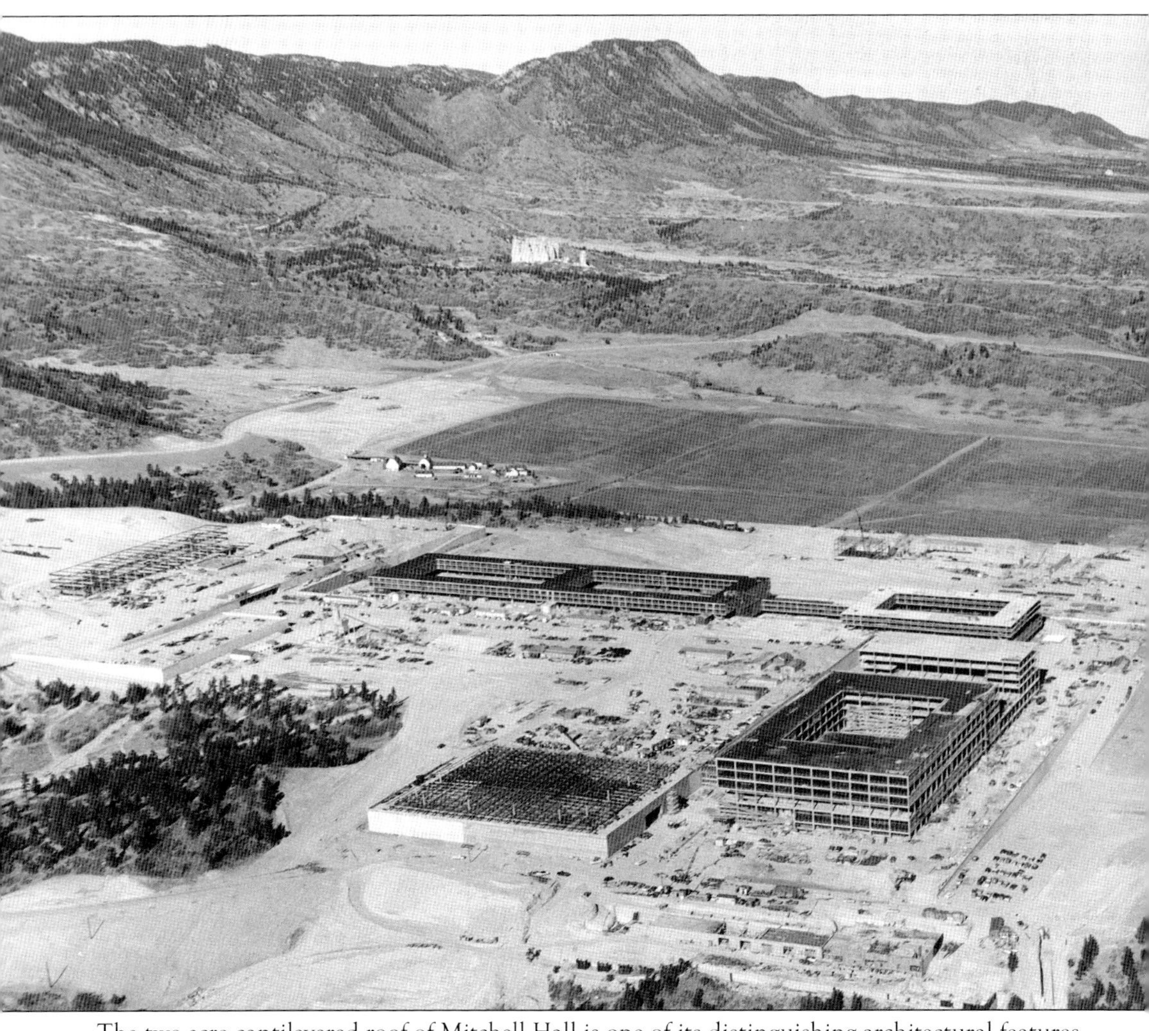

The two-acre cantilevered roof of Mitchell Hall is one of its distinguishing architectural features. The building was designed to achieve an open floor plan for the dining hall, eliminating the need for interior supporting columns. The steel roof was assembled on the ground and then lifted into position with hydraulic lifts by the American Bridge Division of the US Steel Corporation. Once in place, welders were on hand to finish the structural connections to the 16 exterior columns. This innovative method of construction made Mitchell Hall's roof the first of its kind to be lifted into place, and it was the first to use a computer for the structural analysis of the design. This photograph shows the roof prior to being lifted into position. Cathedral Rock Ranch can be seen above the construction site, where the athletic fields will eventually be located. (Photograph by Stewarts Commercial Photographers, © Pikes Peak Library District.)

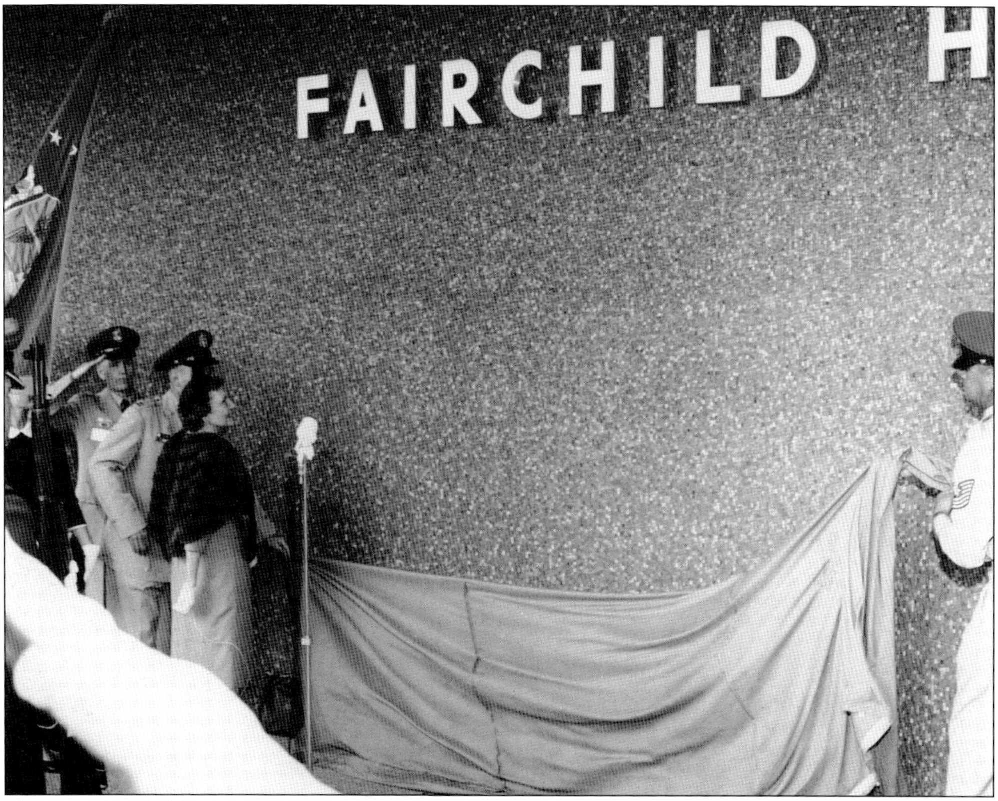

Florence Fairchild, widow of Gen. Muir S. Fairchild, witnessed the dedication of the main academic building in 1959. The McDermott Library is located at the north end of Fairchild Hall and appeared as a separate building when viewed from the Terrazzo level until the 1984 expansion. Fairchild Hall is a six-story freestanding structure connected to the Terrazzo by pedestrian bridges at its third level.

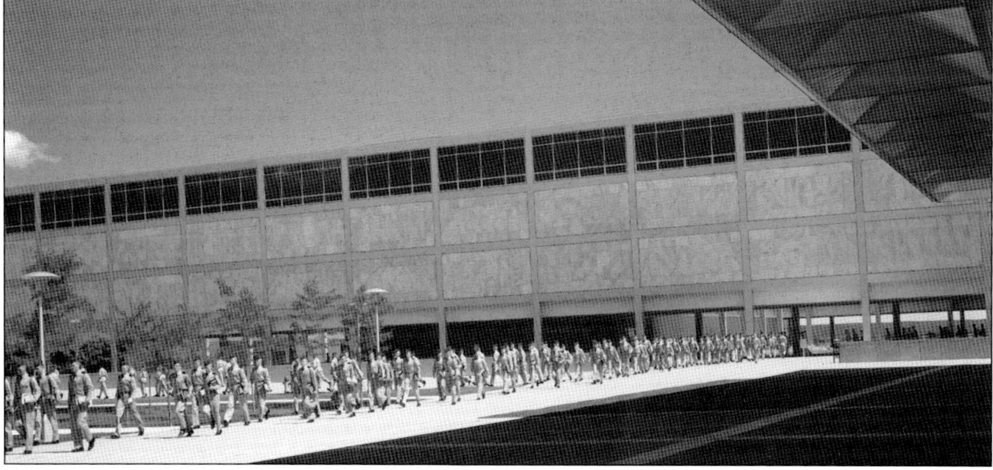

SOM employed a research team during the project to develop new materials and technical methods of construction. The molded, anodized aluminum skin and flush glass walls that clad a complex internal structure exemplify the technological innovations that distinguish the Air Force Academy's construction from the heavy, load-bearing exterior walls of the past. Fairchild Hall houses offices for the dean of faculty and the commandant of cadets as well as academic classrooms and laboratories.

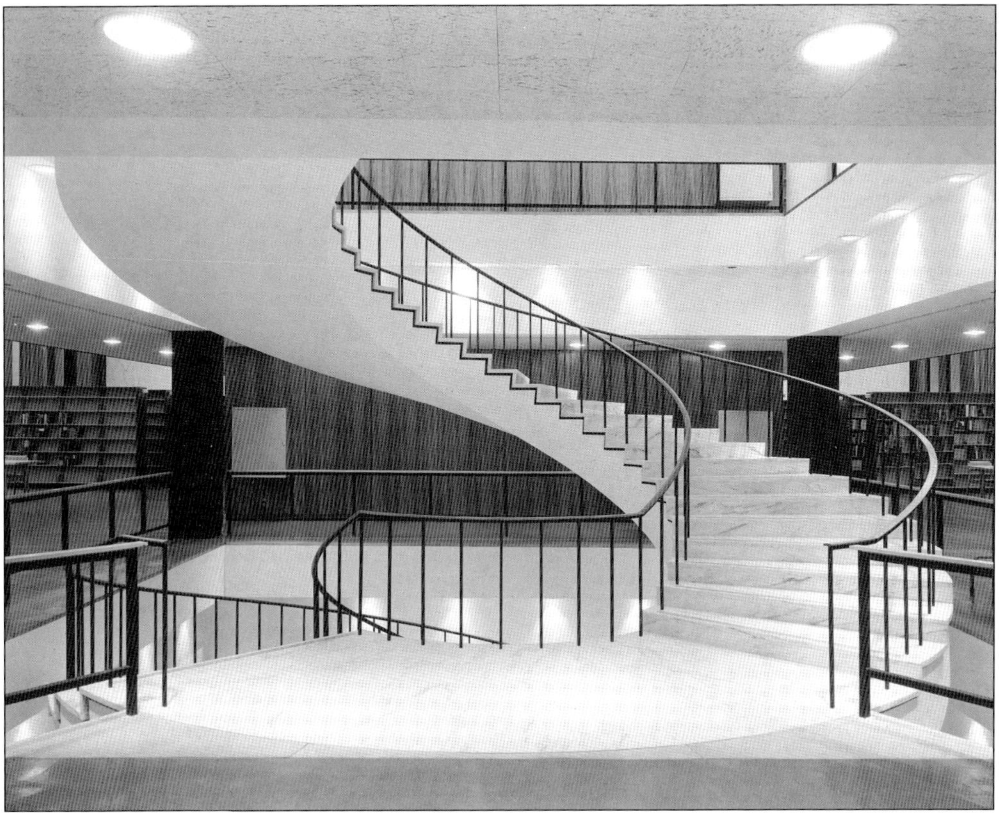

Contrasting the straight lines of the Cadet Area buildings and the Terrazzo, the McDermott Library features a three-story white marble spiral staircase. The freestanding staircase was the central focal point of the original library design, but due to the 1984 expansion of Fairchild Hall, it is now located in the northeastern corner. (Photograph by Stewarts Commercial Photographers, © Pikes Peak Library District.)

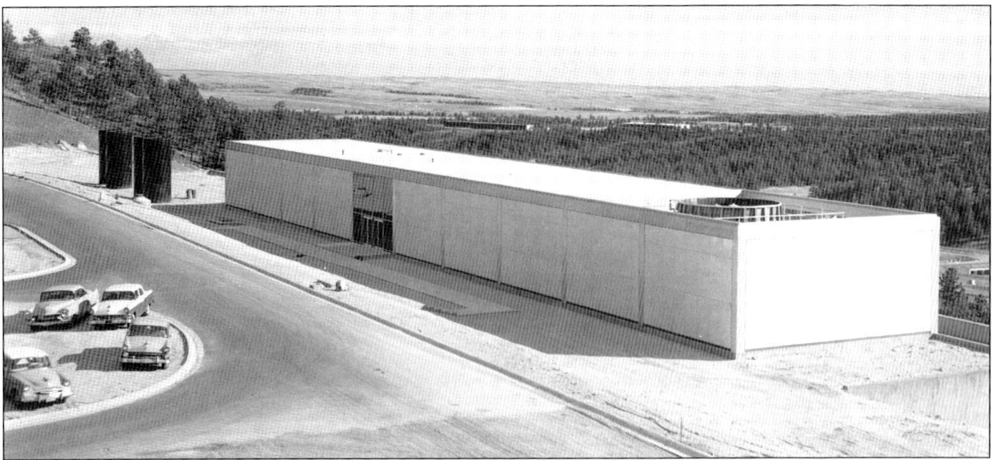

The Air Force Academy established the nation's first department of astronautical engineering. The Aeronautics Laboratory, seen here, serves as a testing facility, with several large bays for heavy testing equipment as well as smaller laboratories, classrooms, and offices. A portion of the south wall is built on tracks, allowing it to open to accommodate large machinery.

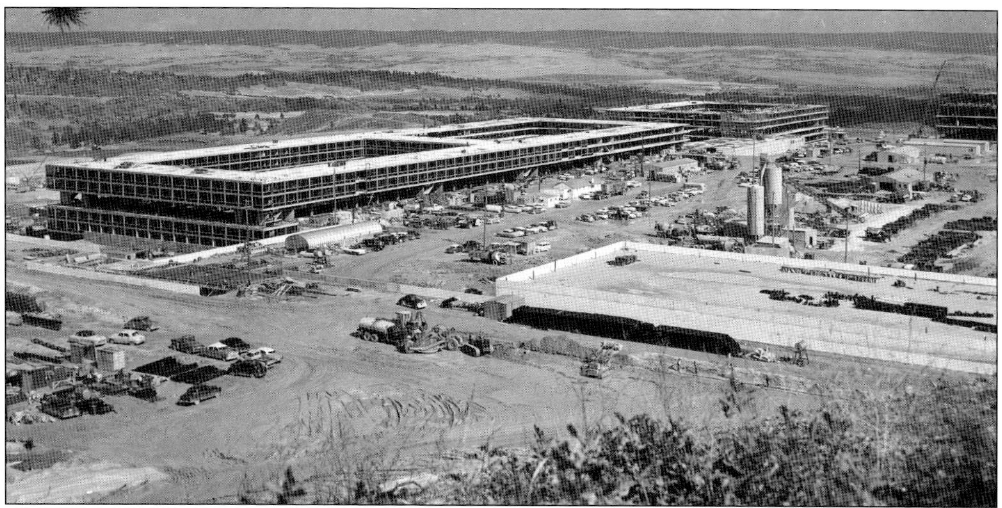

Vandenberg Hall, the six-story cadet dormitory, is a quarter-mile long and covers four acres of the Cadet Area. Vandenberg is the second-largest dormitory in the country behind the Naval Academy's Bancroft Hall, with 1,320 two-person rooms, squadron meeting rooms, a cadet store, a tailor shop, a post office, and offices for cadet activities. Cadet squadrons express their esprit de corps by painting murals depicting squadron heraldry on the walls of their areas.

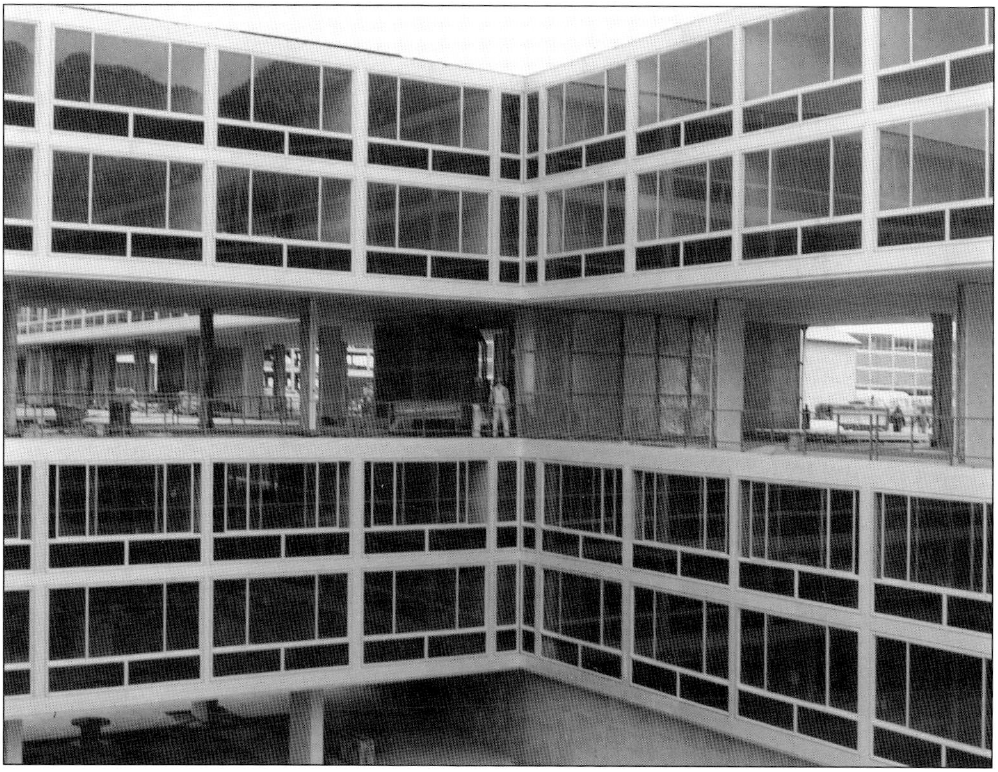

Vandenberg Hall was built so that its midpoint provides access to the Terrazzo level. Floors one and four are open corridors. The interior courtyards were designed by Dan Kiley, intended for gardens that were never constructed. Because the buildings were not air-conditioned, SOM used gray glass of its own invention to limit the amount of light that could penetrate the windows.

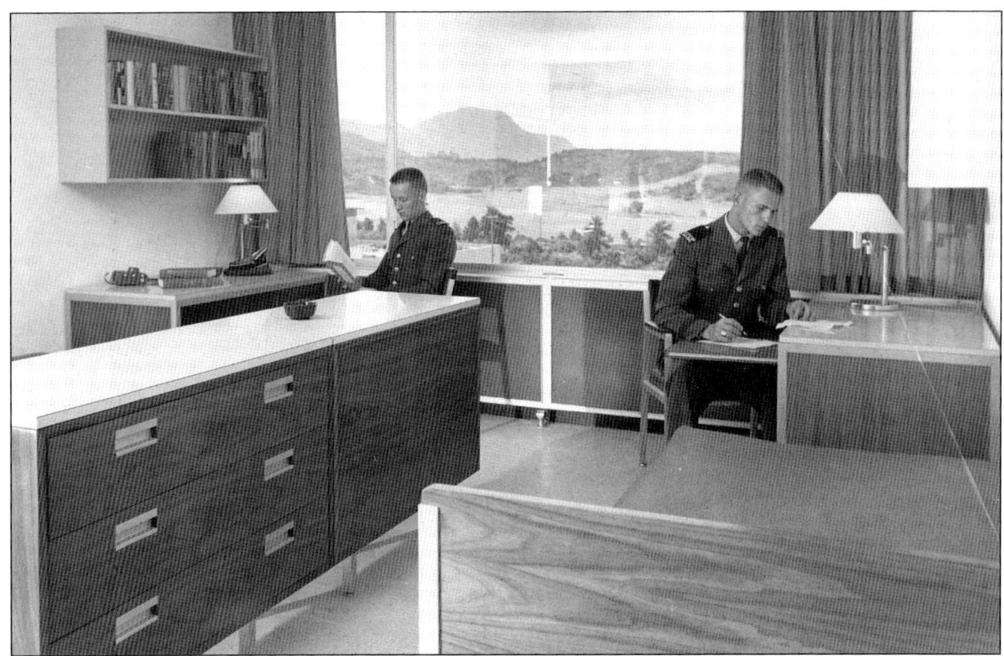

The industrial design firm Walter Dorwin Teague Associates was selected to design the interior furnishings and engineer the equipment for the Air Force Academy buildings. The monumental task required designs that aligned with the unique ways of life at the academy. For example, as fourth-class cadets were required to sit at attention on the edge of their chairs, Teague designed a series of chairs that were forward-balanced to avoid accidental tipping.

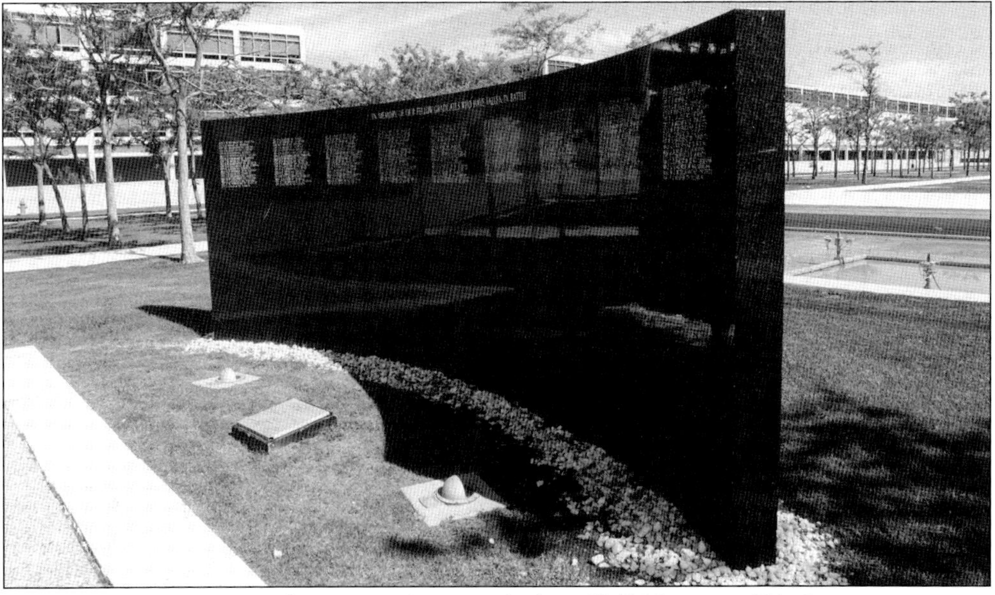

The Graduate War Memorial sits across from Vandenberg Hall. The curved black granite structure honors graduates who gave their lives in service to this nation. The inscription across the top reads, "In memory of our fellow graduates who have fallen in battle." Valmore Bourque, the first cadet to be sworn in on July 11, 1955, became the first combat casualty when his C-123 aircraft was shot down over Vietnam in 1964.

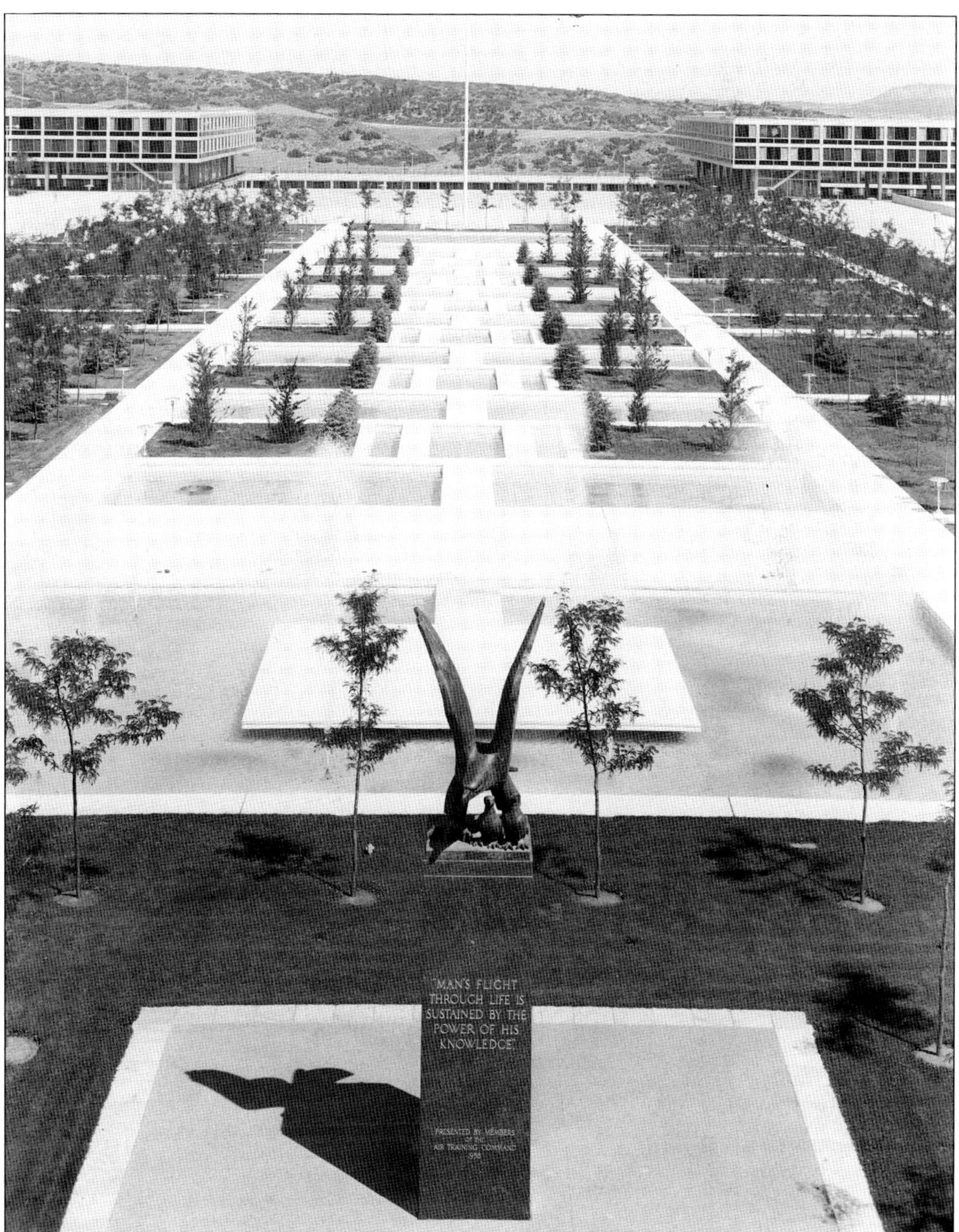

Designed by landscape architect Dan Kiley, the 700-foot Air Garden in front of Fairchild Hall features rectangular lighted pools, sunken grass sections, and a labyrinth of paved walkways lined with honey locust trees, seen here in 1960. To contrast with the rigidly structured life of the cadets, Kiley intended the maze of walkways to prevent them from walking in a straight line. Plagued by drainage issues, the pools were backfilled and covered over in 1975. In 2021, the classes of 1972, 1975, and 1976 and the Joseph and Dorothy Donnelley Moller Trust sponsored the restoration of the Air Garden to its original design. The new Air Garden design includes seating for two outdoor classrooms as well as a 9/11 memorial that features a twisted piece of steel from the Twin Towers. (Photograph by Stewarts Commercial Photographers, © Pikes Peak Library District, 013-6038.)

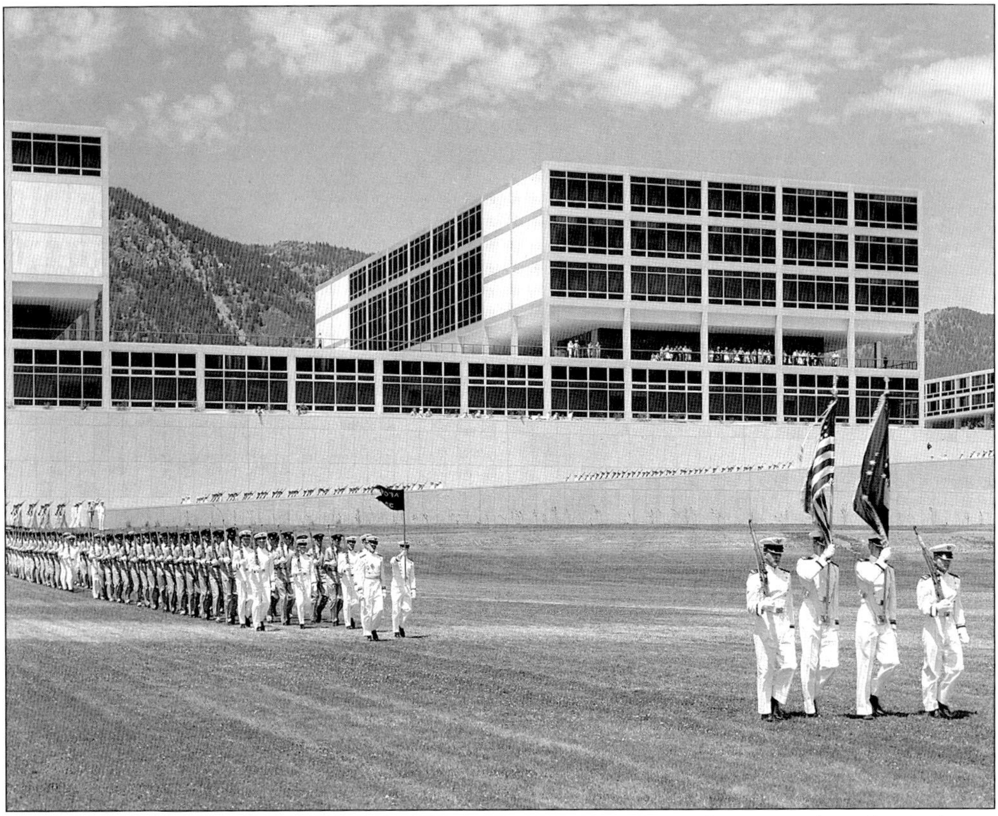

Faculty and staff watch as the Cadet Wing marches down the ramp behind Fairchild Hall onto the Cadet Parade Ground, later named Stillman Field, during a 1959 parade. Graduation was held on Stillman Field from 1960 through 1962. (Photograph by Stewarts Commercial Photographers, © Pikes Peak Library District, 013-4642.)

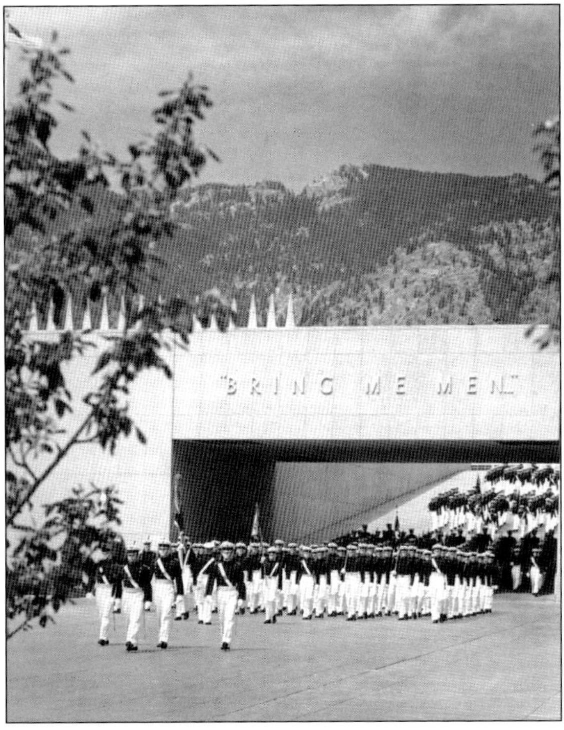

The words "Bring Me Men," from the 1895 Samuel Walter Foss poem "The Coming American," hung above the battle ramp leading up to the Terrazzo from 1964 until 2003. The phrase became controversial after the entrance of women in 1976 and was eventually replaced with the academy's core values: "Integrity First, Service before Self, Excellence in All We Do."

The planetarium was built in 1959 to assist the Department of Navigation in providing celestial navigation training to cadets as well as educational programs for the public. The original Spitz Model "B" projector was capable of recreating 4,000 star patterns across the 50-foot domed screen for an audience sitting in the round. The planetarium was closed in 2004 and remained vacant for 15 years before being refurbished and reopened.

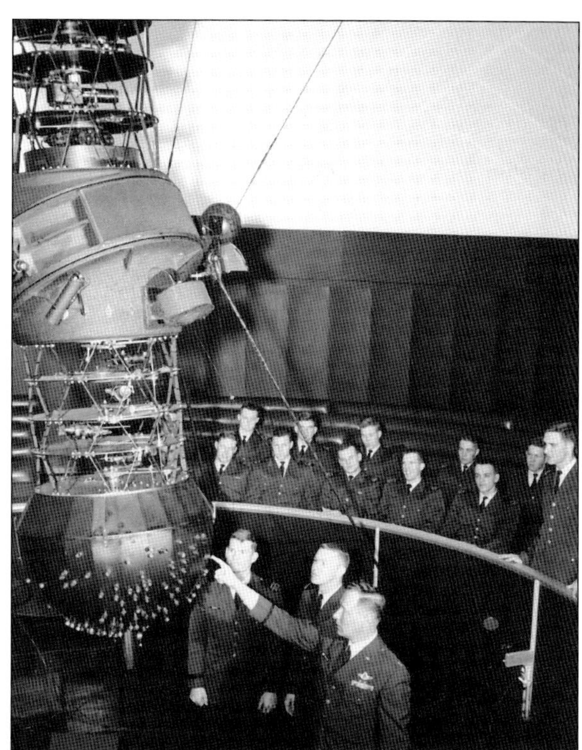

Falcon Stadium was built 2.5 miles southeast of the Cadet Area in a natural bowl-shaped depression in Douglass Valley. The $3.5 million needed to construct the stadium was raised by the Air Force Academy Foundation Inc., a private nonprofit organization. The 40,000-seat stadium opened on September 22, 1962, when a sold-out crowd watched the Falcons defeat Colorado State University (shown below).

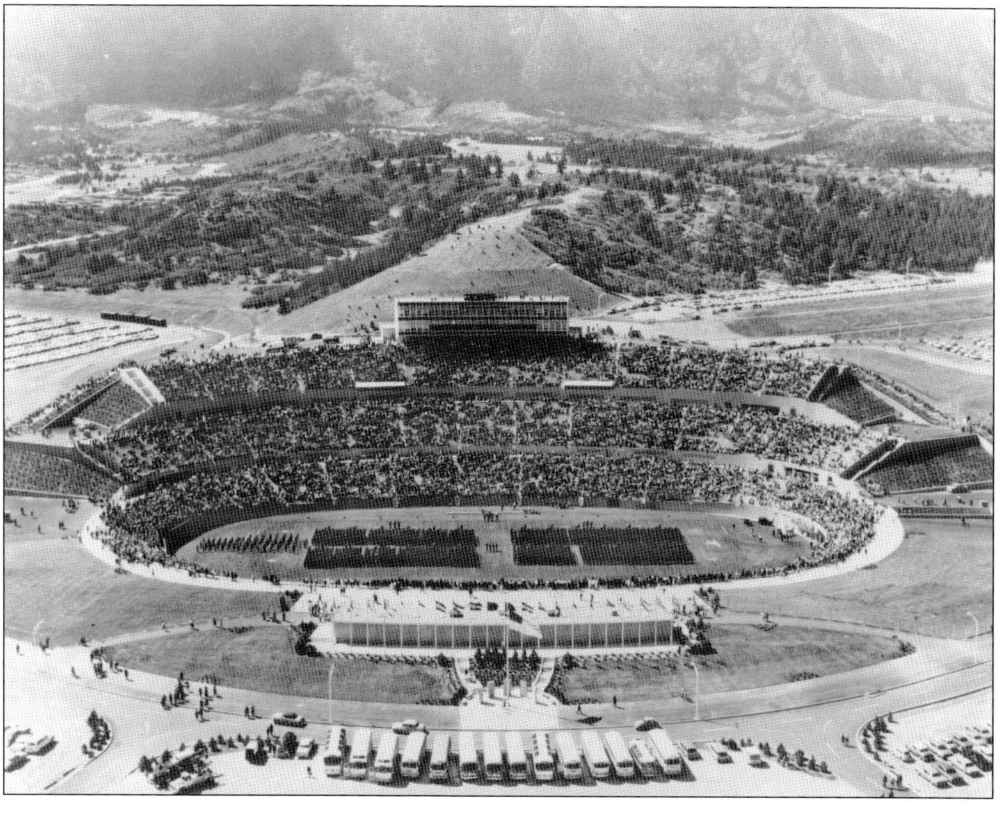

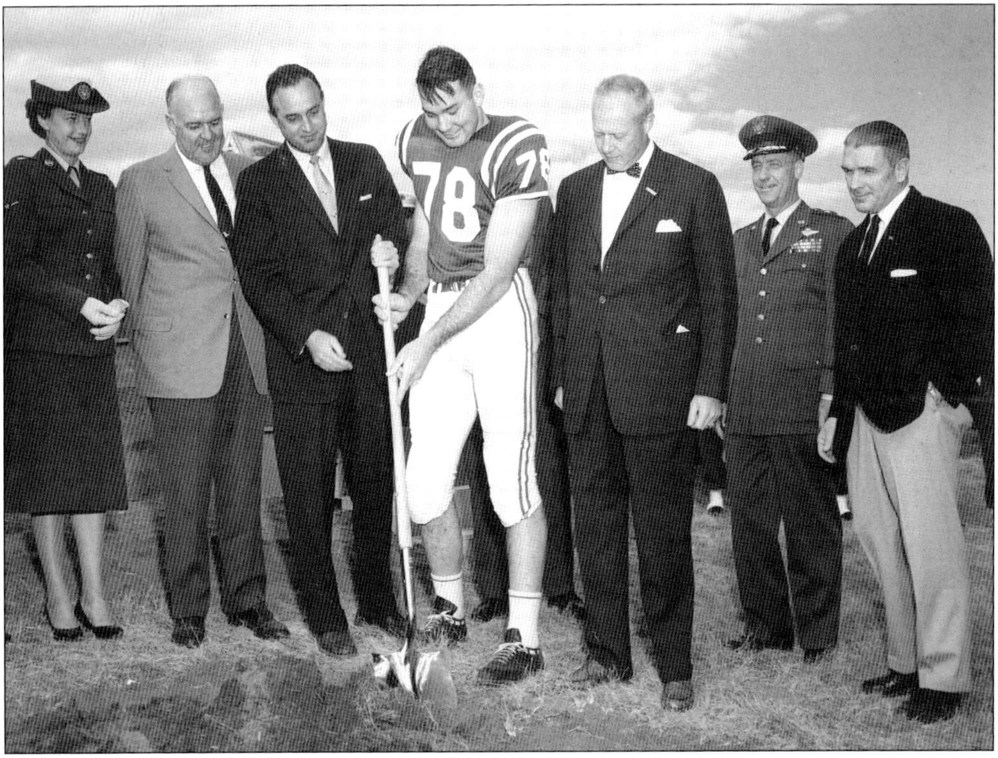

Falcon lineman Neal Rountree, class of 1961, turned over the first shovel of earth during the groundbreaking ceremonies for Falcon Stadium in October 1960. Among the onlookers were, from left to right, A3c. Elizabeth Worcester, Jack Manning representing the Air Force Academy Foundation, football coach Ben Martin, Superintendent Maj. Gen. William Stone, and Colorado governor Stephen McNichols.

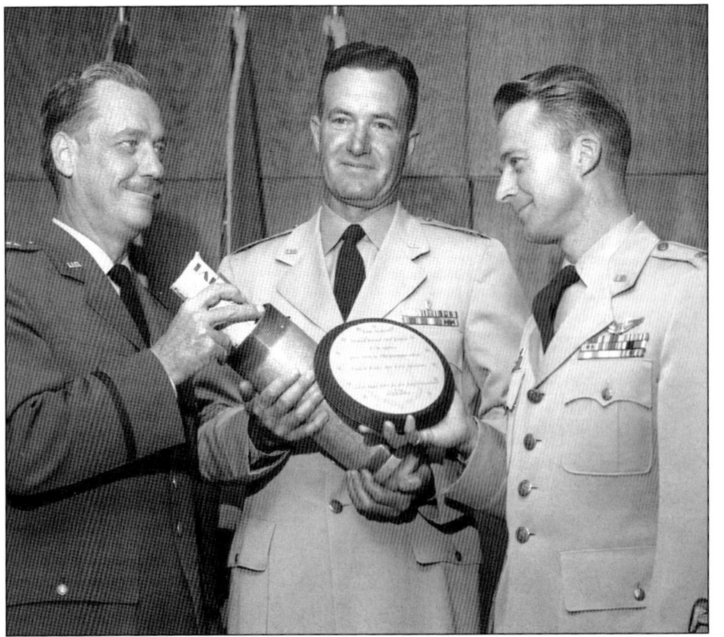

Superintendent Maj. Gen. William S. Stone (left) can be seen here adding a letter addressed to the Air Force Academy superintendent in the year 2060 to the 100-year time capsule buried in the foundation of Falcon Stadium. Also included in the time capsule are a letter from the Cadet Wing commander to his 2060 counterpart and two issues of the weekly base newspaper, the *Falconews*. The capsule was interred near the main entrance to the stadium.

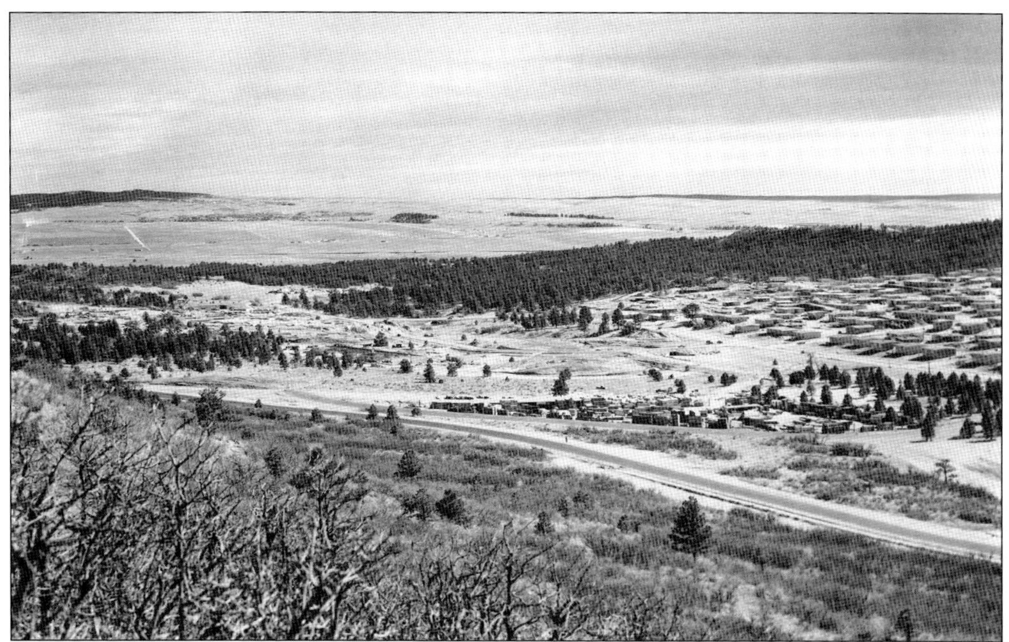

The Douglass Valley housing complex can be seen here to the right, looking east toward Black Forest. In the debate over where to place the Cadet Area on the academy property, Lieutenant General Harmon favored the Douglass Valley site. Located on a mesa between Douglass and Pine Valleys are the community center, base exchange, commissary, post office, recreational and religious facilities, and the Air Force Academy Preparatory School.

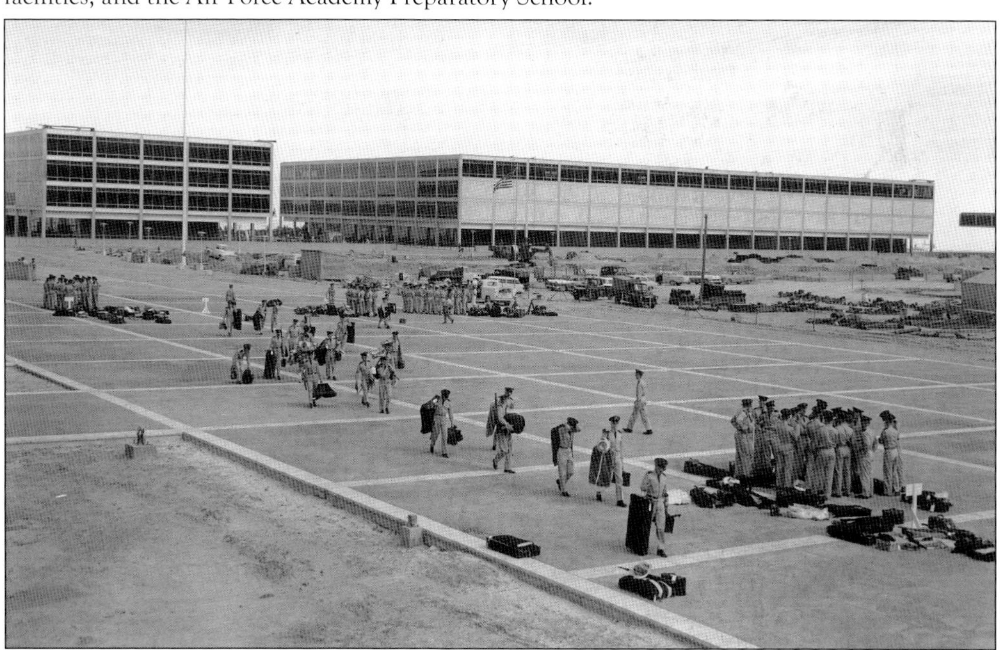

Construction of the Cadet Area was not complete when the Cadet Wing moved from Lowry to its permanent home in August 1958. Parts of Fairchild, Vandenberg, and Mitchell Halls were completed over the following year, while the Cadet Chapel was not finished until 1963. As seen in this photograph, the Cadet Area was still very much a construction site on moving day.

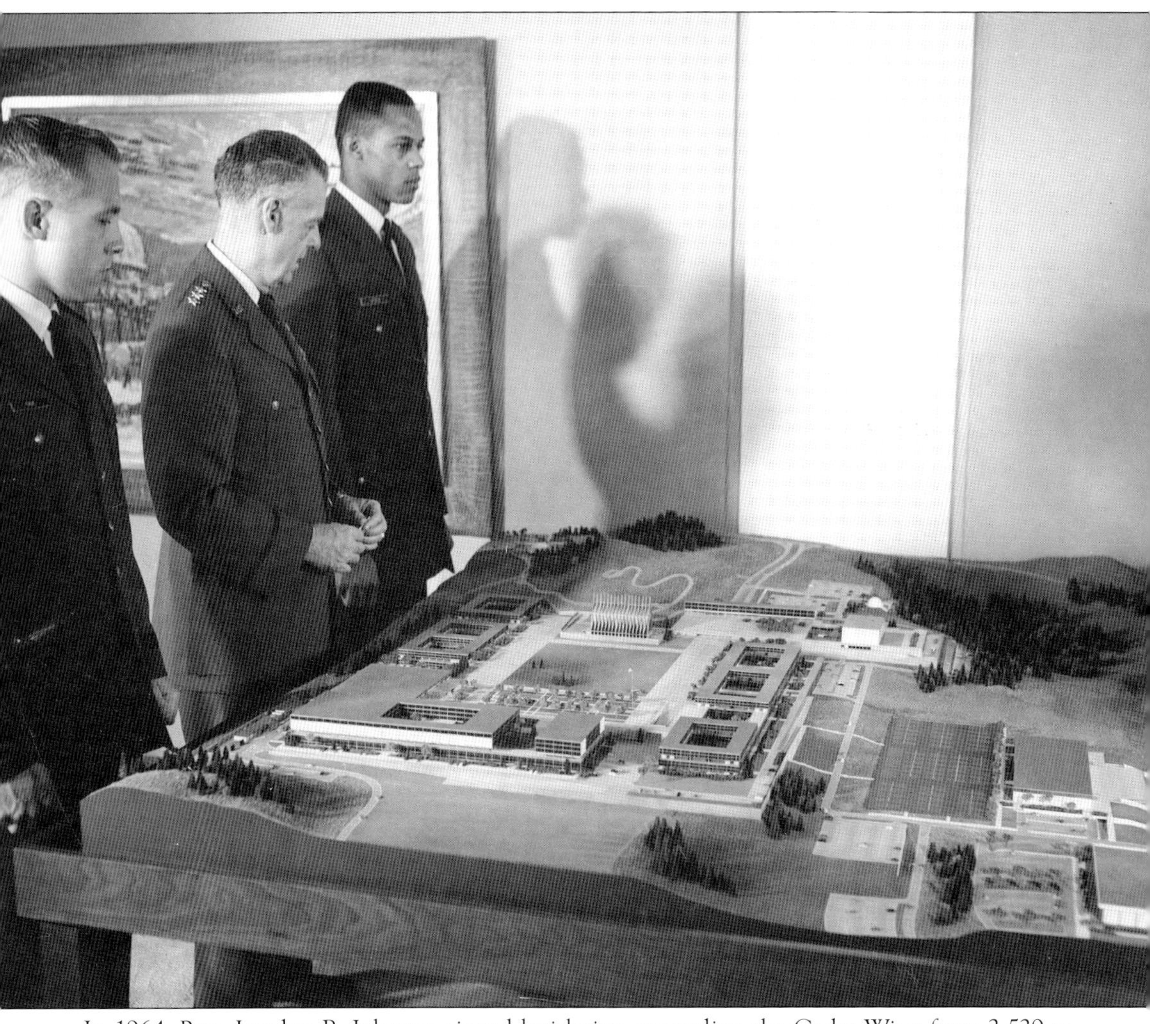

In 1964, Pres. Lyndon B. Johnson signed legislation expanding the Cadet Wing from 2,529 to 4,417 cadets. Superintendent Lt. Gen. Thomas S. Moorman (center) examines a model of the Cadet Area showing planned expansion of facilities to accommodate the increased strength of the Cadet Wing. New construction included a dormitory, a field house, and enlargements of Fairchild Hall, Mitchell Hall, and the gymnasium. The new dorm opened in 1968 and was referred to as the "New Dorm" until 1976, when it was named in honor of Capt. Lance P. Sijan, class of 1965, the Air Force Academy's only Medal of Honor recipient to date. Col. Arthur Witters was instrumental in securing funding for the field house, fulfilling a promise he made to Lieutenant General Harmon in 1955.

Four

The Cadet Chapel

The most iconic structure at the Air Force Academy is undoubtedly the Cadet Chapel. Its 17 spires tower above the academy's Cadet Area, designed to provide vertical relief juxtaposed with the otherwise horizontal aesthetic of the campus. The Cadet Chapel is a geometric wonder that has become a national landmark and the most visited man-made attraction in Colorado. Skidmore, Owings, and Merrill described the ultramodern design that houses multiple faiths within a single building as "a chapel of the future for an Air Force of the future." These visionary architects, using the religious demographics of the Air Force of the 1950s, laid the groundwork for celebrating such diversity in the modern Air Force. Originally, the aluminum, glass, and steel chapel housed Protestant, Catholic, and Jewish worship spaces plus an all-faiths room, but it has since been modified to accommodate permanent chapels for Muslim and Buddhist parishioners as well.

Constructing the chapel proved to be a challenging project from the beginning. Architect Walter Netsch set out to design a singular building that would please not only the religious organizations who would worship there but also a seemingly endless number of highly opinionated individuals, including the secretary of the Air Force and his consultants, senior leadership of the Air Force Academy, various subcommittees of Congress, public interest groups, and famous architects from across the world. All of America seemed to have irreconcilable opinions on every design detail, resulting in the withholding of appropriated funds while debates raged. Colorado governor Edwin C. Johnson called Netsch's "accordion-like" designs an "insult to religion and to Colorado" while openly campaigning for a redesign. With the backing of the partners at Skidmore, Owings, and Merrill and prominent religious leaders, Walter Netsch's design withstood the political quagmire, and the Air Force Academy Construction Agency broke ground in August 1958.

Following the tradition set by West Point and Annapolis, chapel attendance at the Air Force Academy was mandatory until 1972, when the US Court of Appeals voted two to one to end the 150-year-old practice.

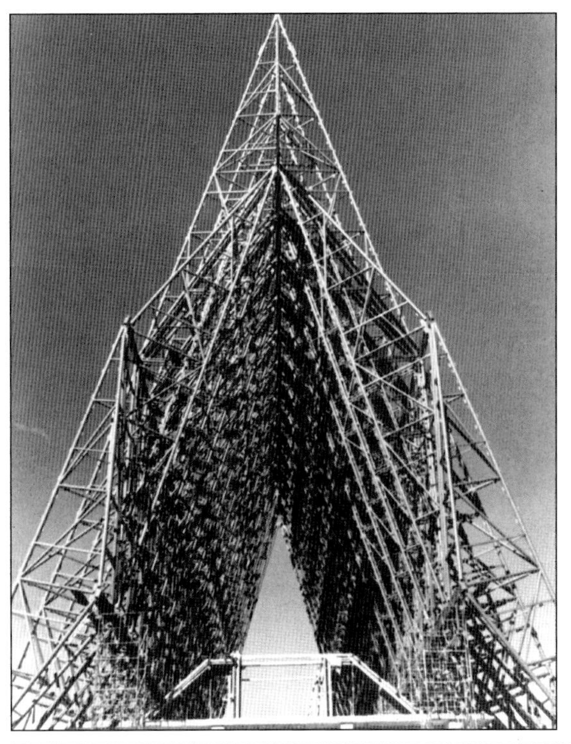

Walter Netsch's chapel design consists of a tubular steel skeleton formed by 100 tetrahedrons, a three-dimensional shape with four triangular faces. Fabricated in Missouri and delivered by rail, each tetrahedron is 75 feet long and weighs five tons. Netsch's original design included 19 spires but was reduced to 17 during the design phase due to budget cuts. People joked that the 17 spires represented the 12 Apostles and the five members of the congressional appropriations committee. A 1955 Air Force design directive required the ramp to the chapel from the Terrazzo level to be wide enough to accommodate the Cadet Wing to march to chapel three abreast.

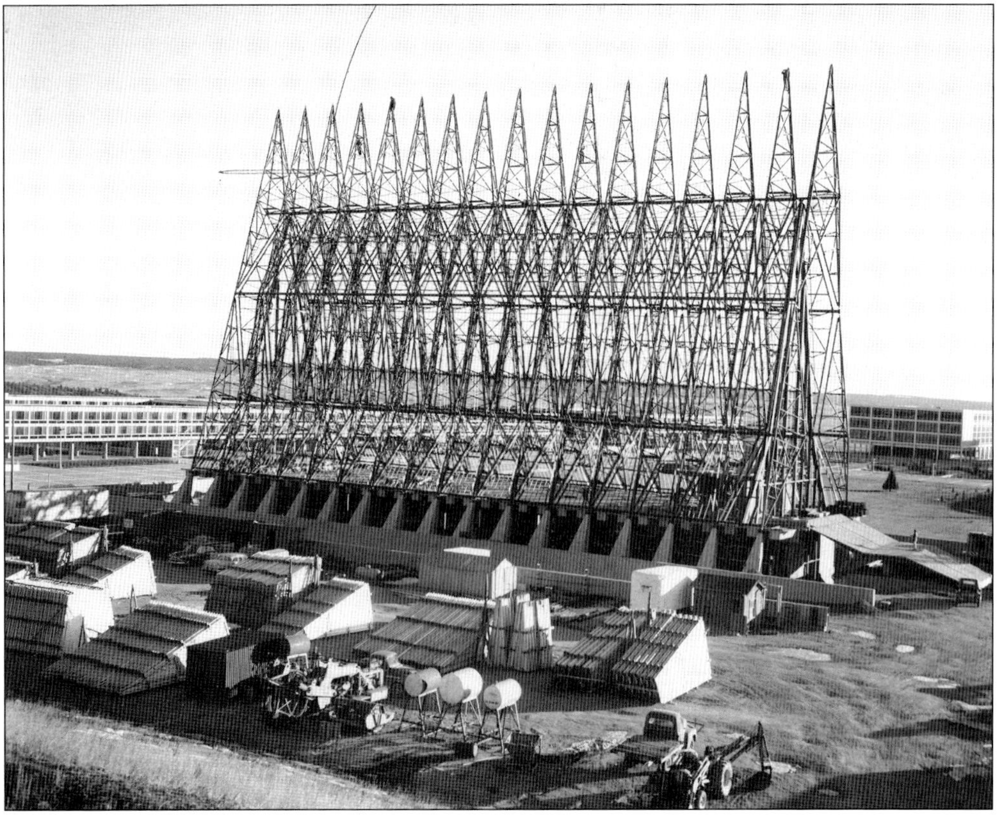

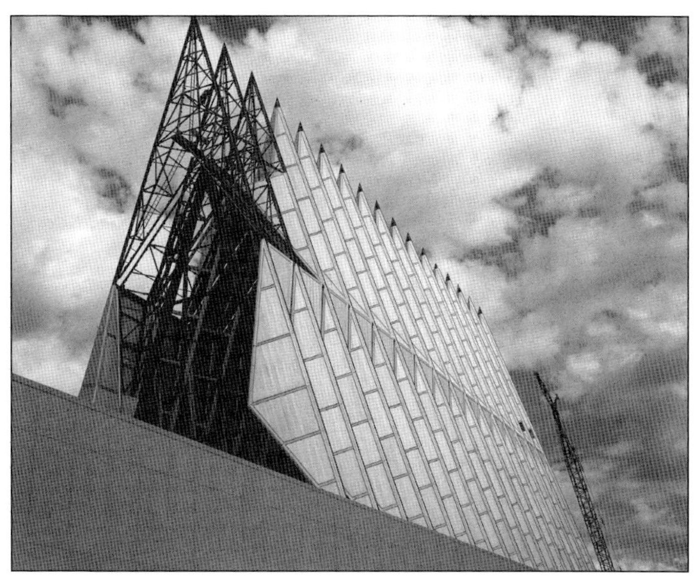

The chapel's exterior is clad in embossed aluminum. Walter Netsch designed a sophisticated drainage system to prevent water damage from expansion and contraction due to Colorado's high winds and varying climate. However, budget cuts forced the use of caulk, which has failed to withstand the environment. Since its completion in 1962, the Air Force Academy has dealt with a leaky roof. This 1962 photograph shows 14 of the 17 spires completed.

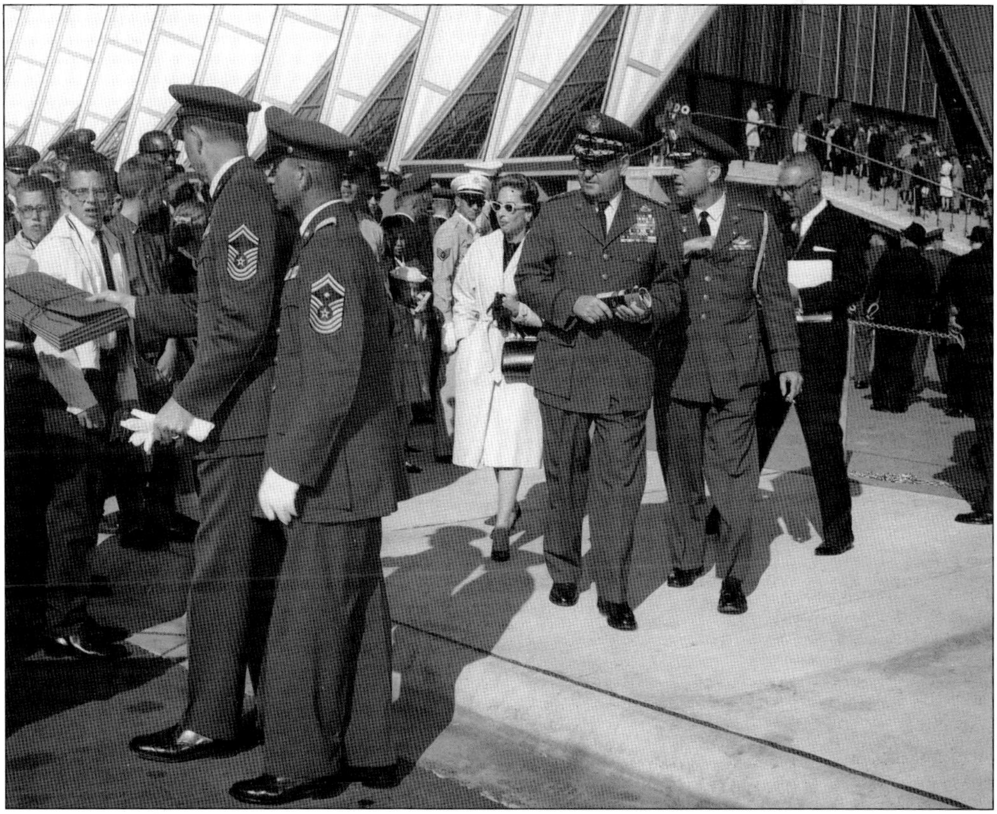

Gen. Curtis E. LeMay (center), chief of staff of the Air Force, is shown leaving the chapel following the dedication ceremonies on September 22, 1963. The fall dedication was too late to host the flurry of post-graduation weddings for the class of 1963. Since its opening, the Cadet Chapel has hosted more than 100 weddings per year, peaking in the days following graduation, when it hosts several per day.

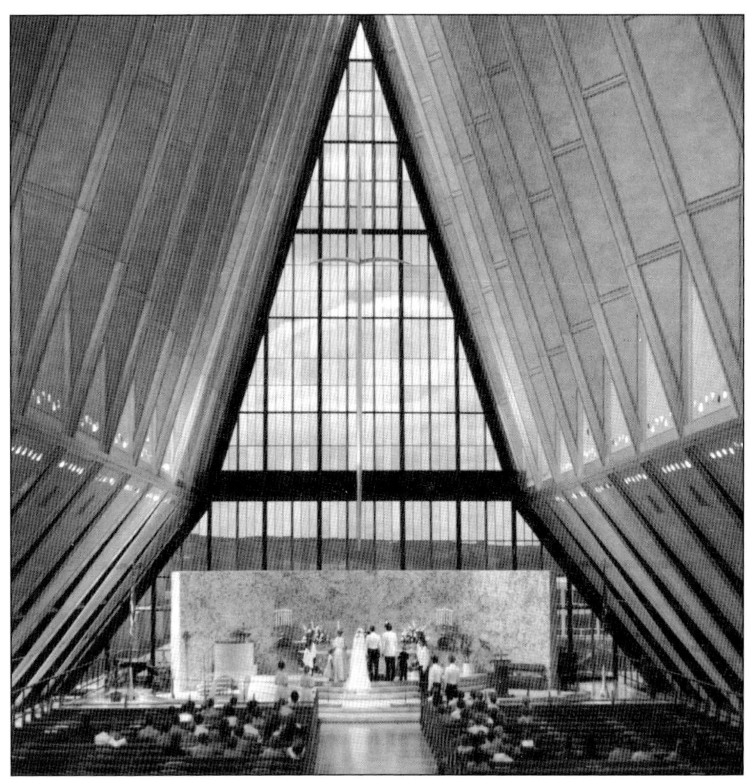

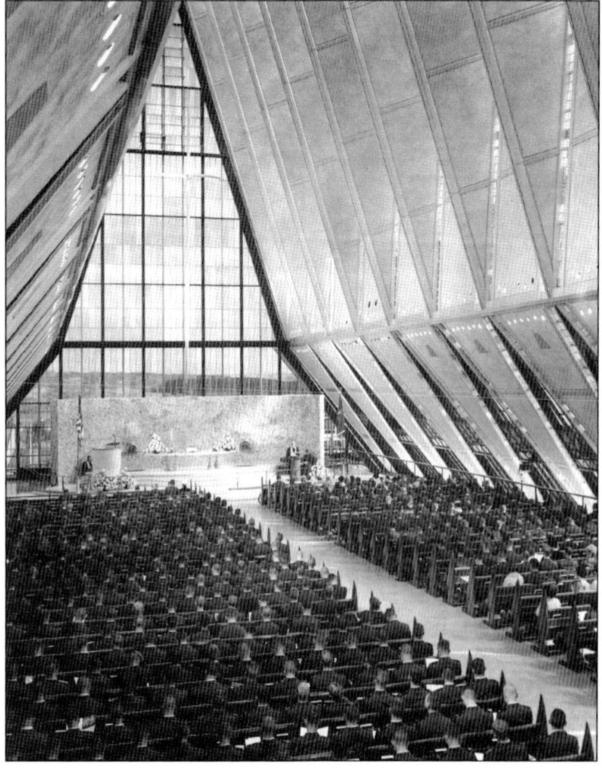

The Protestant Chapel, the largest of the separate chapels at 1,260 square feet, features a 15-foot Italian marble altar. Behind it, a curved reredos adorned by semiprecious stones and Venetian glass suggests the open arms of God. A saber-shaped aluminum cross, measuring 46 feet tall, 12 feet wide, and weighing 1,200 pounds, hangs above the chancel. The ends of the walnut and mahogany pews are sculpted to resemble the propeller of a World War I aircraft, and the backs are capped with a strip of aluminum, symbolizing the edge of a modern fighter aircraft wing, bringing old and new together. Walter Netsch disliked the aviation-themed pews and the saber-like cross but failed to convince the Council of Churches, which provided financing for the furnishings, to change the design.

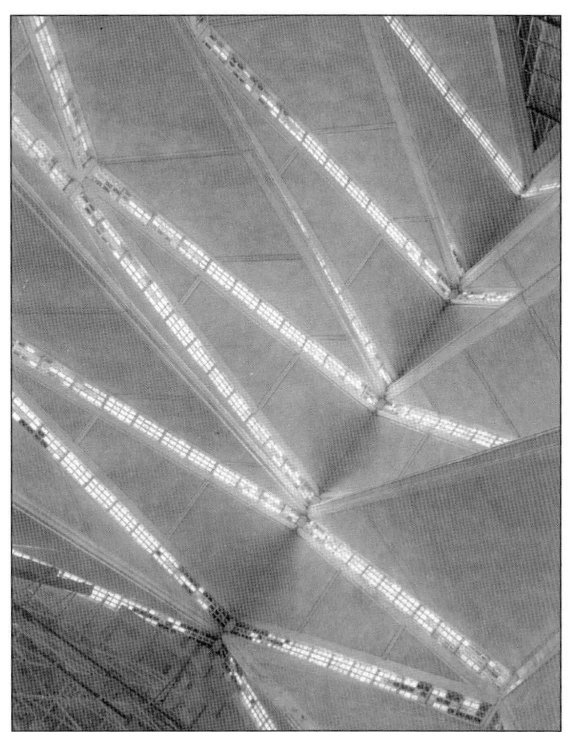

This 1962 photograph captures the ceiling of the Protestant Chapel, highlighting Netsch's remarkable design. Between each tetrahedron is a one-foot space filled with Dalle de Verre stained glass. Netsch positioned each piece of faceted stained glass to, as he described, saturate the chapel in a "symphony of color." The colors gradually shift from purples near the entrance to reds and gold over the altar, expressing the Creation story through light.

Until the Cadet Chapel opened in 1963, chaplains had to find space around campus to hold services for their cadet congregations. As shown in this 1958 photograph, Protestant cadets gathered for Sunday services in Mitchell Hall, the cadet dining hall. Catholics met in Fairchild Hall, and Jewish services were held in Vandenberg Hall.

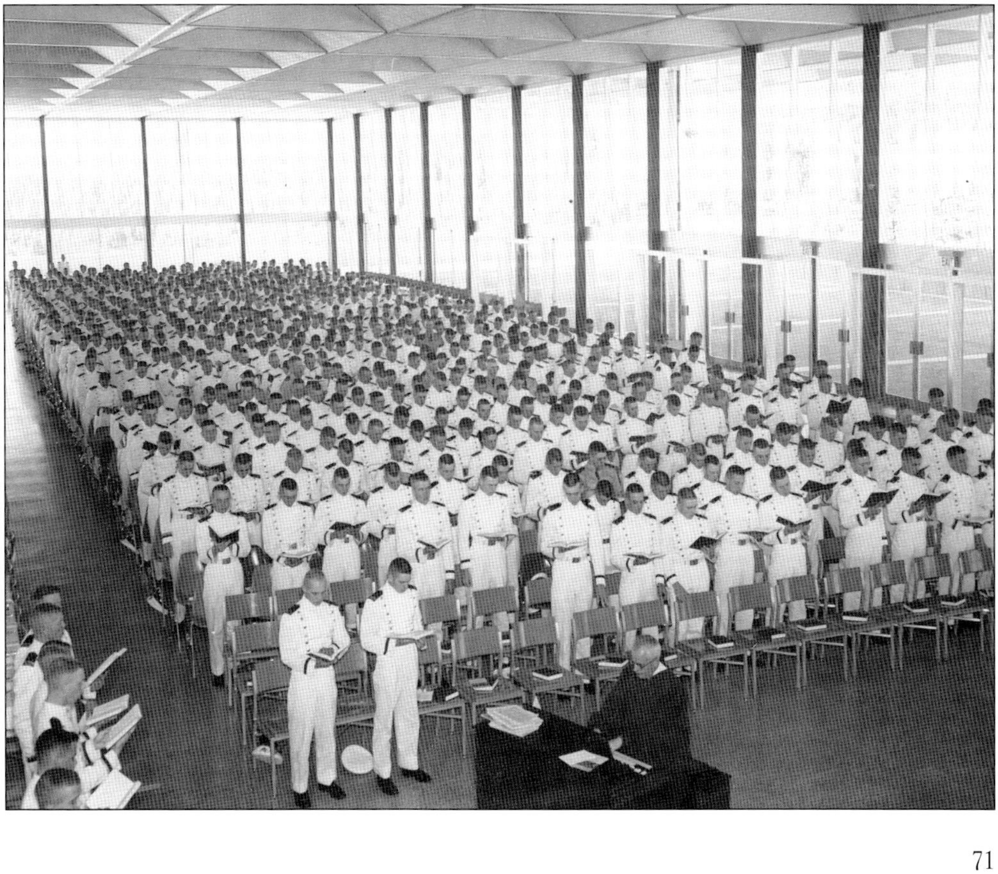

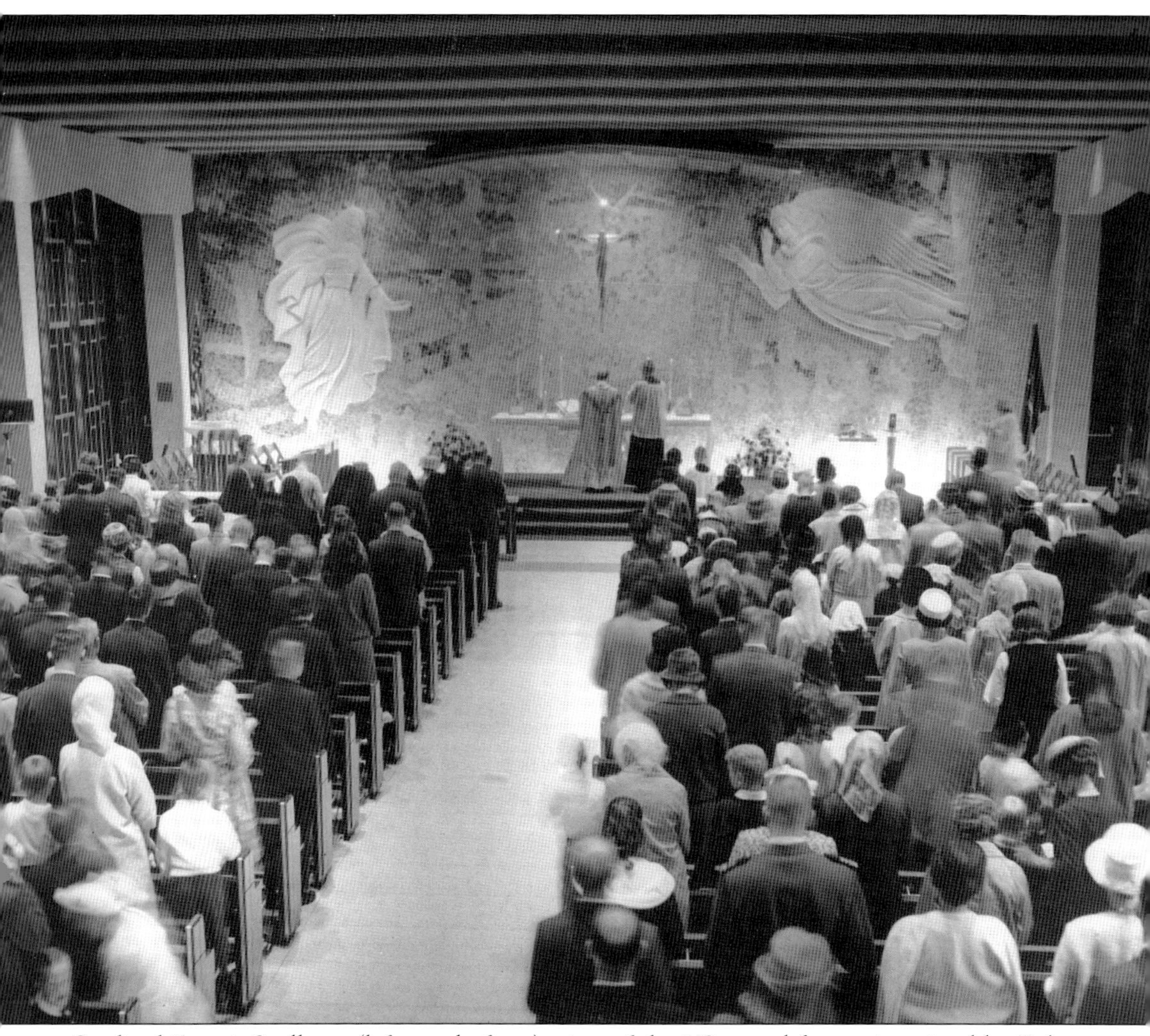

Cardinal Francis Spellman (left on platform), vicar of the US armed forces, is assisted by Col. Constantine Zielinski, the first Catholic chaplain, at the mass attended by cadets and guests on dedication day, September 22, 1963. The focal point of the 500-seat chapel is an enormous Italian glass and marble reredos behind the altar. The bas-relief features marble sculptures of Our Lady of the Skies (the Blessed Mother) on the left; a guardian angel on the right; and a dove symbolizing the Holy Spirit in the center against a blue, turquoise, rose, and gray mosaic background, providing an abstract portrayal of the heavens. The angel and Mary figures each weigh 1.5 tons and are carved from the same marble quarry Michaelangelo used for the Medici Chapel in Florence, Italy.

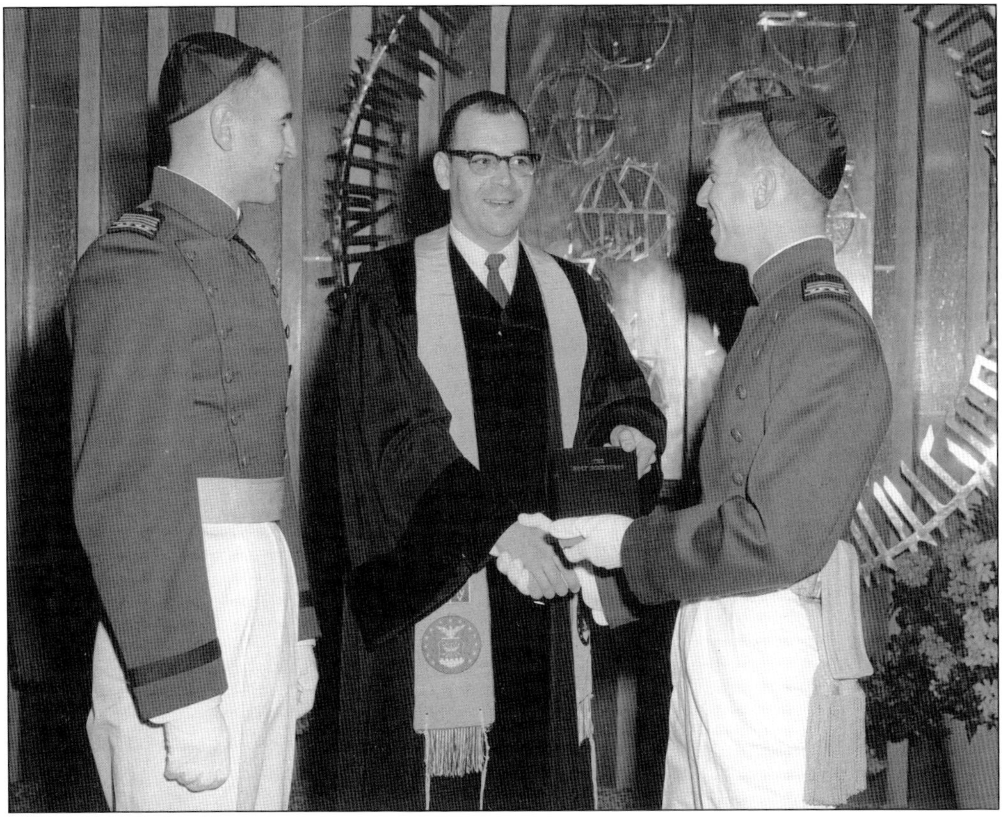

Unique among the three chapels is the circle-within-a-square Jewish Chapel. Designed to evoke the desert tents of the 12 tribes of ancient Israel, the worship space is a freestanding circle of alternating cypress wood uprights and opalescent glass. The square foyer surrounding the worship space is paved with 1,631 pieces of Jerusalem stone donated by the Israeli Air Force. The Jewish Chapel was the first place specifically created for Jewish worship in the US Air Force, and Chaplain Martin L. Labinger, pictured above, was the first Jewish chaplain in a full-time capacity at any US service academy.

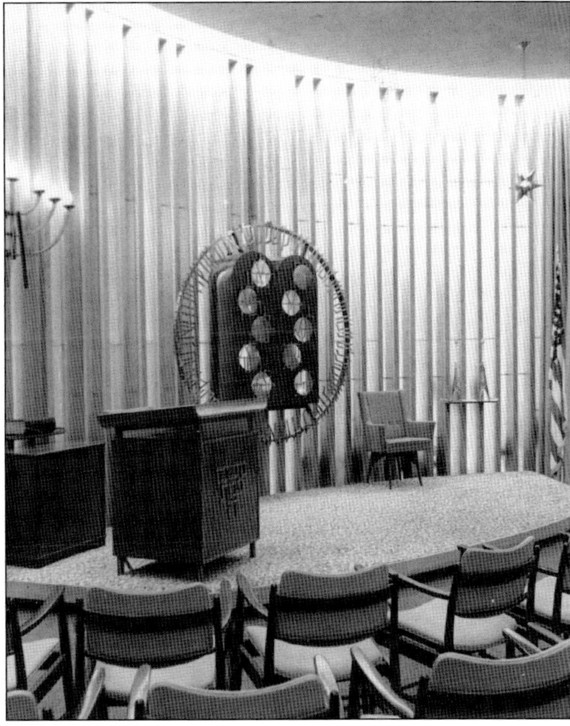

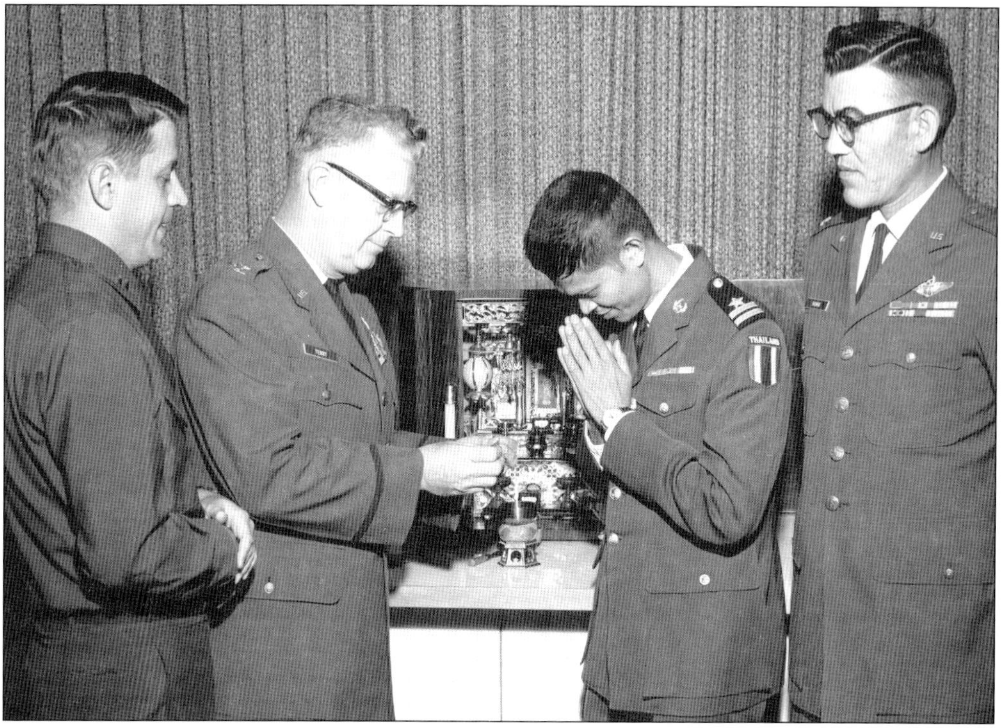

The Cadet Chapel boasts the first Buddhist chapel constructed on a US military base. This 300-square-foot chapel with bamboo floors and Port Orford cedar walls was constructed in the early 2000s. Upon the altar sits a Burmese Buddha figure. Services are conducted in the Zen tradition; however, all forms of Buddhist observance are welcome in the space. Before the Buddhist chapel was constructed, cadets of the Buddhist faith could worship at the Buddhist shrine located in the interfaith chapel. In these 1968 photographs, Capt. Prasit Pongprudhanon of the Thai Air Force Academy presents a Buddhist image for the shrine to Col. Roy M. Terry, Air Force Academy command chaplain.

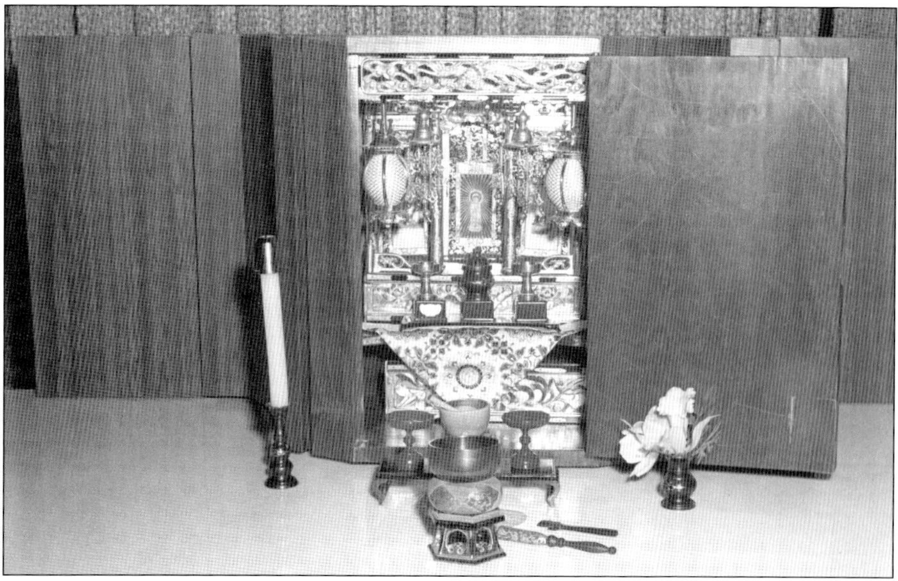

Five

The Academy Mission

The mission of the United States Air Force Academy is "to educate, train and inspire." Lieutenant General Harmon, the academy's first superintendent, wanted the academy to be more than a technical training school merely turning out second lieutenants. He stressed to his staff that the academy should produce second lieutenants with the potential to become general officers. An innovative admissions system, introduced with the selection of the class of 1959, measured a nominated individual's academic excellence and physical aptitude as well as their leadership abilities and provided the foundation for the academy philosophy of producing well-rounded professional officers for the Air Force and the nation. The Air Force Academy's mission is accomplished through a rigorous and comprehensive blend of academic, athletic, and military training programs.

The academic program was designed from the beginning to set itself apart from the traditional military education style of West Point, which rigidly taught the same courses to all cadets and left no room for academic majors or electives. In response to the inflexible education he received at West Point, Dean McDermott introduced an "enrichment program" to offer advanced electives to cadets as well as offering academic majors. Both initiatives have since been adopted by the other US service academies. The strength of the academic program led to the Air Force Academy receiving academic accreditation prior to graduating its first class.

The academy curriculum requires that all students receive physical conditioning through physical education classes and competitive sports. All cadets must participate in intercollegiate, competitive club, or intramural athletics.

The rigorous military training program, executed under the commandant of cadets, occurs throughout a cadet's four years at the academy, including summer programs. Basic cadets learn military customs and courtesies, followership, and servant leadership during an intense six-week period before their freshman academic year. Successive summer programs and academic years are essentially learning laboratories where, given more and more responsibilities, cadets hone their leadership skills to prepare themselves to be successful leaders after graduation as second lieutenants.

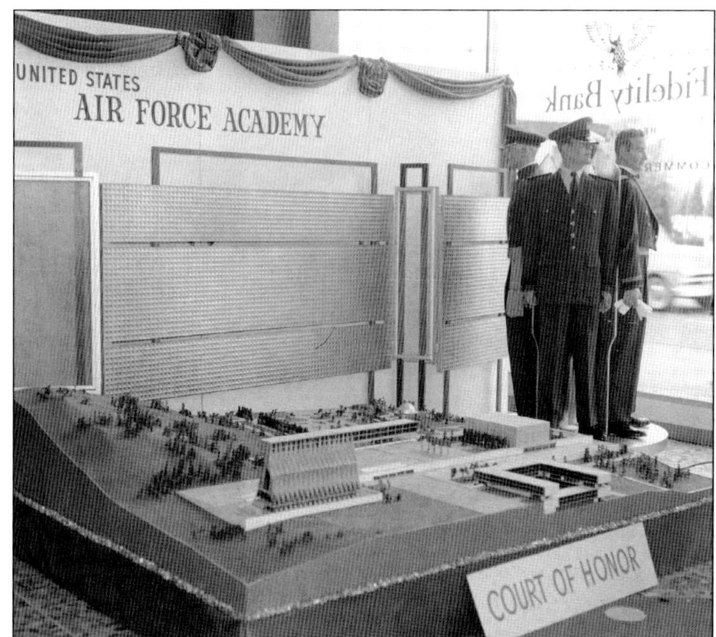

The class of 1959 received over 6,000 applications for appointments; however, the Air Force Academy grew to its original authorized strength slowly to maintain roughly equal class sizes. If all appointing sources filled available slots at the outset, the class of 1959 would have been roughly triple the size of the classes of 1961, 1962, and 1963. Recruitment exhibits appeared in public places across the country, such as this Fidelity Bank window display.

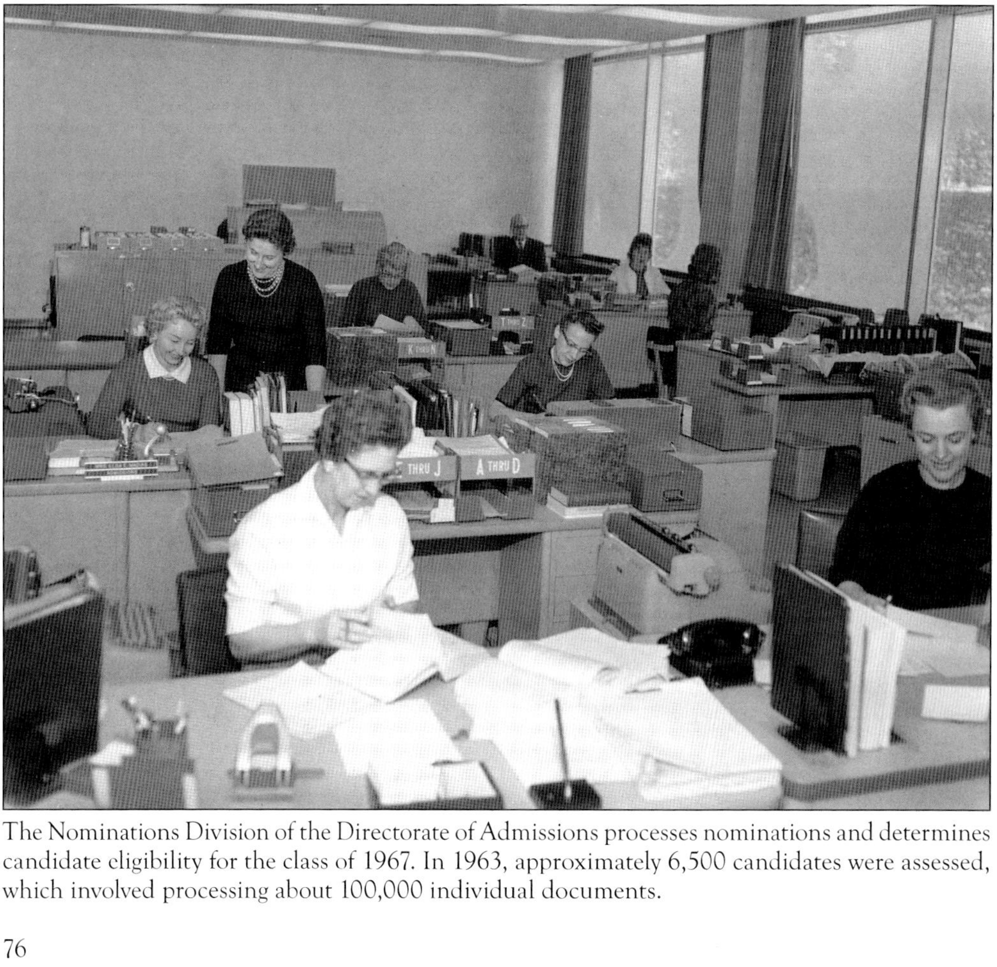

The Nominations Division of the Directorate of Admissions processes nominations and determines candidate eligibility for the class of 1967. In 1963, approximately 6,500 candidates were assessed, which involved processing about 100,000 individual documents.

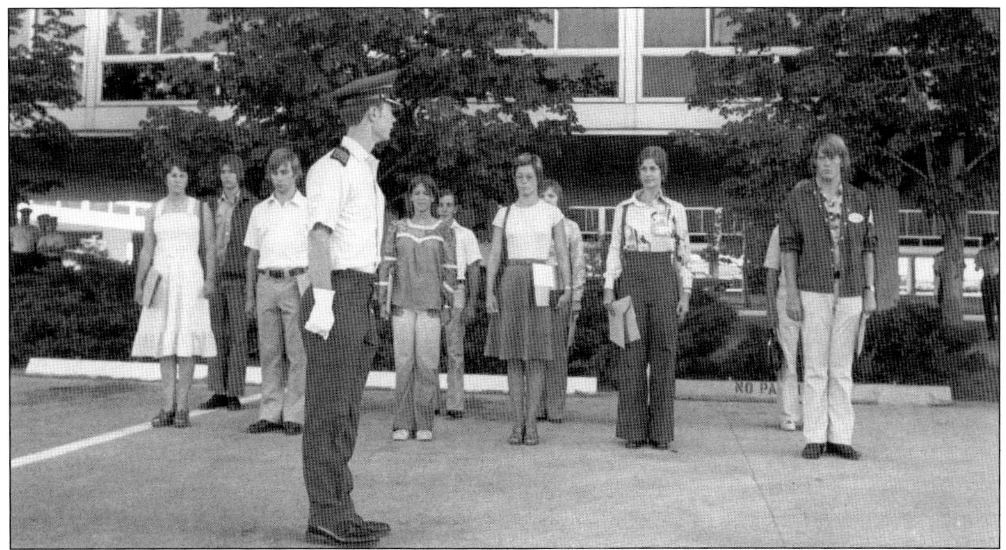

Every June, appointees arrive at the academy to begin Basic Cadet Training, abbreviated as BCT but commonly pronounced "beast." In-processing Day, also known as I-Day, marks the transition from civilian to cadet. Cadet Cadre, consisting of junior and senior cadets, leads BCT, allowing them to hone their leadership abilities. Here, appointees line up on the Footprints at the base of the "Bring Me Men Ramp" in 1976. (Courtesy of Marianne LaRivee, class of 1980.)

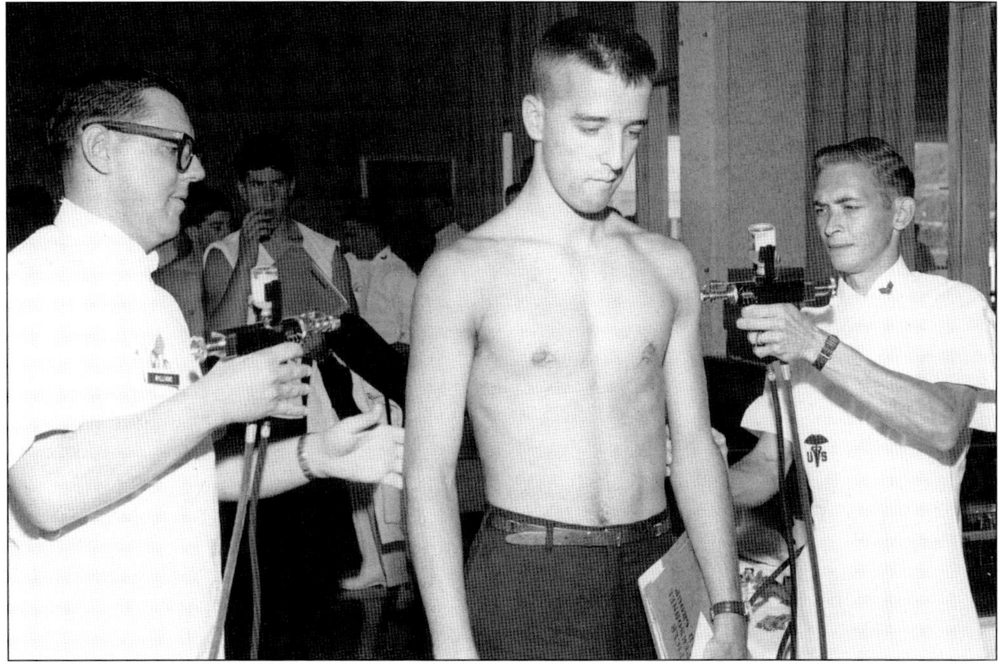

On In-processing Day, appointees maneuver through various records processing stations, receive haircuts and vaccinations (shown here), and are issued uniforms and equipment. They will attend orientation briefings before raising their right hands to take the oath of office, where they officially become basic cadets. Currently, basic cadets are assigned to one of eight summer squadrons for the duration of BCT: Aggressors, Barbarians, Cobras, Demons, Executioners, Flying Tigers, Guts, and Hellcats.

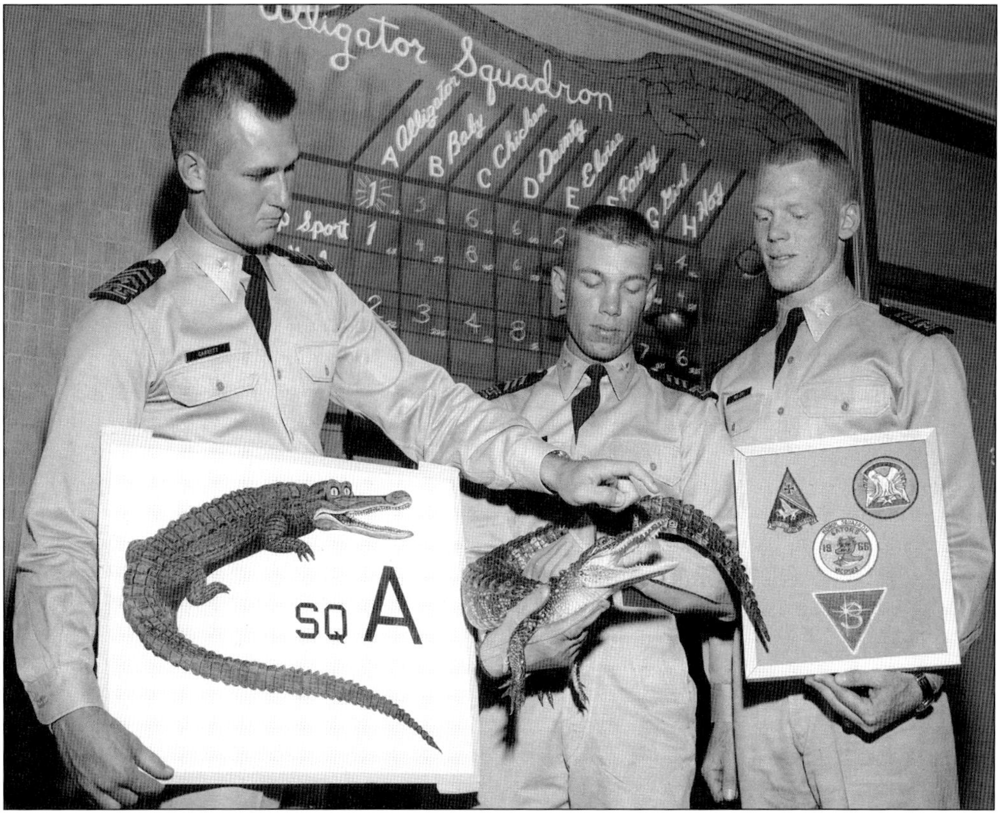

In 1963, cadets proudly display Albert, their toothy squadron mascot. Before becoming the Aggressors, Basic Cadet Squadron A was nicknamed the "Alligators." This three-foot, seven-inch reptile from Louisiana was cared for by, from left to right, Bill Garrett, Dave Williams, and Stephen Muller, all from the class of 1964. Although the class of 1964 hoped the cranky creature would become a mainstay of the squadron, his stint at the academy was brief.

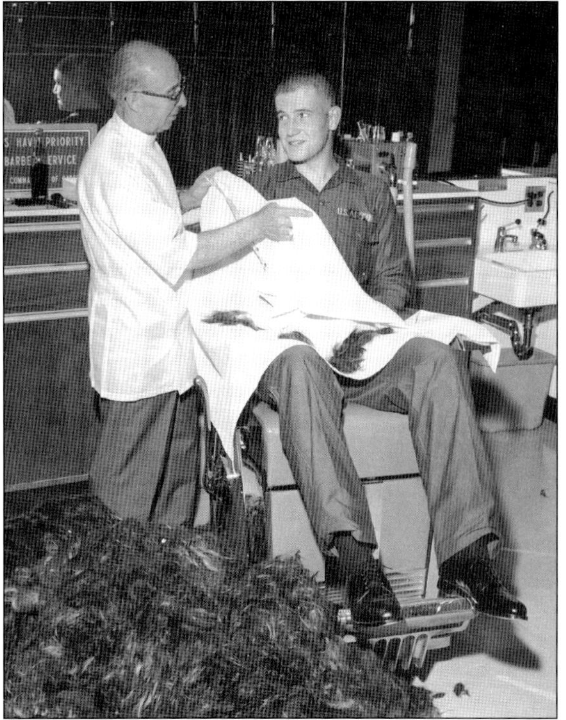

Appointees are encouraged to arrive with their hair meeting traditional military standards, but the barber is never without clients on In-processing Day. As seen here, the class of 1962 lost a collective total of 62 pounds of hair on their first day at the academy. Women can wear their hair in an approved style and are no longer required to cut it short.

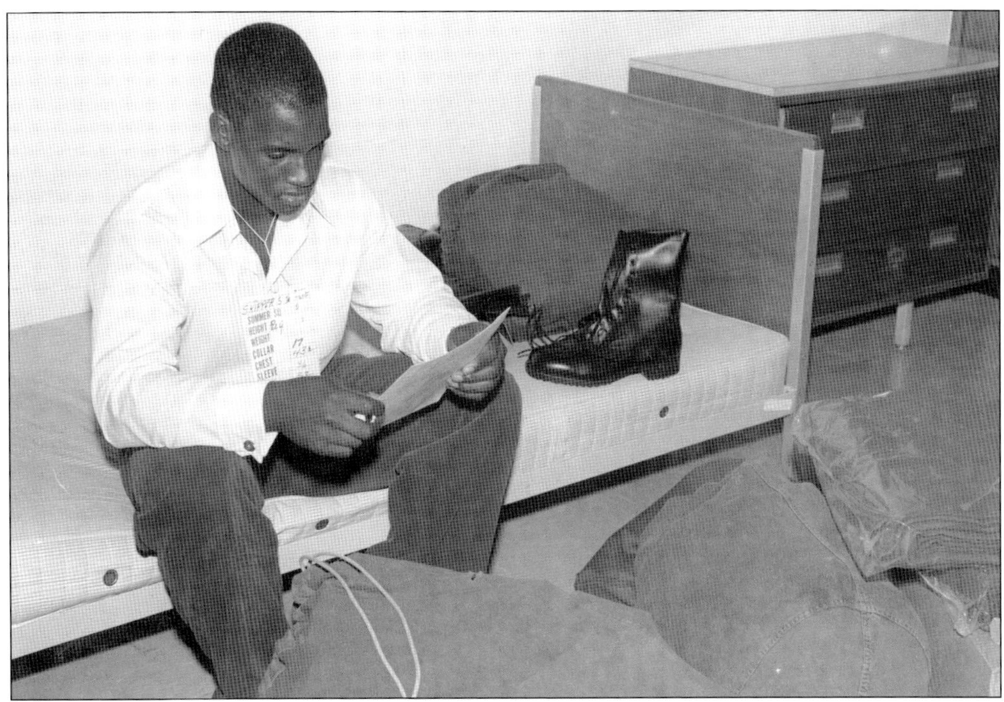

During uniform issue, appointees receive stacks of uniform items according to their measurements identified on the hangtag worn around their necks, as seen here. On In-processing Day, appointees receive their physical training uniforms as well as the operational camouflage pattern uniform, which replaced the airman battle uniform.

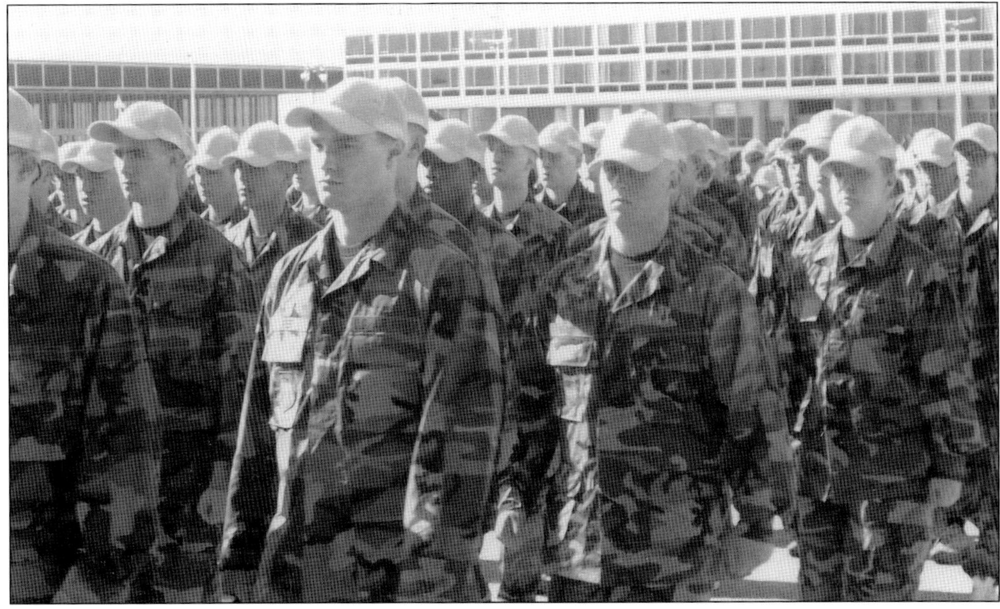

Each basic cadet is issued a baseball cap in their official class color. The class colors rotate between gold, blue, silver, and red. Here, the class of 2011 marches through the Cadet Area during BCT in 2007 wearing their gold class caps. (Photograph by WebGuy; courtesy of the United States Air Force Academy Association of Graduates.)

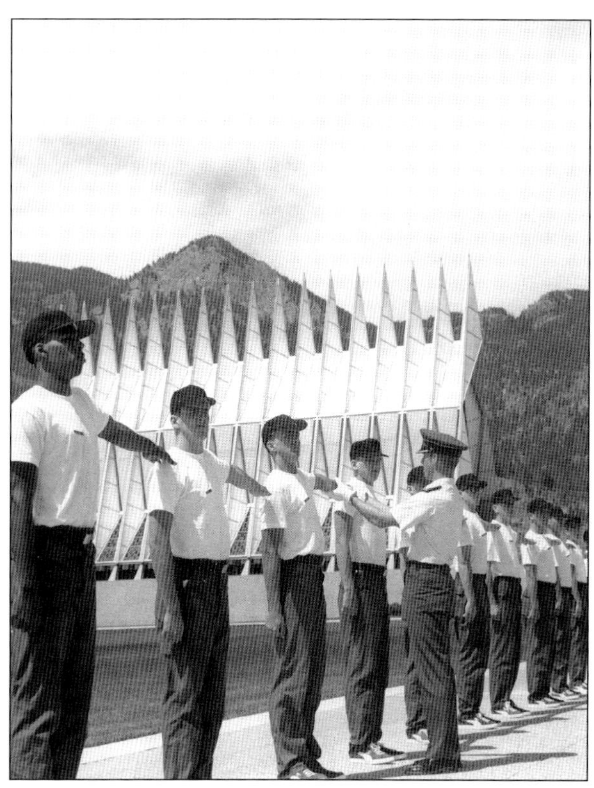

Basic Cadet Training is divided into two sections. The first section is held in the Cadet Area and focuses on Air Force customs, courtesies, regulations, and heritage as well as marching, drill, and living by the Air Force Academy Honor Code. Here, cadets learn "dress right, dress," which establishes proper formation alignment and spacing.

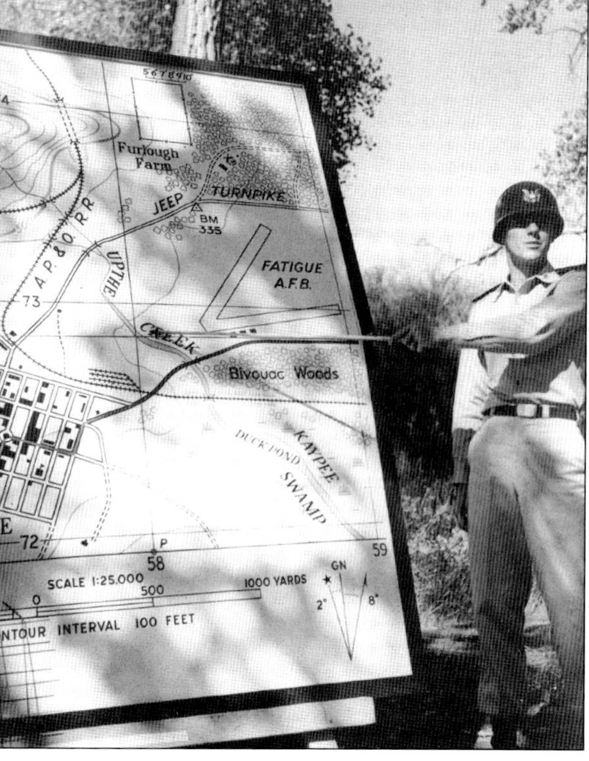

Upperclassmen during the early-summer bivouacs instructed in the use of the lensatic compass, map reading, emergency communications, marksmanship, and defense against chemical, radiological, and bacteriological warfare. Near the end of the summer bivouac, the Air Force put on a display of aerial firepower. Jets flew over the assembled cadets to drop bombs and fire rockets on the bombing range.

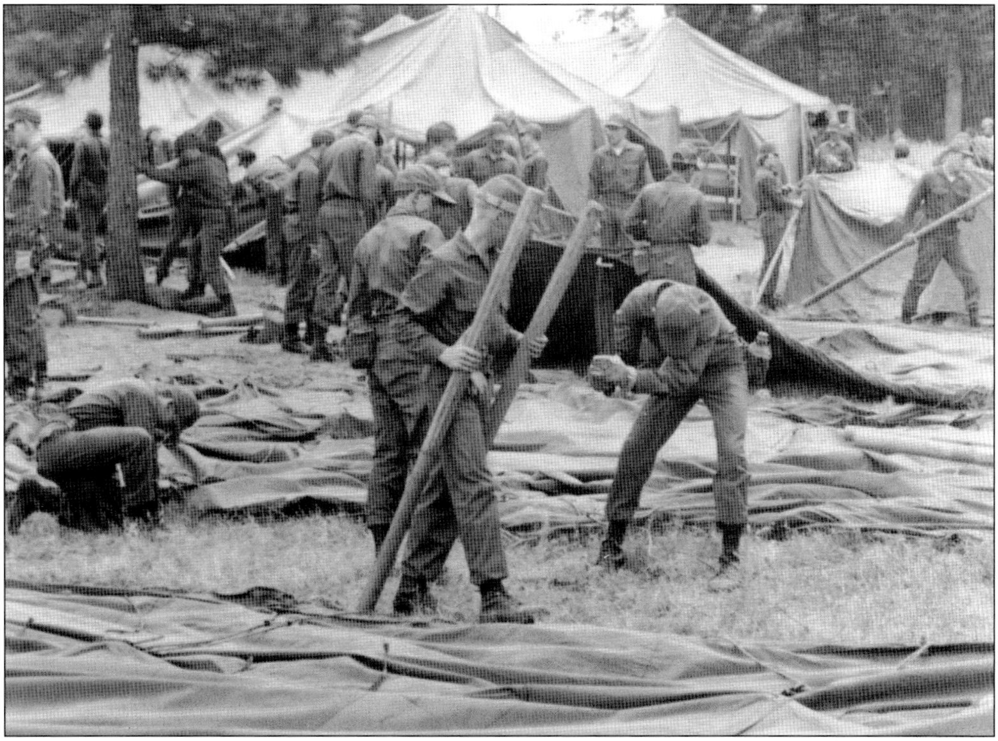

A new training program at Jacks Valley was introduced in 1966 under the leadership of Lt. Gen. Louis T. Seith, commandant of cadets, as a response to the situation in Vietnam. The program required basic cadets to construct an encampment where they would live and work for their two-week stay. Cadets are trained in base defense, counterinsurgency, and reconnaissance patrolling techniques; they are charged with defending their encampment against guerrilla attacks, infiltration, and sabotage staged by upperclassmen. Jacks Valley is the northernmost of the valleys on the academy property and is named after Cleo and Zelda Jack, who owned a 480-acre cattle ranch in the area before the Air Force Academy moved in.

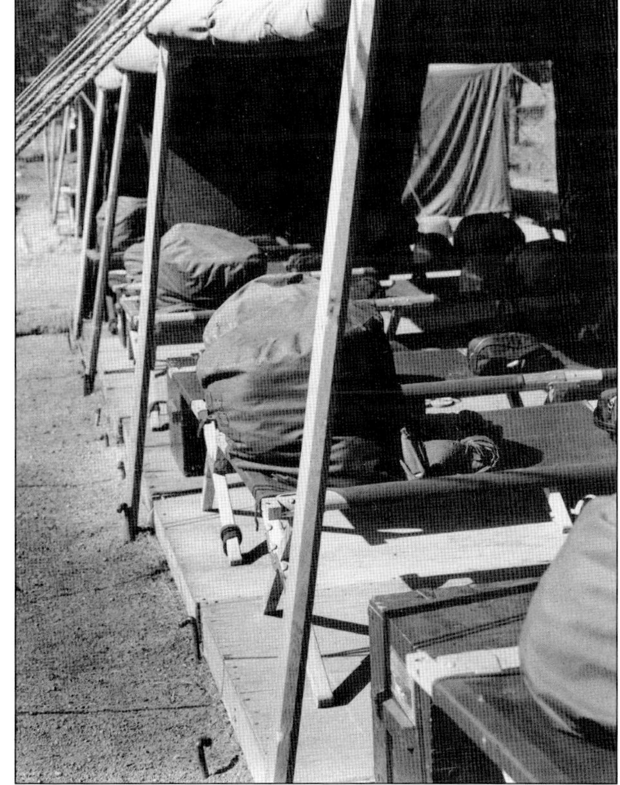

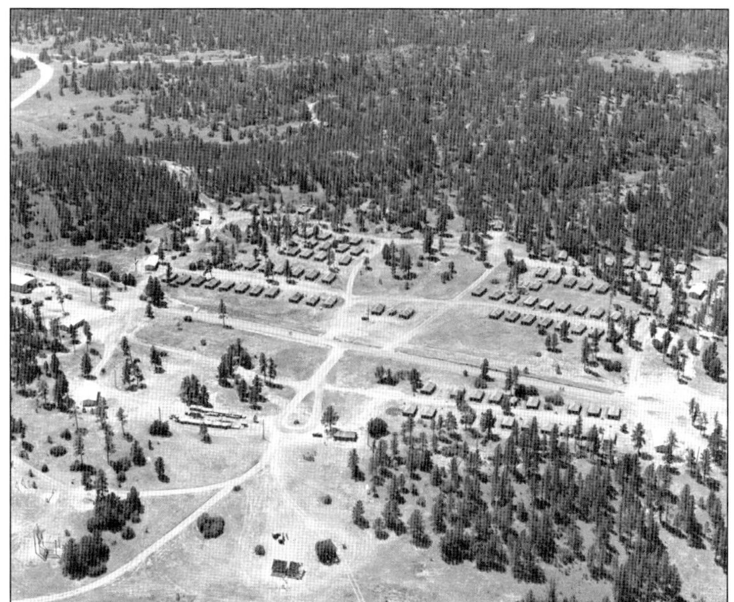

The Jacks Valley Training Complex is located five miles north of the Cadet Area and houses the Basic Cadet Training Encampment. It is also home to the Leadership Reaction, Assault, Confidence, Obstacle, and Land Navigation Courses as well as the Combat Arms Training Compound. Before Jacks Valley was opened, basic cadets completed their field training at Saylor Park, part of the Pike National Forest.

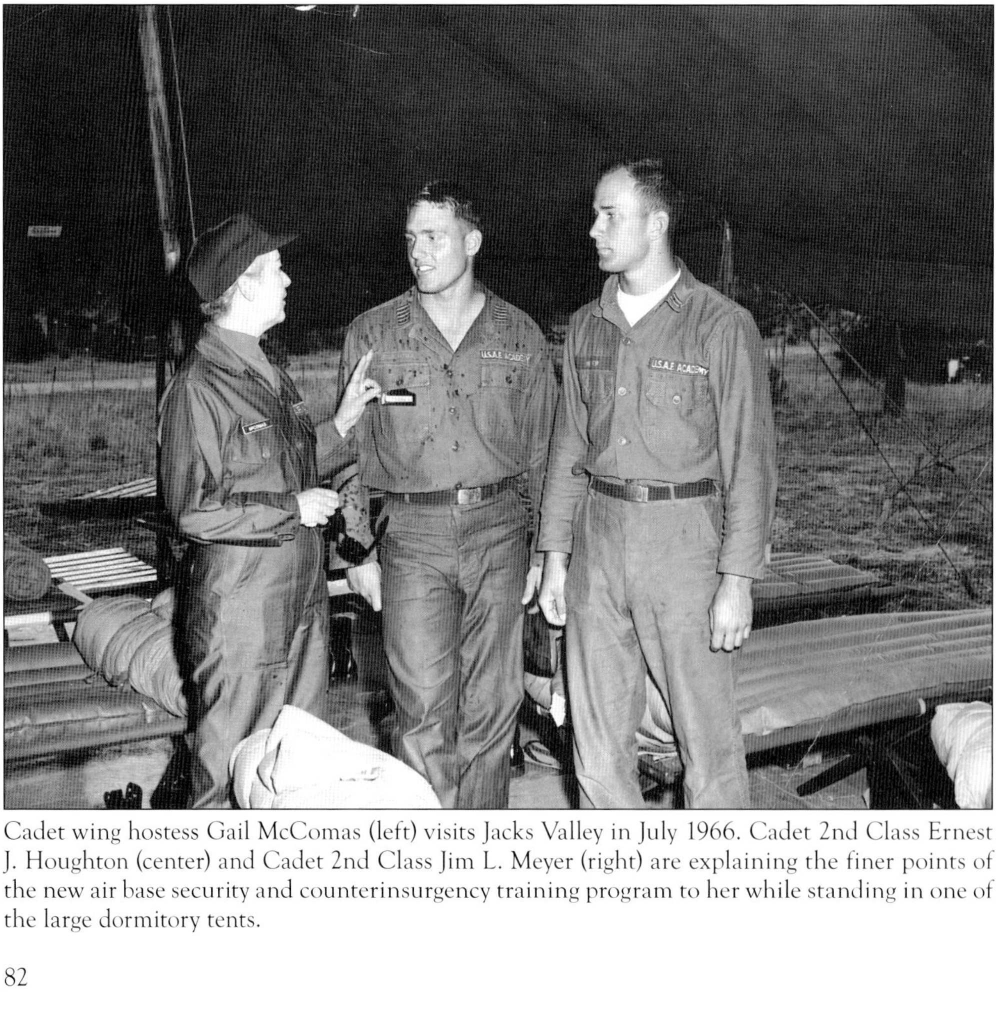

Cadet wing hostess Gail McComas (left) visits Jacks Valley in July 1966. Cadet 2nd Class Ernest J. Houghton (center) and Cadet 2nd Class Jim L. Meyer (right) are explaining the finer points of the new air base security and counterinsurgency training program to her while standing in one of the large dormitory tents.

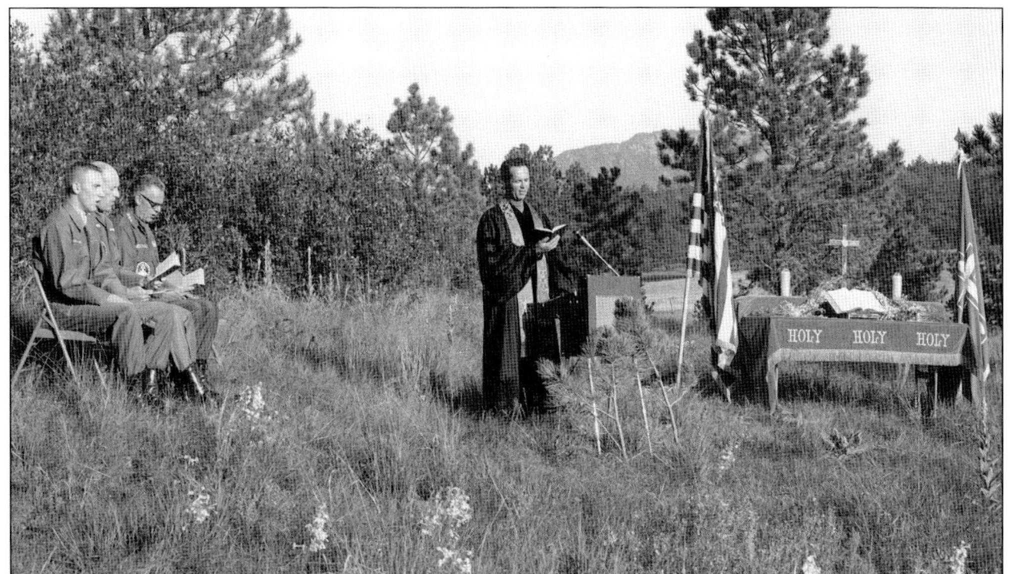

Tending to his flock wherever it may be, Air Force Academy command chaplain Col. Harold D. Shoemakers conducts Sunday services in Jacks Valley during the Air Base Defense Training Program on August 16, 1966. Attending this service are the superintendent, Lt. Gen. Thomas S. Moorman, and the commandant of cadets, Brig. Gen. Louis T. Seith.

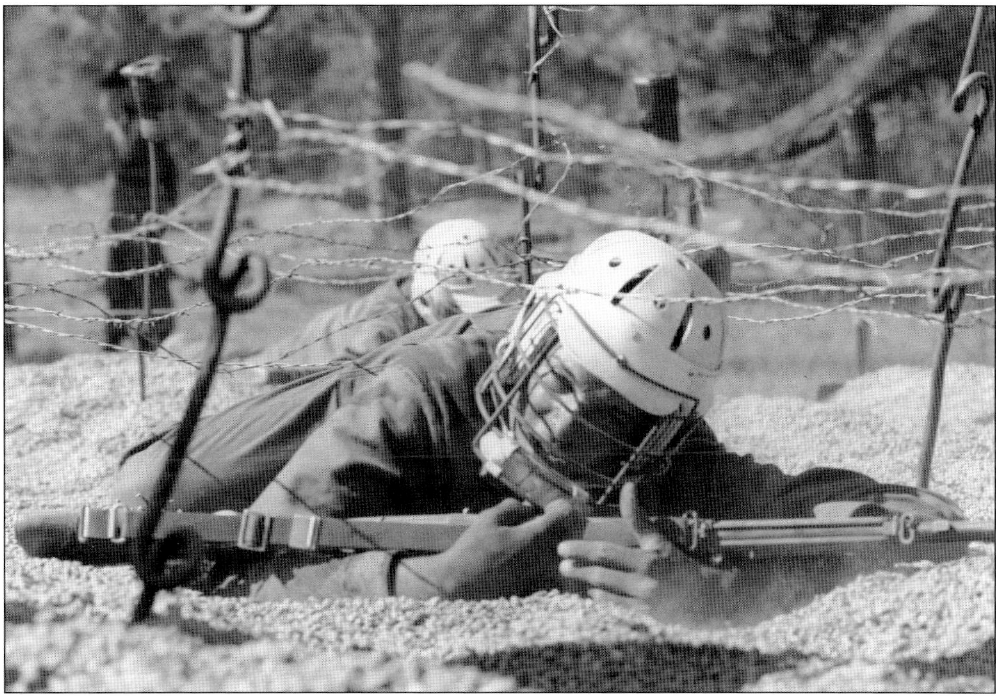

Basic cadets crawl through barbed wire as part of the Assault Course at Jacks Valley. The Assault Course consists of a variety of obstacles designed to replicate combat situations, complete with simulated small-arms fire and artillery explosions. Prior to running the course for a competitive time, cadets are trained in both armed and unarmed combat skills that they will need to exhibit along the way.

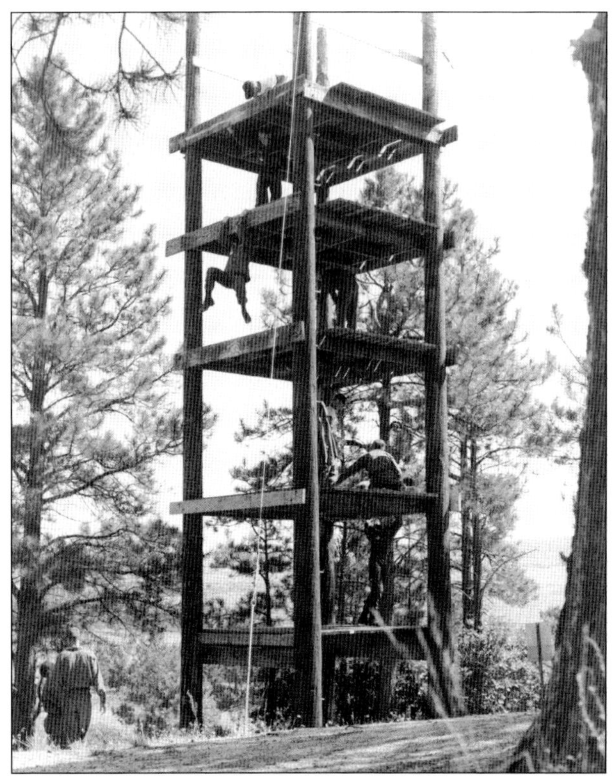

Physical conditioning and confidence building are crucial parts of BCT. At Jacks Valley, the Confidence Course requires cadets to navigate a challenging series of elevated obstacles requiring teamwork, balance, and courage to complete. In this 1975 photograph, basic cadets scale a 40-foot tower known as the "Tiltin' Hilton." The tower was modified in 2009 to include safety nets. As of 2022, the obstacle is no longer in use.

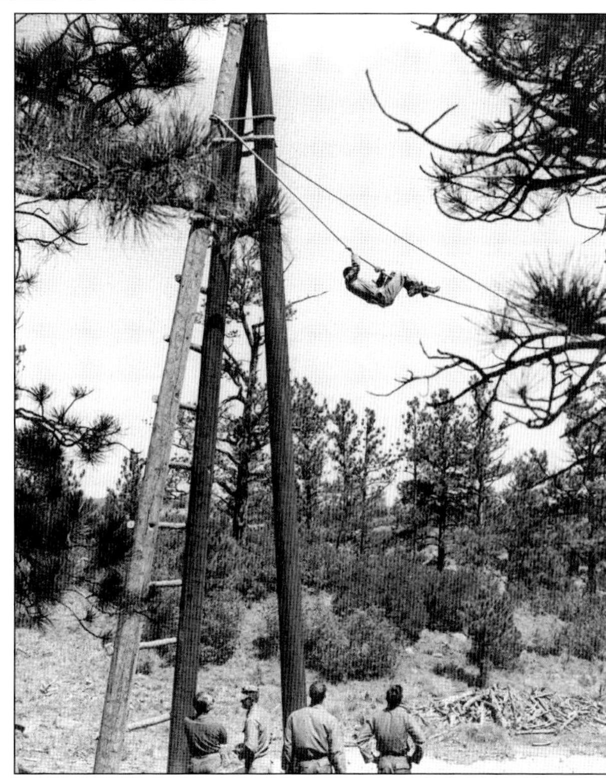

The "Slide for Life" was one of the early obstacles on the Confidence Course. Like the "Tiltin' Hilton," this obstacle is no longer in use.

Cadet 1st Class Edward Rice, class of 1978, grabs a plate during the midday meal while serving as Cadet Cadre during basic training. During the field training portion of BCT, basic cadets are offered 4,000–4,500 calories per day due to the intense physical requirements demanded and eat their meals in a Quonset hut nicknamed "Mitch's" after the dining hall in the Cadet Area.

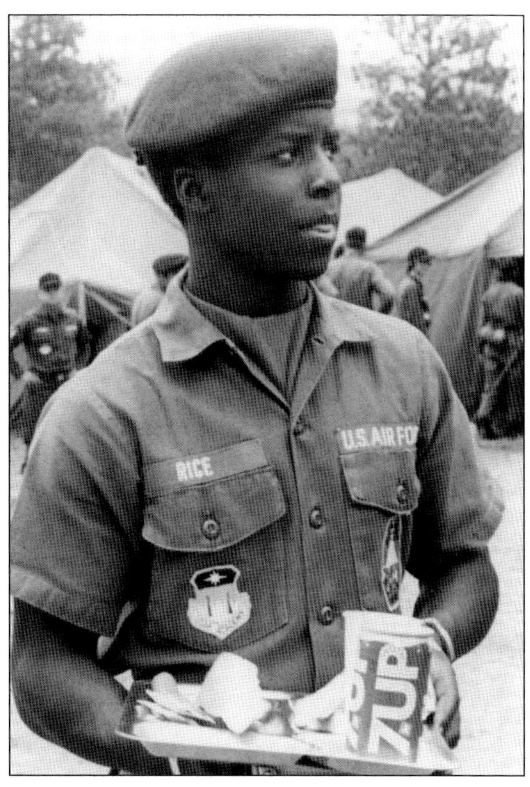

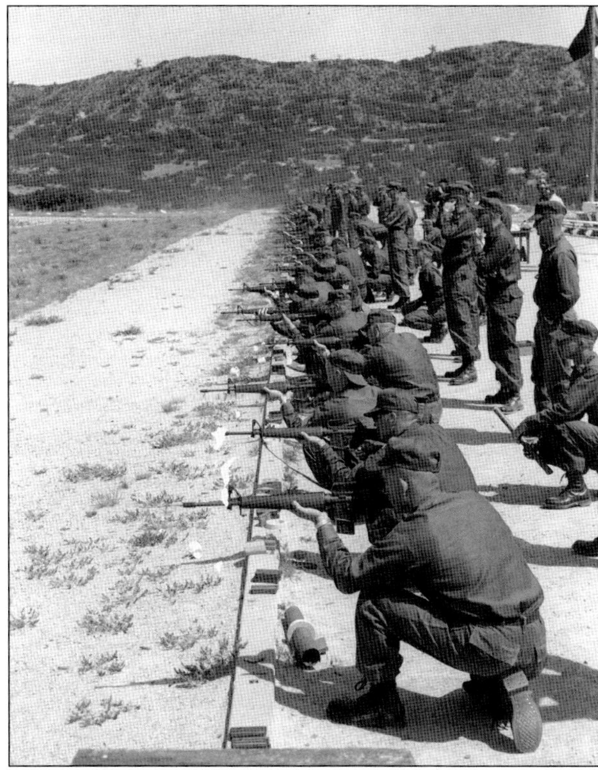

Weapons training is a fundamental component of the Basic Cadet Training program. Basic cadets are schooled in the use of the M-16 rifle, shown here, as well as the .38-caliber pistol. The M-16 was introduced in the late 1960s to replace the older M-1.

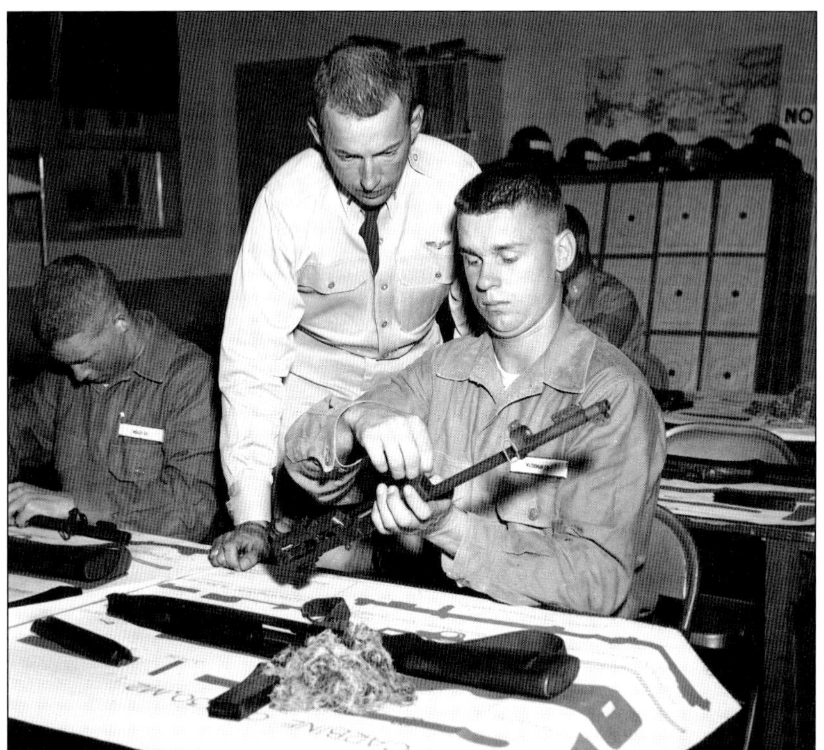

Here, a cadet in the class of 1959 assembles an M-2 carbine under the watchful eye of an ATO. Cadets receive combat arms training and are able to practice firing rifles, machine guns, carbines, and pistols.

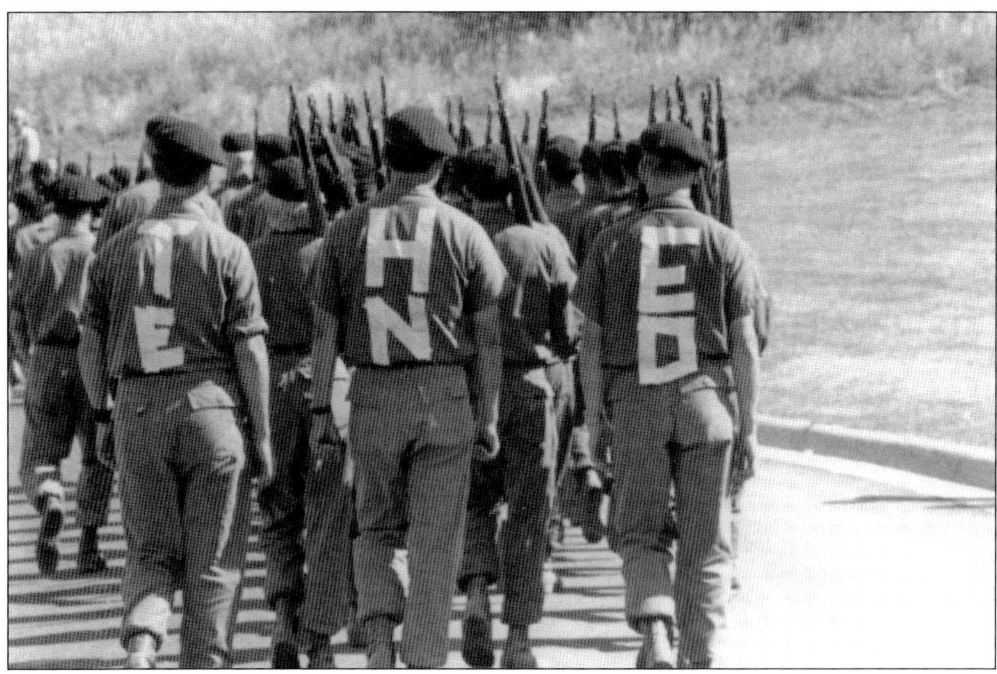

Cadet Cadre brings up the rear of the formation during the march back from Jacks Valley. Graduates from earlier classes often meet the cadets at Jacks Valley and march with them back to the Cadet Area, a tradition that highlights the bond of the Long Blue Line, the graduate community that the basics will join after their four years at the academy are complete.

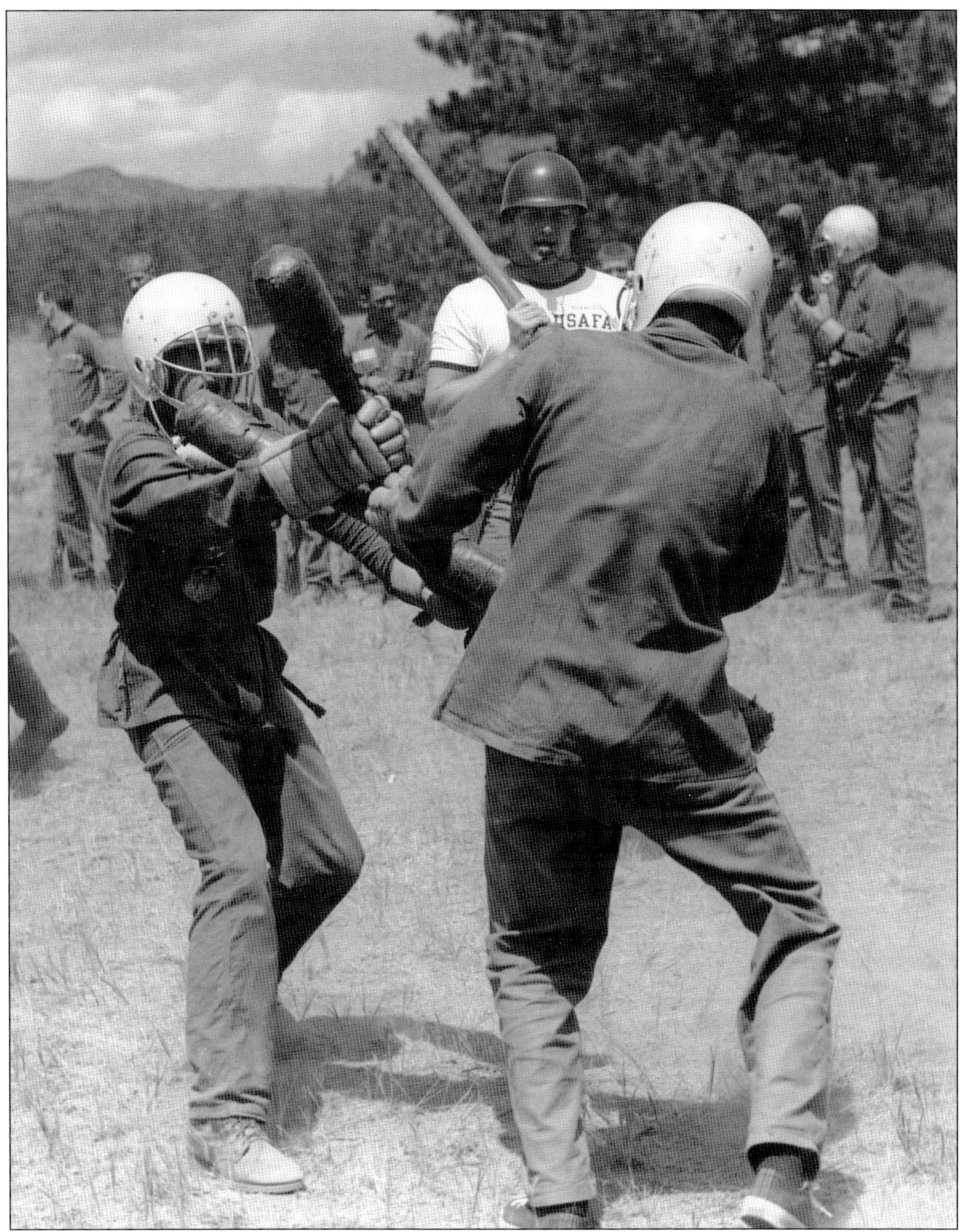

Two basic cadets engage in combat with pugil sticks, four-foot-long military training weapons with padded ends. Pugil sticks have been used since the 1940s for hand-to-hand combat training by the US Army and replaced bayonet training at the Air Force Academy. At Jacks Valley, cadets battle their squadron mates as part of the Assault Course. Near the end of the two-week encampment, each basic cadet squadron sends its top male and female cadets to the Big Bad Basic Tournament, a fierce one-on-one combat event where each pugilist seeks the title of "Big Bad Basic." Winners are named in three divisions: men's heavyweight, men's lightweight, and women's overall.

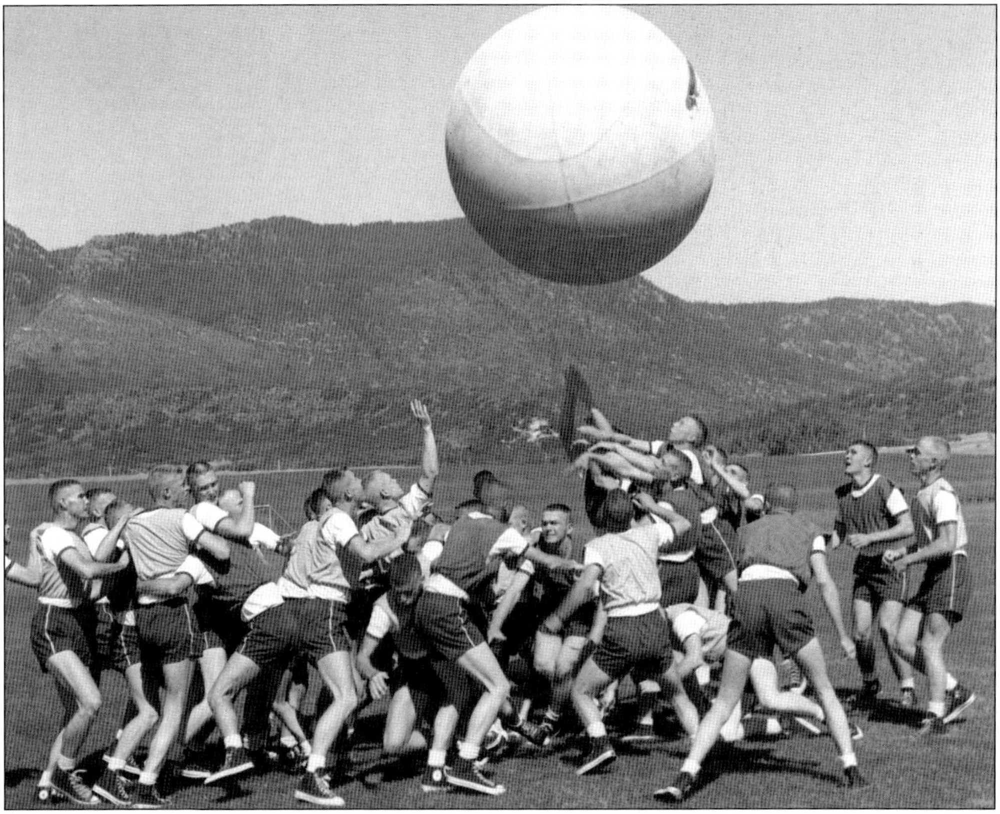

In the past, cadets concluded BCT with a field day competition between basic cadet squadrons. Push-ball, played with 30 cadets on each side, was a highlight for the 1,000 spectators who came to watch the games in 1963. The objective was to get the ball over the enemy's goal line. Body blocks, shoulder blocks, and tackling were illegal; however, the game was aggressive, exhausting, and allowed for no time-outs.

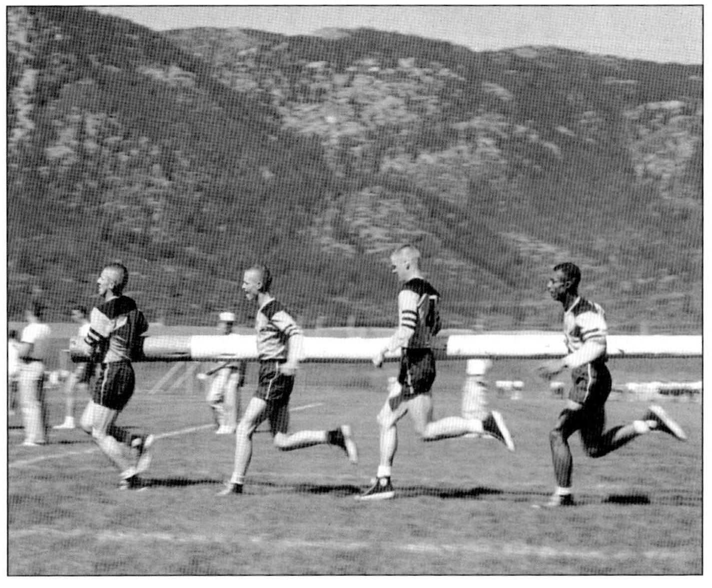

Dashing for the finish line in the log relay, these cadets are carrying a 300-pound, 30-foot ponderosa pine log from the Air Force Academy grounds. Other events such as relays, a distance run, a pentathlon, a wall climb, an obstacle course, log rolling, and tug-of-war gave cadets opportunities to bring victory to their squadron during the field day on August 6, 1965.

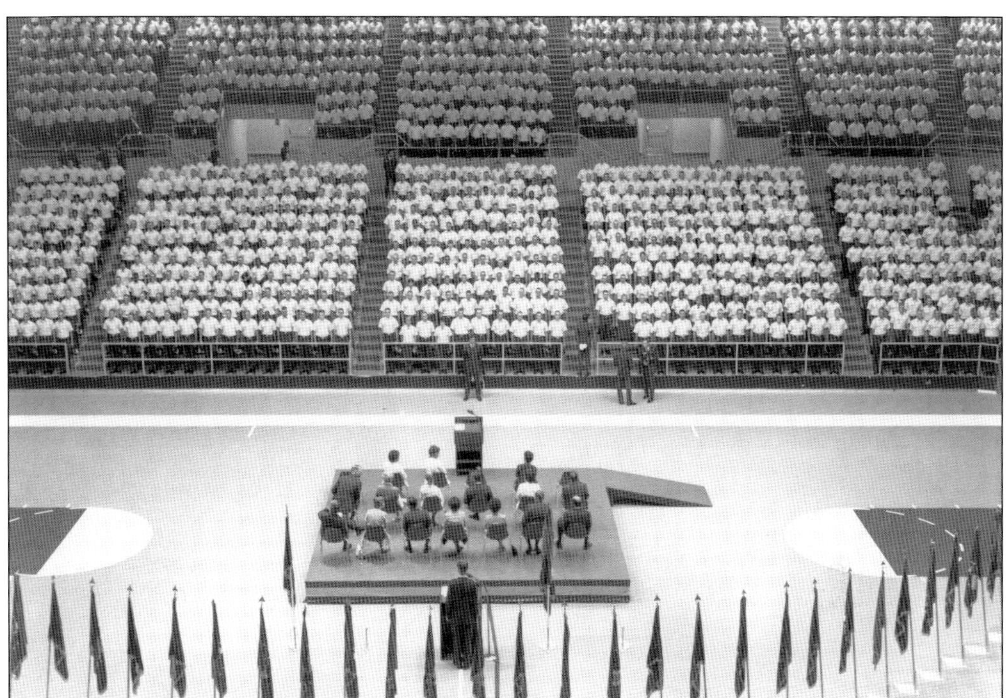

In this image, basic cadets take the Honor Oath during an Acceptance Day ceremony in Clune Arena, formally accepting the Air Force Academy Honor Code. Adopted in 1984, the oath states: "We will not lie, steal, or cheat, nor tolerate anyone who does. Furthermore, I resolve to do my duty and to live honorably, (so help me God)." Administered by the Cadet Wing, the Air Force Academy Honor Code reflects each cadet's commitment to honor.

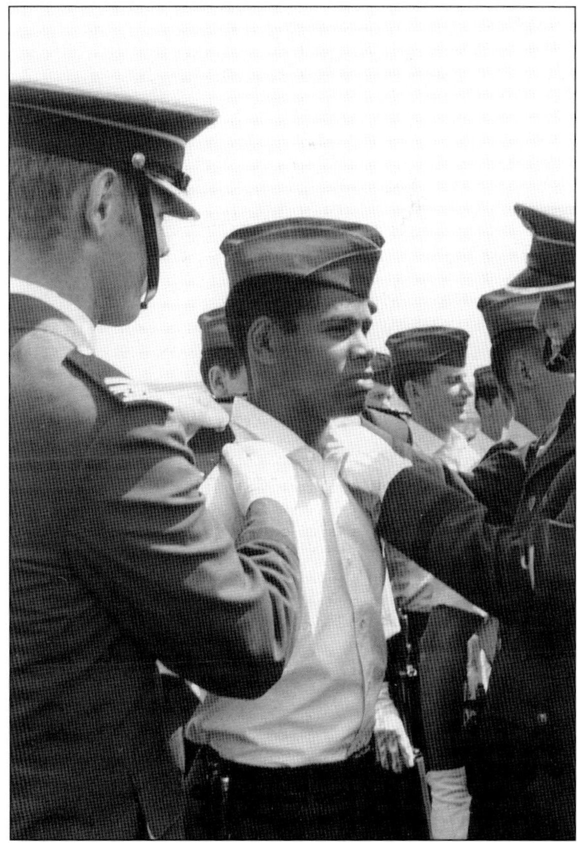

Upperclassmen place fourth-class shoulder boards on a newly accepted member of the Cadet Wing following the Acceptance Day Parade in 1978. Acceptance Day celebrates not only the successful completion of Basic Cadet Training but also the beginning of the academic year. The ceremony is a significant occasion and represents the first opportunity for cadets to see their families since In-processing Day.

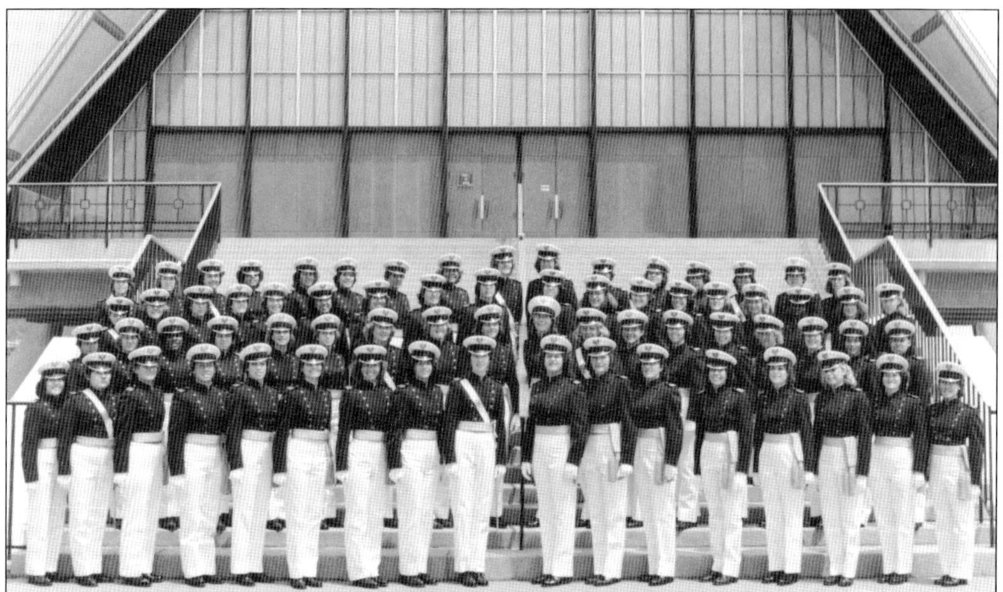

The most significant change at the Air Force Academy came with Pres. Gerald Ford's signing of Public Law 94-106 on October 7, 1975, opening US service academies to women. Members of the class of 1980, above, made history when they arrived at the base of the "Bring Me Men Ramp" to begin BCT. Over 1,000 women received nominations, but only 157 were selected to join the more than 1,400 men in the inaugural coed class. Despite facing challenges and some resistance, the women exceeded the expectations of academy leadership and earned their place. Ninety-seven of these women graduated with their class, more than any other service academy that year, and one became the Air Force's first female four-star general. The photograph below, taken by T.Sgt. Herman J. Kokojan, won the Military Picture of the Year Competition in 1976. (Below, courtesy of Marianne LaRivee, class of 1980.)

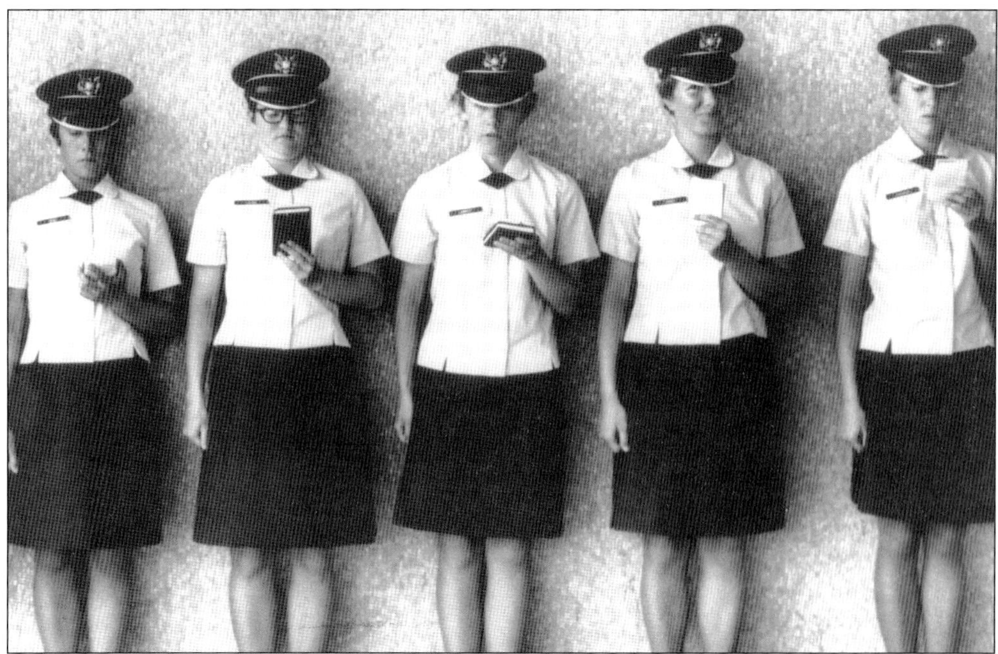

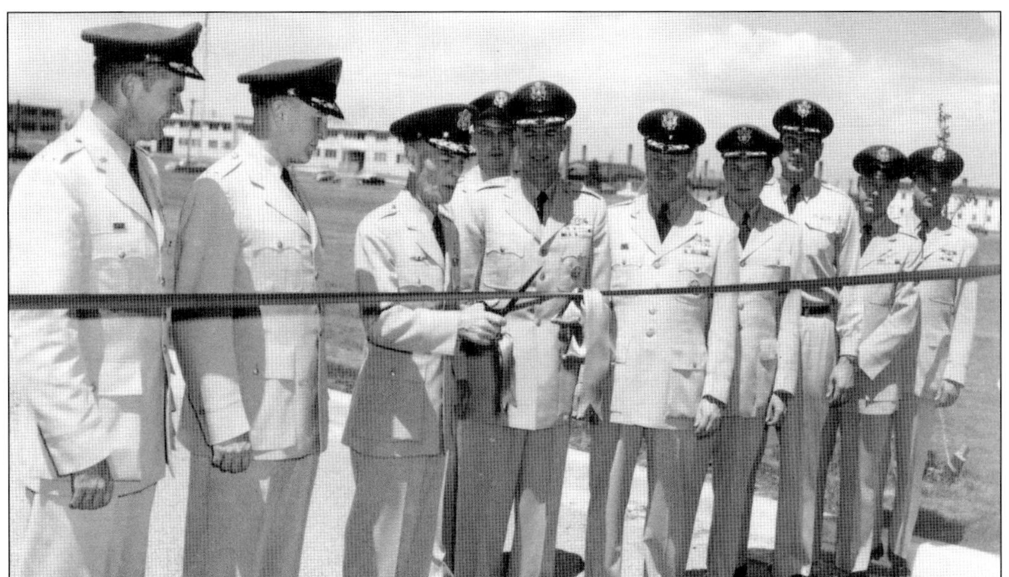

In 1955, Lieutenant General Harmon, surrounded by members of the first faculty, cut the ceremonial ribbon signifying the opening of the Air Force Academy's first academic year. The faculty at the academy is composed primarily of uniformed officers. The integration of civilians into the faculty began in the early 1990s, and they have since grown to roughly 30 percent of the faculty.

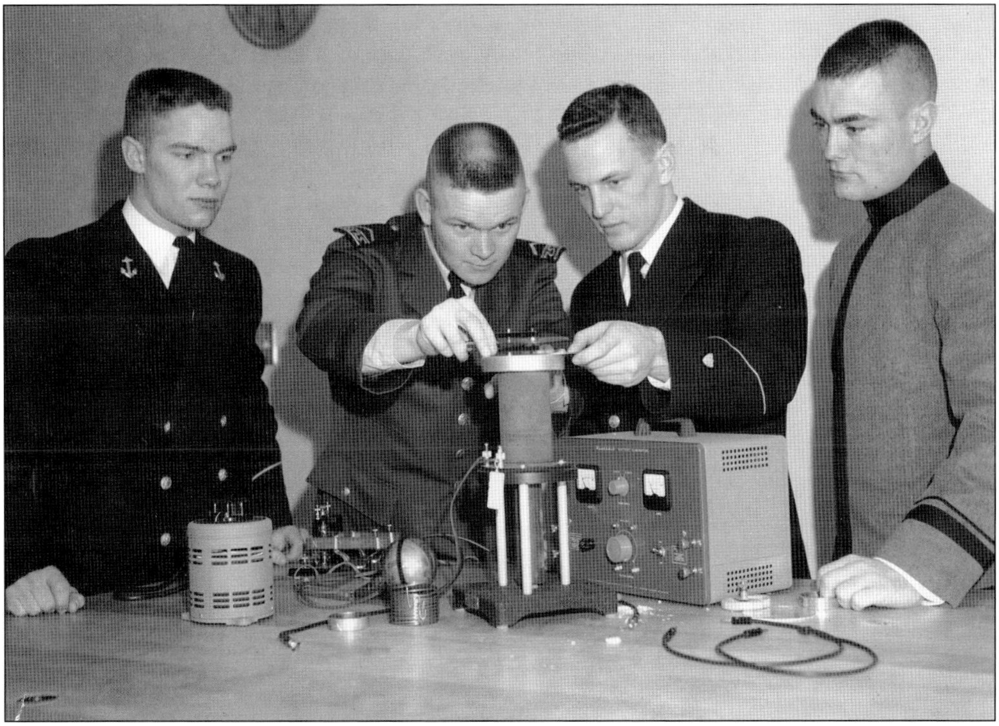

US Military Academy and Coast Guard Academy cadets and a Naval Academy midshipman work on an experiment in magnetism with an Air Force Academy cadet in the chemistry lab at Lowry Air Force Base. The visiting cadets were part of the first exchange program between the four institutions in 1960. Air Force cadets now can complete semester-long exchanges with other service academies.

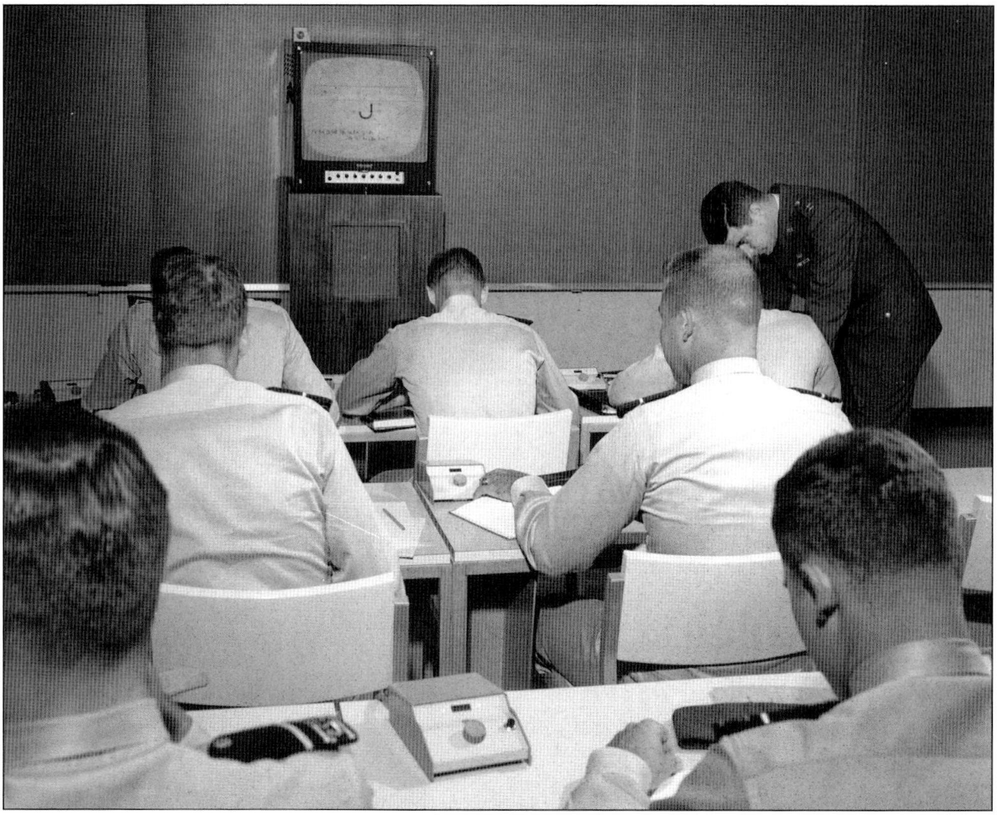

During the 1960s, the Air Force Academy enhanced classroom instruction by implementing a closed-circuit television system. Educational programs could be broadcast from the television studio and distribution center located in Fairchild Hall to 335 classrooms over 12 channels. Here, Capt. John Baldner, an assistant professor in the Department of Aeronautics, teaches in a television-equipped classroom where cadets answer questions about diagrams displayed on the monitor via response stations at each desk.

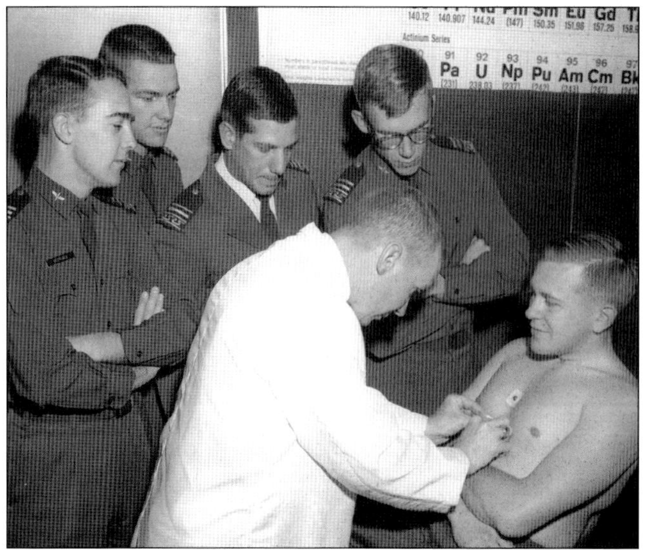

The Air Force Academy offers cadet instruction and research opportunities in multiple fields. In a unique bioengineering class, an interdisciplinary course offered by the Department of Life Sciences and the Department of Electrical Engineering, cadets researched peripheral circulation problems experienced by astronauts during space flight. In this 1966 photograph, electrocardiograph electrodes are attached to Cadet 1st Class Robert Mestemaker to gather crucial data as part of a physiological monitoring laboratory for the course.

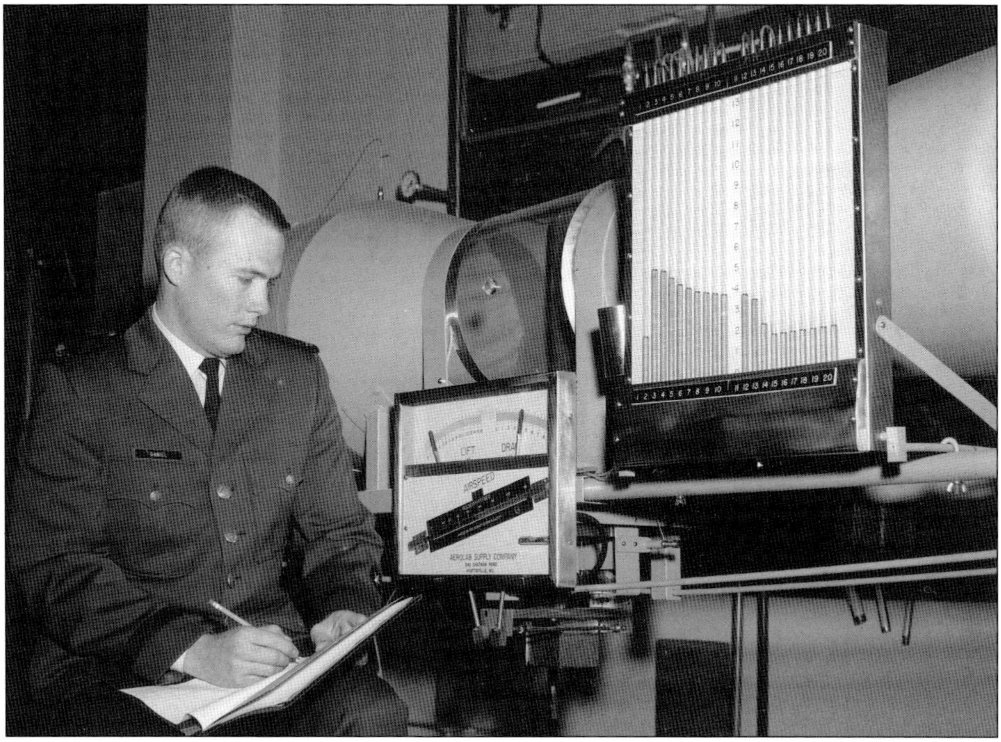

Seen here, Cadet Edward Daniel, class of 1967, notes lift and drag readings on a wind tunnel machine in the Aeronautics Laboratory. Wind tunnels are used to study the aerodynamic flow of air as it moves over a model placed inside the machine. Decades later, cadet research has expanded, utilizing the Air Force Academy's world-class wind tunnels to conduct innovative research on aircraft and weapon models at transonic and hypersonic speeds.

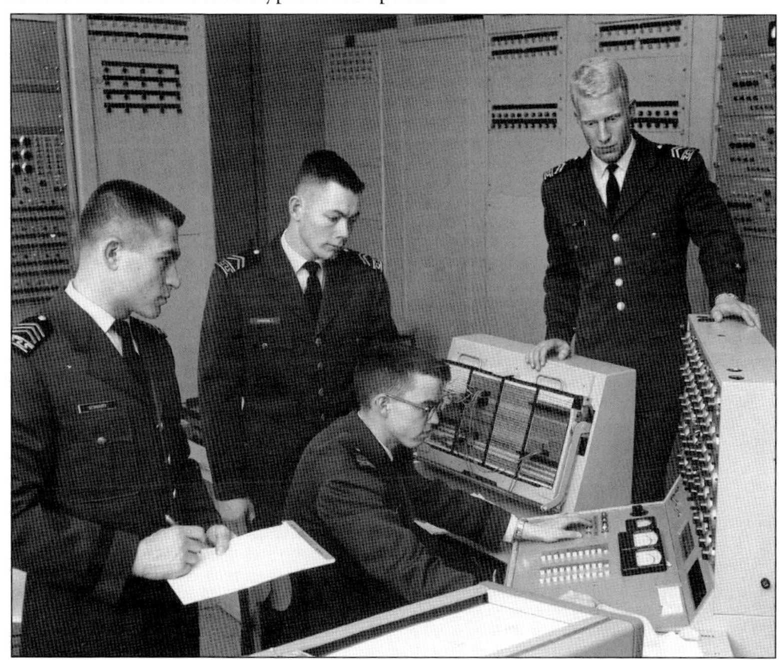

Three members of the class of 1962 watch fellow cadet Robert Harrison Weight operating an analog computer. Demonstrations of analog computer operations were offered to the public in Fairchild Hall during the open house on September 22, 1962.

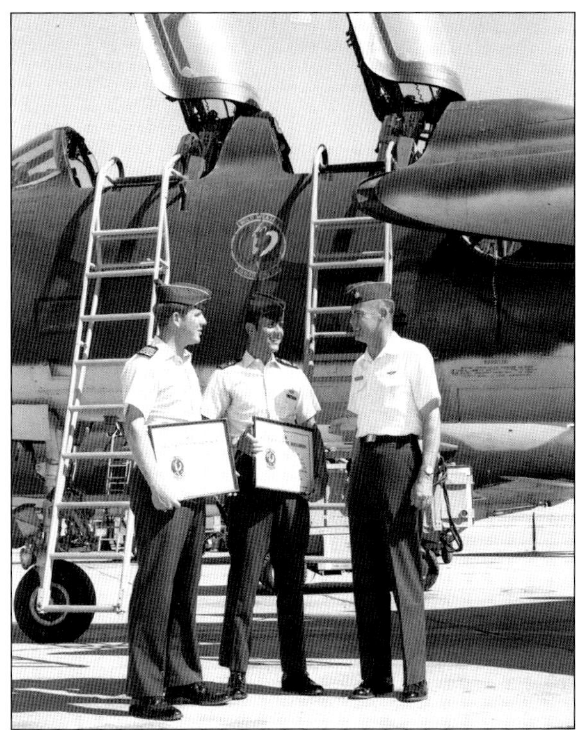

The Operation Third Lieutenant program, introduced in the late 1950s, allowed cadets to experience temporary duty (TDY) at host units in the Air Force's combat commands: Strategic Air Command, Tactical Air Command, and Air Defense Command. Cadets William Looney (left) and Larry Faher (center) were made honorary Wild Weasels upon completing their TDY with the 66th Fighter Weapons Squadron at Nellis Air Force Base in the summer of 1971.

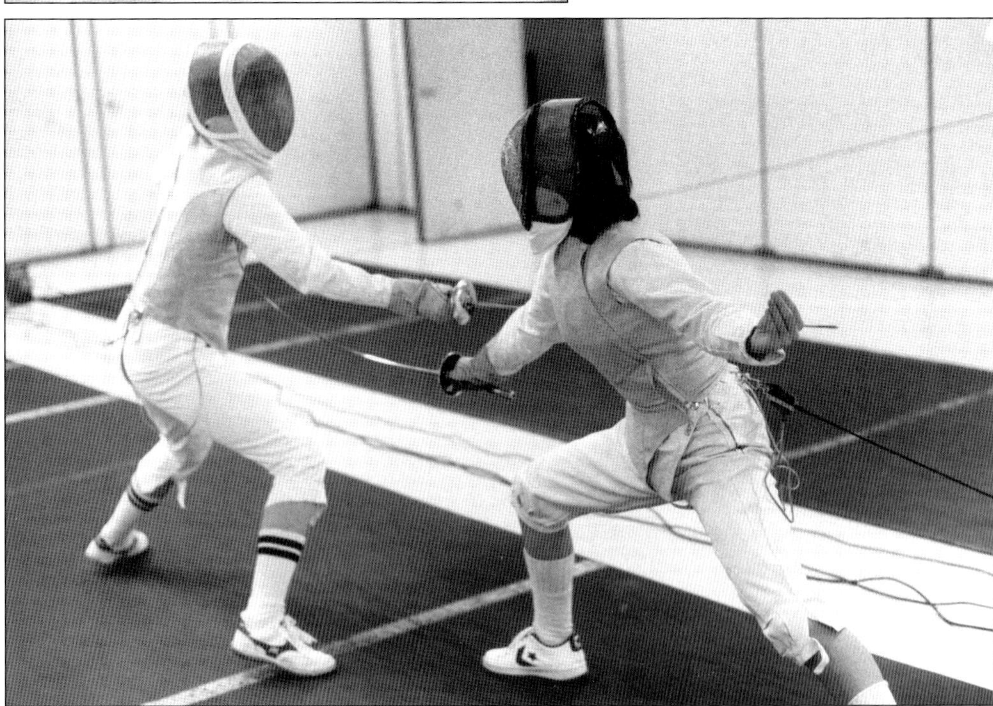

The physical education curriculum was adjusted with the entrance of women into the Air Force Academy in 1976 but was organized to match the men's program as much as possible. For some physical education courses, the grading curve varied to reflect effort rather than strength for female cadets. Fencing was taken in place of boxing for female cadets.

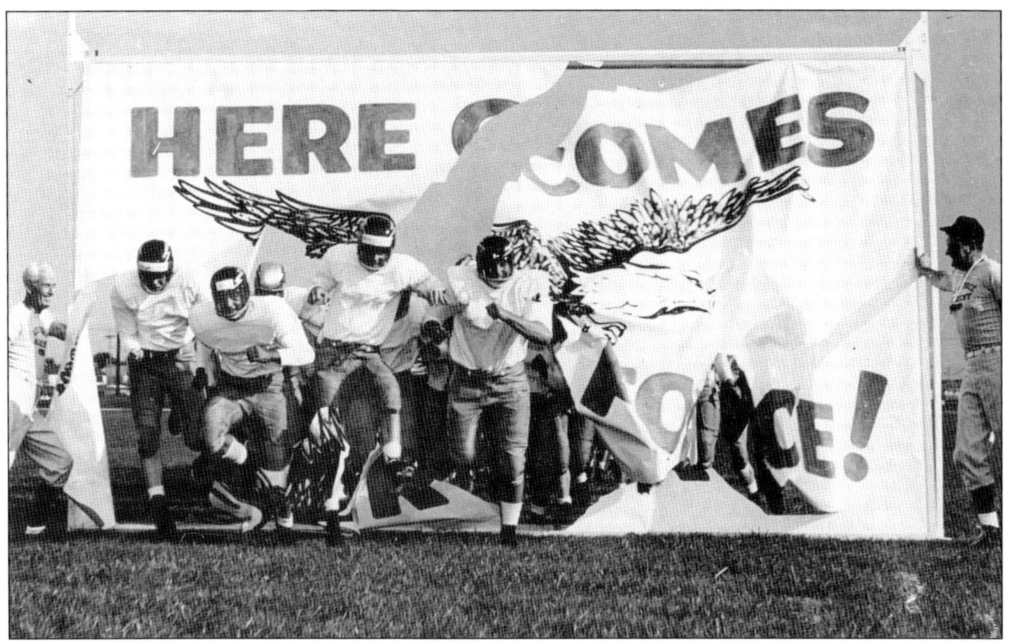

Air Force Academy director of athletics Col. Robert V. Whitlow (right) and Lawrence T. "Buck" Shaw (left), the team's civilian consultant, stand clear of a charging band of cadets during tryouts for the first football team on September 7, 1955.

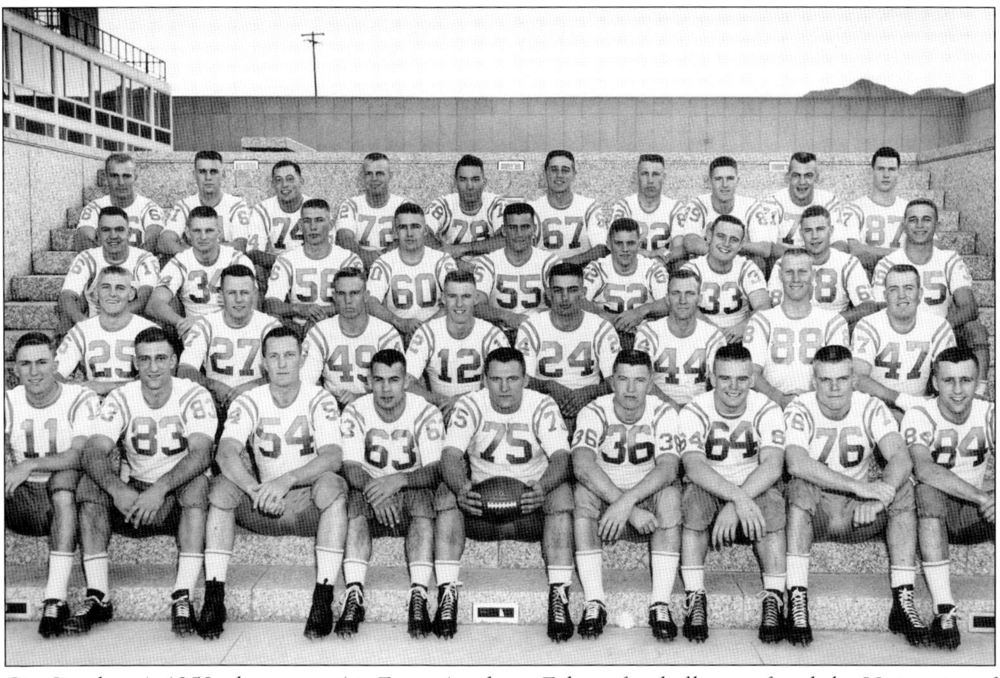

On October 4, 1958, the young Air Force Academy Falcon football team faced the University of Iowa Hawkeyes, the reigning champions of the Big Ten Conference, a landmark game in Air Force Academy football history. The Falcons held their own, ending the game in a 13-13 tie. The 1958 Falcons, pictured here, went on to have an undefeated season, culminating in an invitation to the Cotton Bowl, ending in a 0-0 tie.

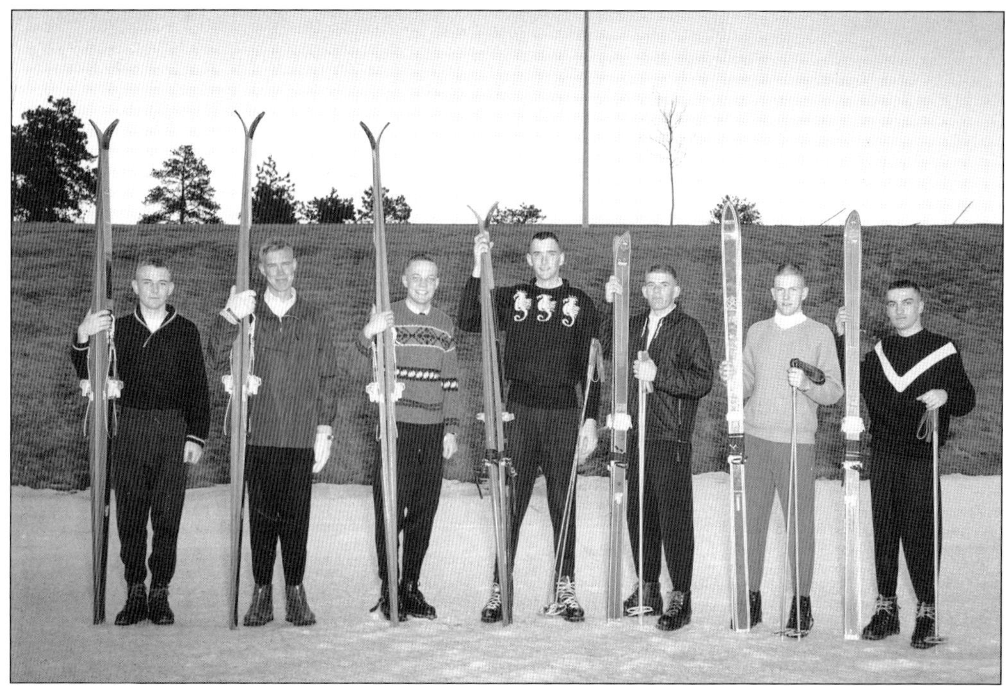

Shown here are members of the 1960–1961 academy ski team. During the Lowry years, the ski team practiced at Winter Park, 60 miles to the west. In the early 1960s, the academy community built a small ski hill near Pine Drive equipped with a rope tow lift. However, the venture was short-lived. Varsity skiing was dropped in favor of water polo in 1971 due to a lack of sufficient training facilities.

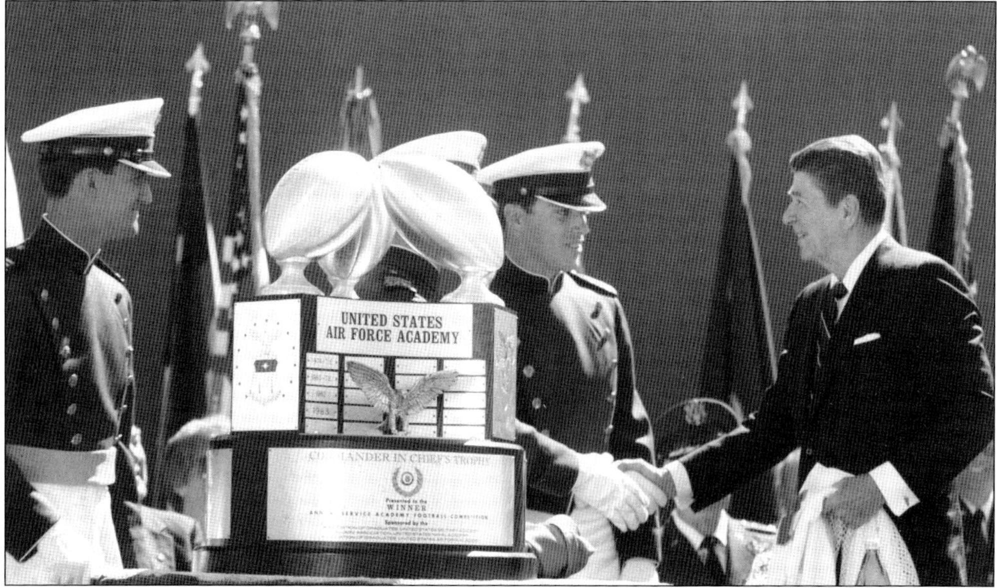

Sponsored by the alumni associations of West Point, Annapolis, and the Air Force Academy, the Commander in Chief's Trophy is awarded annually to the best-record holder of a three-game series. The trophy was conceived by Col. George Simler, the Air Force Academy's second athletic director. As of 2024, the Air Force Academy holds the record for the most wins. Here, Pres. Ronald Reagan presents the trophy during the 1984 graduation ceremonies at Falcon Stadium.

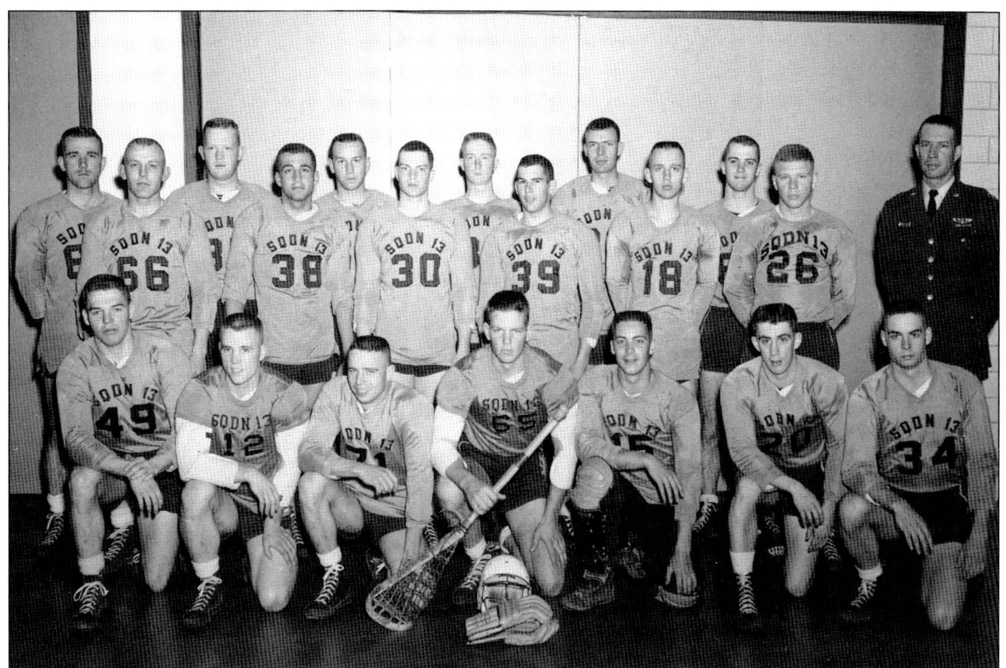

Shown here are members of the 13th Squadron intramural lacrosse team, winners of the 1962 Spring Intramural Wing Championship, who defeated 10th Squadron 2-1. Each semester, four to five sports are offered, and every squadron fields a team. The Malanaphy Trophy is awarded annually to the top performing squadron in intramural athletics. The trophy was named for an ATO killed in an F-86 crash at Lowry Air Force Base.

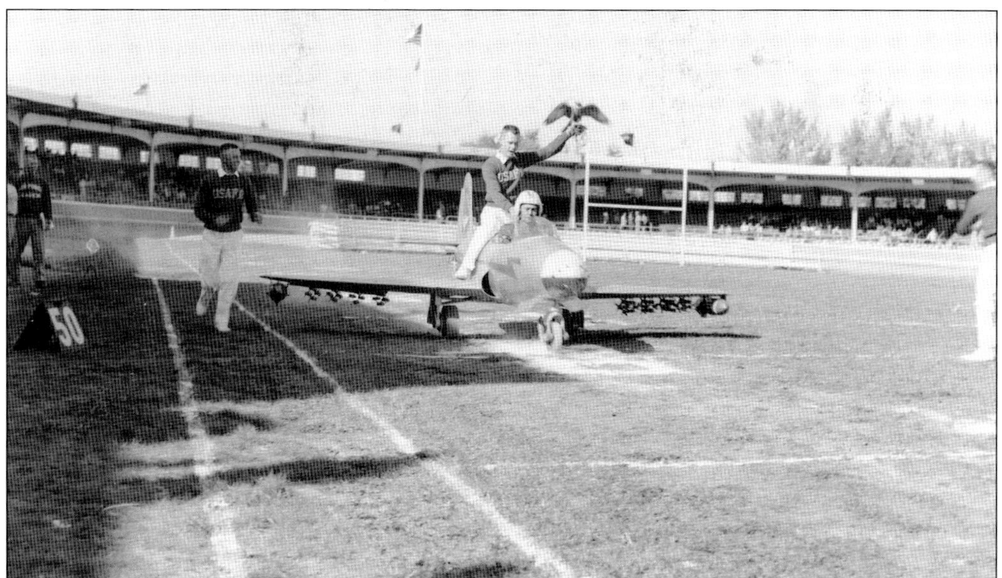

Before Falcon Stadium was built, football games were hosted in other venues, such as Penrose Stadium. As a rodeo stadium, there was no "field" to play on, requiring the Air Force Academy to sod the playing area before the game, remove it afterward, and borrow goalposts from nearby Fort Carson. Here, in a 1956 halftime presentation, the mascot is being "flown" around the stadium on the arm of his cadet handler.

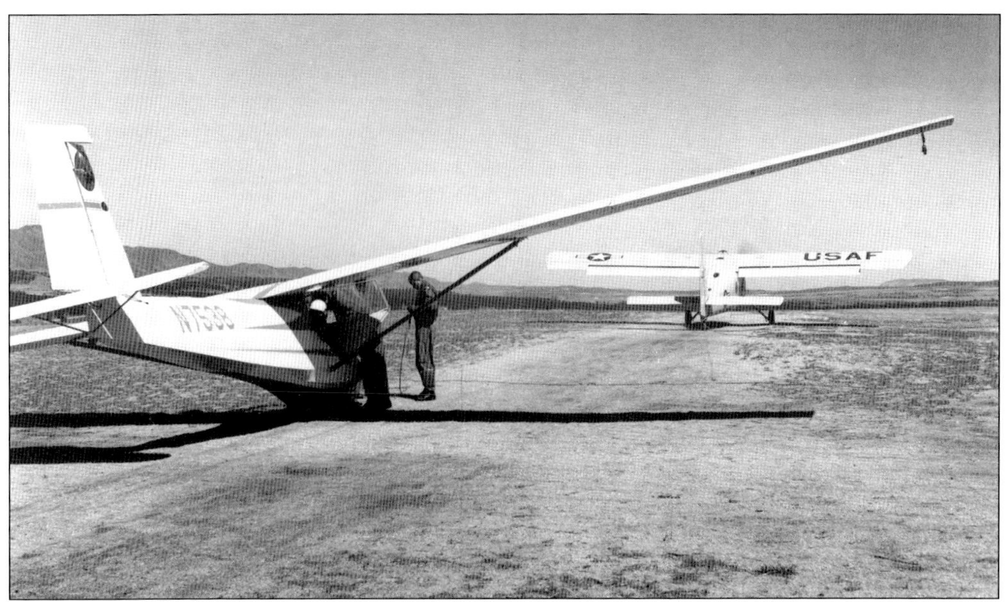

Soaring began as a club in 1956 and has evolved into the largest soaring program in the world. In the early 1960s, it became part of the Airmanship Program, giving all cadets the chance to fly gliders as freshmen. Interested cadets can earn their glider pilot wings and become cadet instructor pilots, who conduct most glider flight instruction. In this image, two cadets prepare for a glider flight on the grassy runway at the academy airfield in 1974.

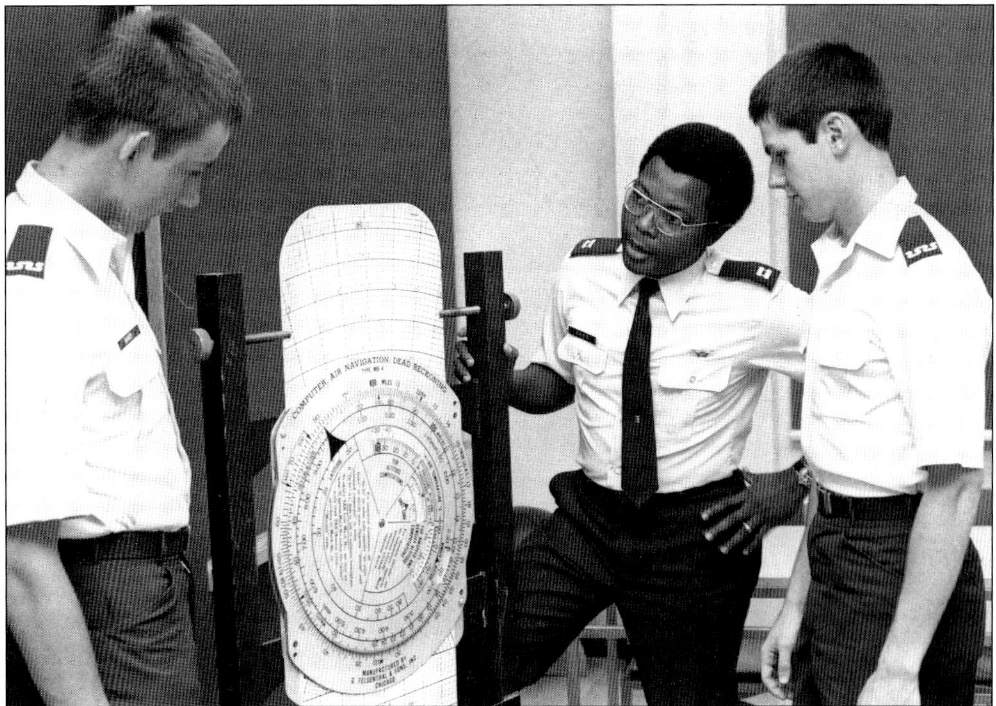

As part of the Airmanship Program, cadets are seen here receiving a navigation lesson on a large-scale model of an EB6 flight computer, otherwise known as an Air Navigation Dead Reckoning computer, or, by pilots, a "whiz wheel." This circular aluminum slide rule is used for flight planning.

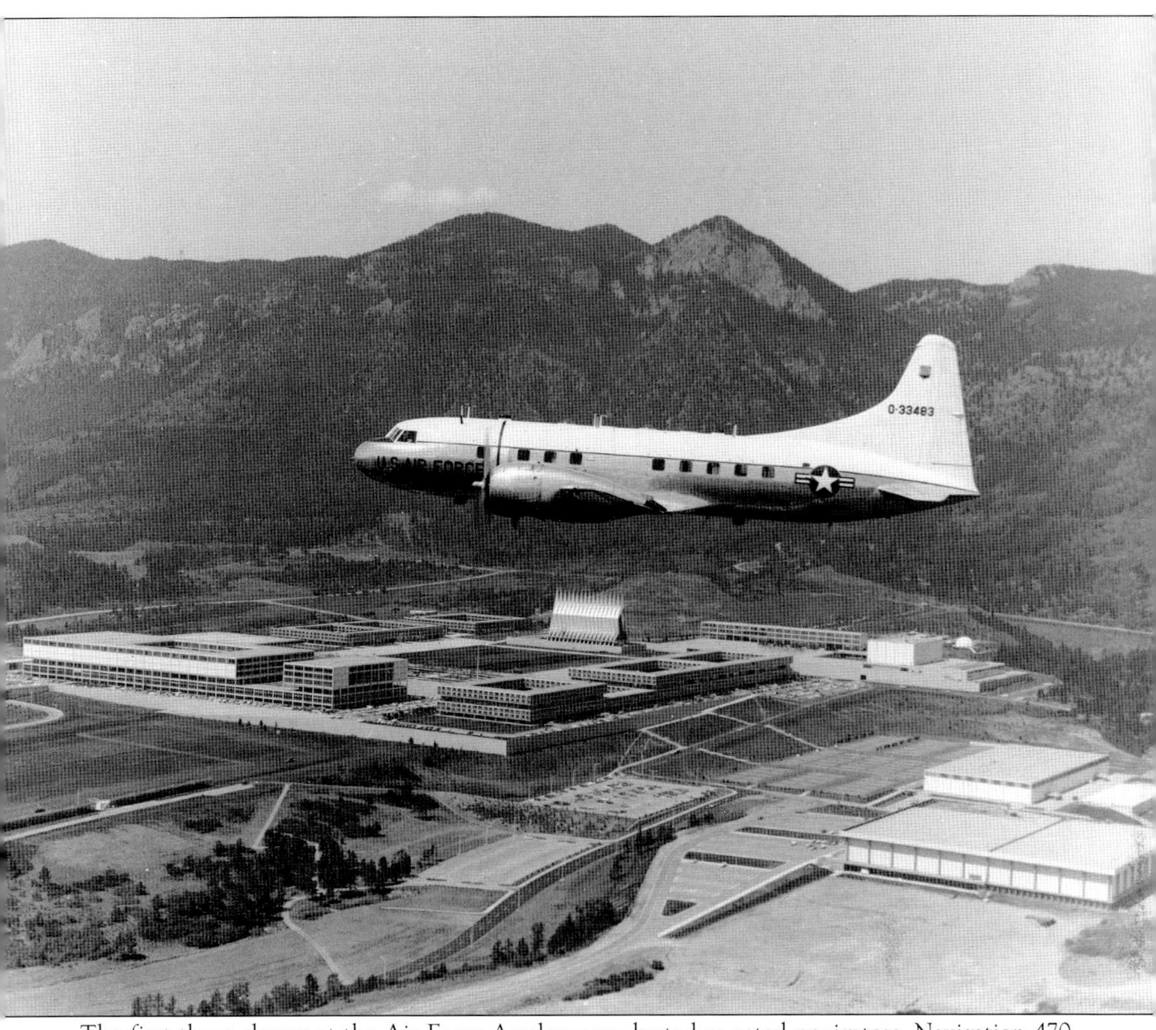

The first three classes at the Air Force Academy graduated as rated navigators. Navigation 470 included classroom instruction, simulator training, and six five-hour flights aboard the T-29 "flying classroom," seen here flying over the Cadet Area. The interior of the T-29 was configured with rows of consoles equipped with navigation instruments for celestial, radar, and dead reckoning navigation training as well as map reading. The T-29s did not move to the academy with the cadets in 1958, requiring cadets and their instructors to travel to Lowry and later to Peterson Airfield for training, which became untenable given the cadets' already packed schedules. After 16 years and 70,000 flight hours of training cadets, the final T-29 cadet navigation mission was flown in May 1975. The Air Force Academy's airfield operations expanded in 1973 with the construction of new operations buildings, hangars, two runways, and a new control tower. This development supported an expanded Airmanship Program and reduced crowding at Peterson Field. In 2019, the airfield was named Davis Airfield after Gen. Benjamin O. Davis Jr., a Tuskegee Airman and World War II pilot.

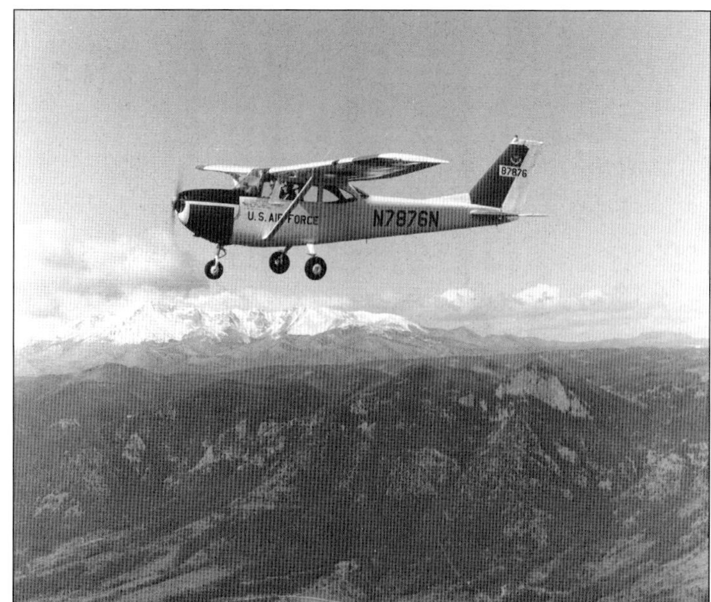

Powered flight became part of the academy program in 1968 with the introduction of the Pilot Indoctrination Program, which offered cadets classroom instruction and 36.5 hours of flying training in a T-41 aircraft. On January 8, 1968, Cadet 1st Class Frederick E. Bassett copiloted the program's inaugural flight with instructor pilot Lt. Col. Joe Price. During the first year of the program, 223 cadets learned to pilot the single-engine propeller aircraft.

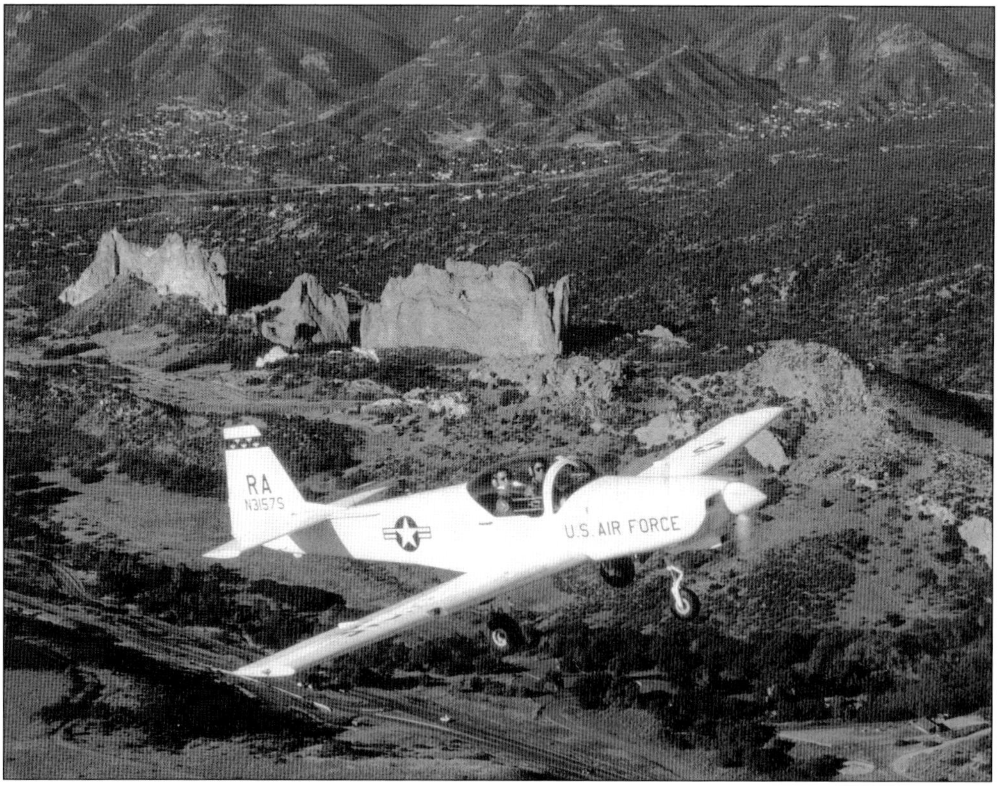

In 1994, the T-41 was replaced by the Slingsby Firefly T-3A, pictured here in flight over the Garden of the Gods near Colorado Springs. The aircraft proved to be unsuitable for the flying training mission. After three fatal accidents claimed the lives of three Air Force Academy cadets and their three instructor pilots between 1995 and 1997, Air Education and Training Command permanently grounded the entire fleet.

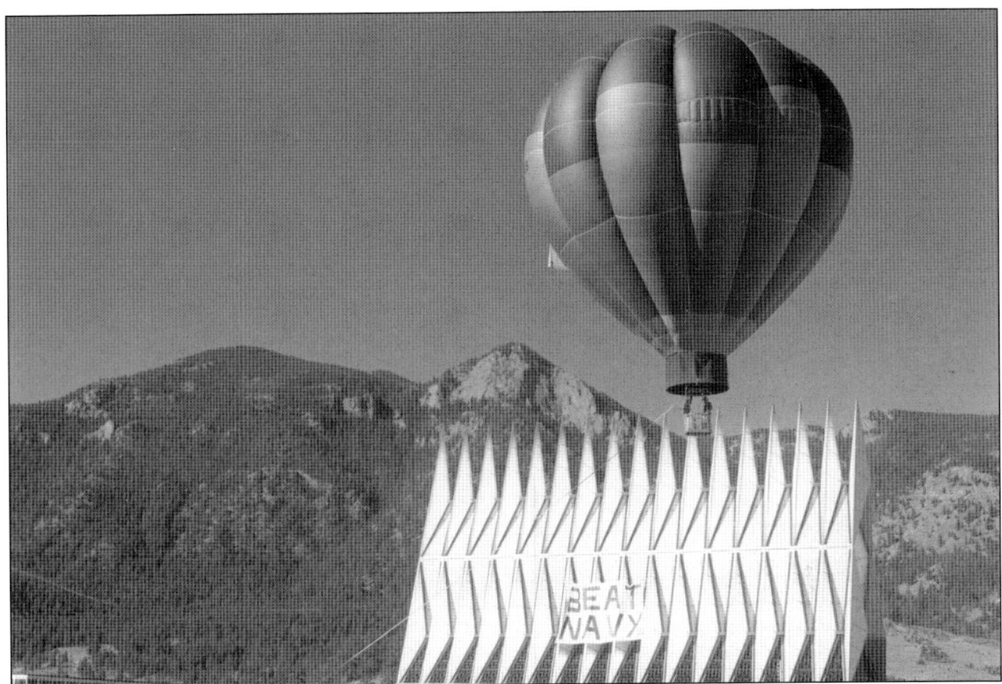

Parasailing, hang gliding, and hot-air ballooning were incorporated into the Airmanship Program in 1975. However, parasailing and hang gliding were quickly discontinued, while the ballooning program continued until 1978, when it was cancelled due to the high cost per cadet, a lack of interest in participation, and safety issues. Before it was cancelled, cadets participated in the February 1978 St. Valentine's Day Balloon Massacre Festival in Albuquerque, New Mexico.

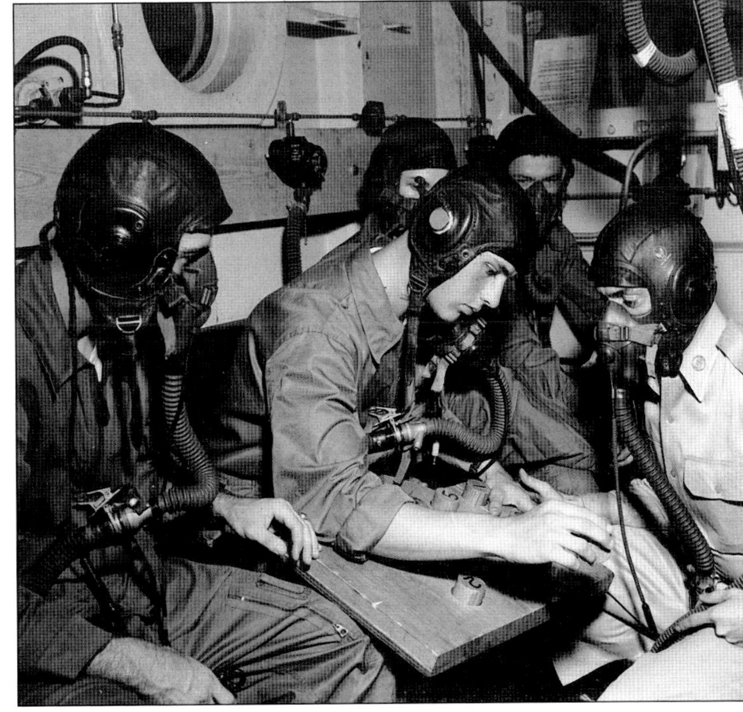

At Lowry, cadets utilized an altitude chamber to simulate the high-altitude, low-oxygen environment of flight at 35,000 feet. During training, cadets completed a puzzle or wrote a dictated message while their oxygen supply was cut off briefly to demonstrate how the body reacted at high altitude. In this photograph, a cadet is working on fitting the right pegs in the right holes. (Courtesy of Special Collections, Pikes Peak Library District, 001-4660.)

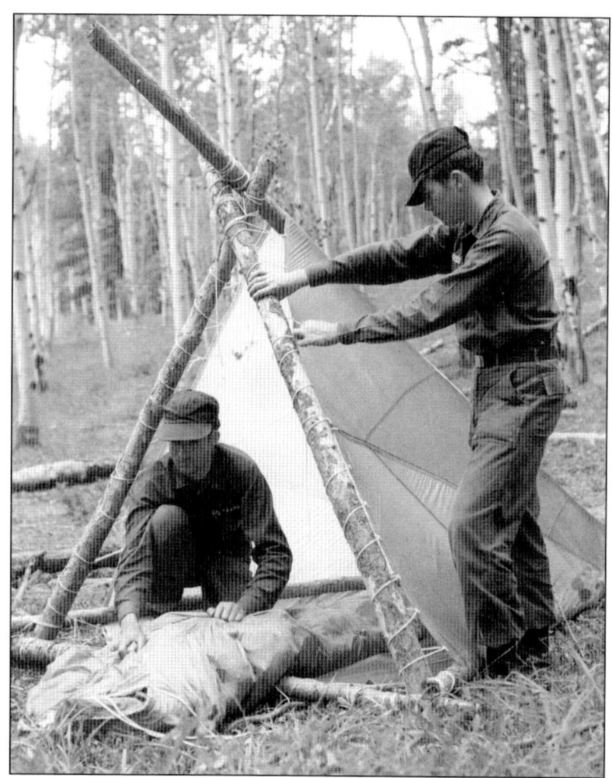

SERE, the Survival, Escape, Resistance, and Evasion program, teaches cadets advanced survival skills through classroom instruction, a water survival course, and field exercises. In this photograph, cadets prepare their shelter during an intense survival exercise in Saylor Park in the Pike National Forest. The exercise requires cadets to live off the land, evade capture by the "enemy" upperclassmen, and resist as a prisoner of war if captured.

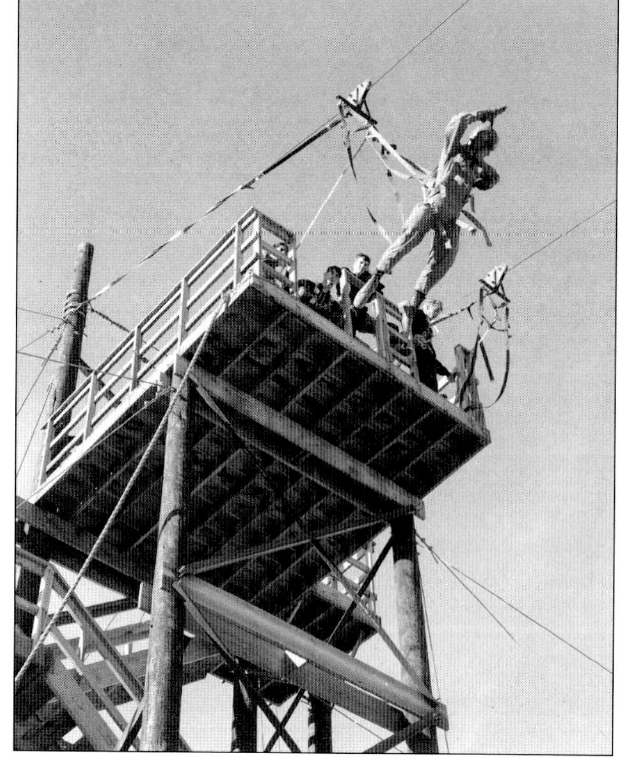

As part of the Airmanship 490 course, Basic Freefall, this cadet has just jumped off the 34-foot training tower near the academy airfield and is seen suspended by the wire in the freefall position. He is reaching for his rip cord after counting 10 seconds of freefall. Once he pulls the cord, it will simulate opening shock, and the trainee will slide down the wire to simulate a parachute landing fall.

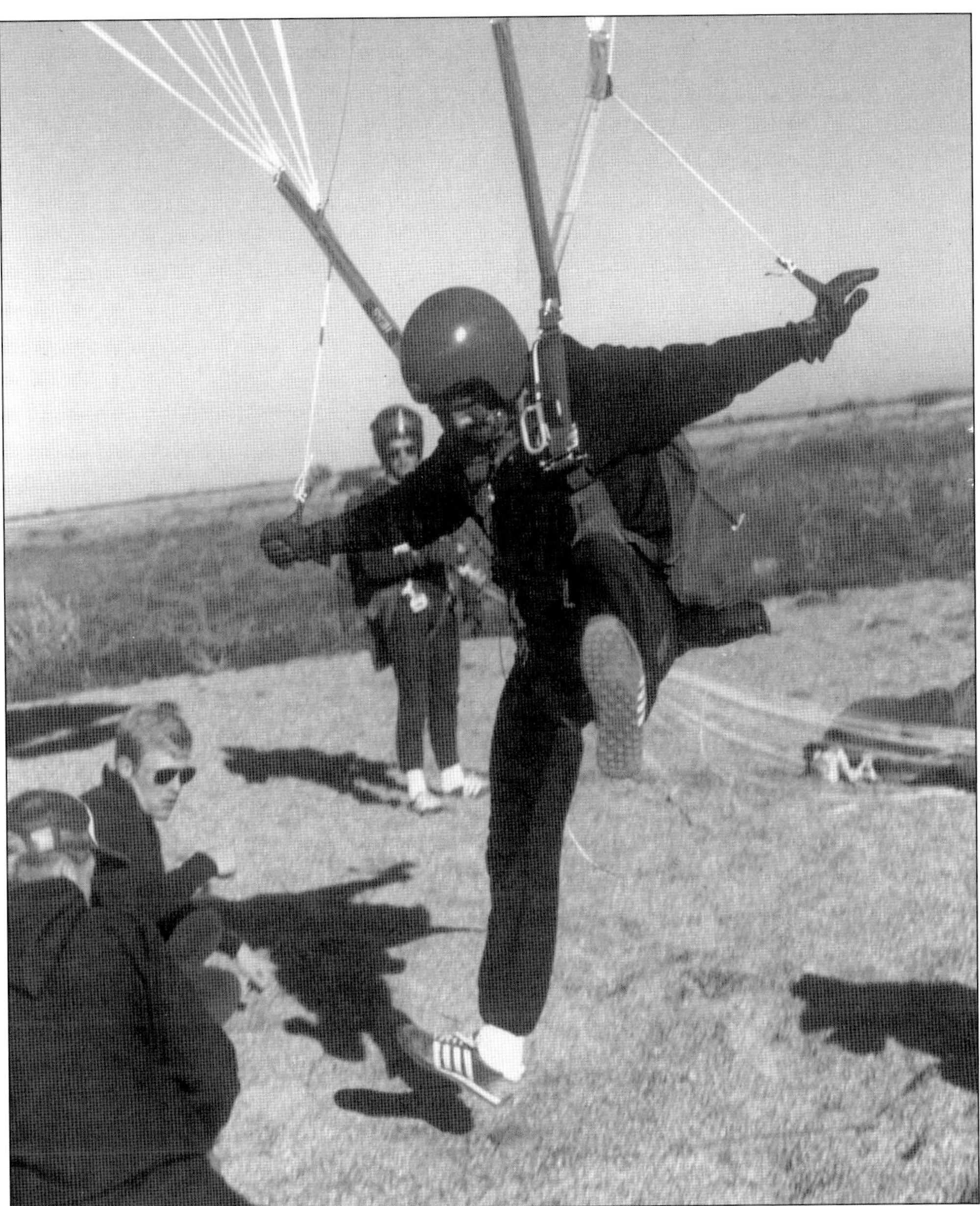

Parachuting at the Air Force Academy began in 1962 with a group of cadets making unsanctioned jumps using local aviators and old SERE equipment. Two years later, the parachute team gained club status. In 1966, the team was established as an official competitive unit, and it was renamed the Wings of Blue in 1976. The Wings of Blue has a demonstration team as well as a competition team. They also serve as jumpmasters and instructors for Airmanship 490, the academy's Basic Freefall parachuting course. Derek Hess is seen here landing on a 10-centimeter-wide target while practicing for the accuracy competition in 1978. Cadets Jim Crump (left with back to camera) and Bob Chapman (second from left) are scoring his landing, while Frank Ott (in back) looks on; all four are members of the class of 1980. The Wings of Blue competition team dominated the 1978 Collegiate Invitational Parachute Competition, held in Deland, Florida, winning the National Collegiate Championship for the 10th year straight. The team continues to excel to this day.

The United States Air Force Academy
Class of 1981
Heartily Invites the Class of 1980
to Attend the Joyous Festivities of
"Hell Week".
The Fun Starts at
1915 on 21 May, in the Year of Our Lord
Nineteen-Hundred and Seventy Eight.
Dress Appropriatly and do not be Late.

WE WILL BE THERE. PO

R.S.V.P.

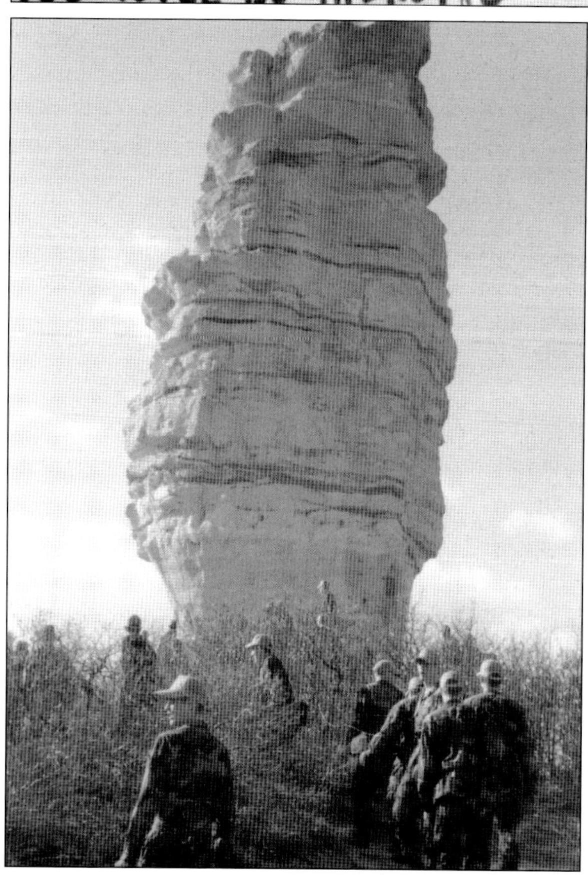

During the spring semester of their fourth-class year, cadets participate in Recognition, a strenuous military and leadership assessment that tests them both mentally and physically, allowing them to become "recognized" members of the Cadet Wing. While officially called Retraining Week, this challenging time was known to early classes as "Hell Week." In a cheeky move, the class of 1981 issued this formal invitation to their upper-class trainers.

Recognition at the Air Force Academy has evolved over the years, but it typically closes with a five-mile run to Cathedral Rock. First-class cadets join the fourth-classmen in the "Run to the Rock," a time-honored tradition that strengthens each squadron's esprit de corps. After completing the run, fourth-class cadets earn the right to wear the upper-class cadet Prop and Wings insignia.

Six

Life at the Academy

Men and women come to the Air Force Academy for a variety of reasons. When asked why they chose to pursue admission to the academy, cadets often give answers nodding to attractive academic programs, patriotism, and solid career opportunities. Some, however, choose to attend a service academy because of its promise of camaraderie and lifelong fraternity among its graduates. These cadets see that the rigor of the academy experience builds and transforms into the spirit of excellence that binds graduates together over time.

Many cadets will say right before graduation that the best view of the Air Force Academy will be in the rear-view mirror. This sentiment, alluding to the challenging nature of a cadet's four years, is usually short-lived. Graduates are quick to realize that the relationships they built at the academy serve them well throughout their peacetime and wartime service in the Air and Space Forces and beyond.

Life at the Air Force Academy is not all hitting the books or dropping and giving 'em 20. Before his retirement, Lieutenant General Harmon told the cadets to "take your duties seriously, but not yourself." Judging by decades of graduate "war stories" of spirit missions and hijinks, many generations of cadets have taken his words to heart. Cadet life is an intangible, but essential, addition to the formal training that finishes that unshakable foundation to a graduate's character. This final chapter is dedicated to some of the moments that build esprit des corps in the Cadet Wing, define its heritage, and elucidate its traditions. What follows here offers a mere glimpse of the Air Force Academy experience that builds a lifetime of memories for the Long Blue Line.

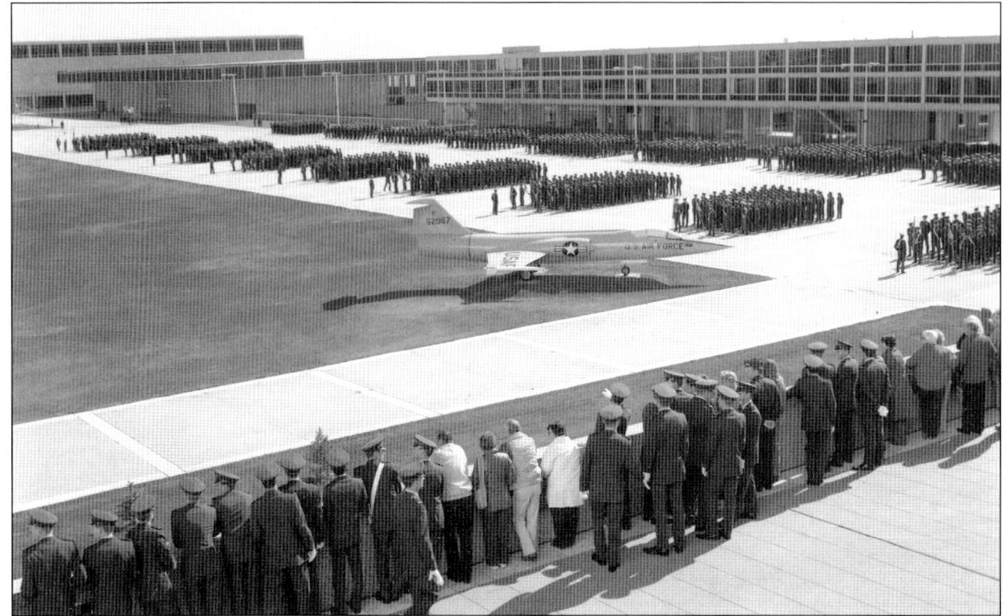

The Air Force Academy is often referred to as "The Zoo" or "Blue Zoo." The name comes from the feeling cadets experience when they see spectators looking at them from the top of the chapel wall, seen here during a noon meal formation. Wanting the academy to have a popular name like West Point or Annapolis, President Eisenhower suggested it be called Manitou, after a nearby town, a name which was never adopted.

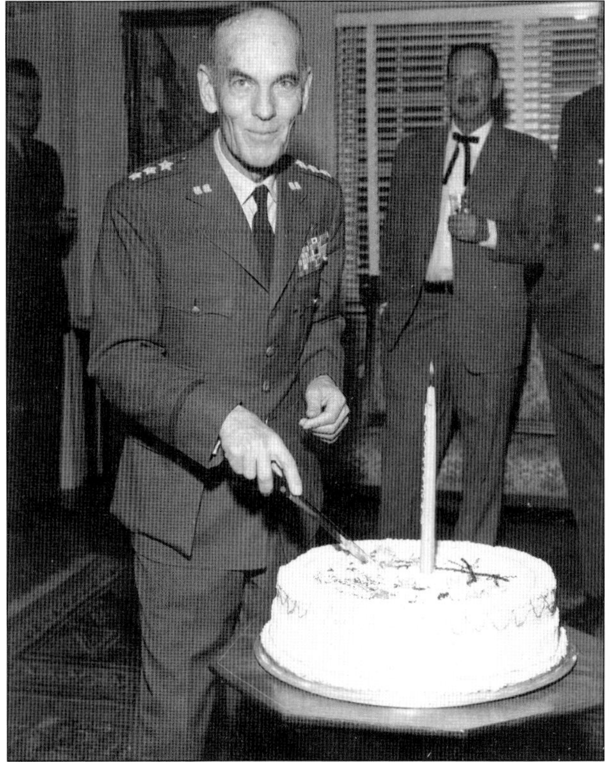

Superintendent Harmon, known to his fellow West Pointers as "Doodles," celebrates the first anniversary of the signing of the Air Force Academy Act on April 1, 1955. Harmon passed away shortly after handing leadership of the Air Force Academy to Lieutenant General Briggs. His visionary leadership during the planning and organization of the Air Force Academy defined the institution, and he is remembered as the "Father of the Air Force Academy."

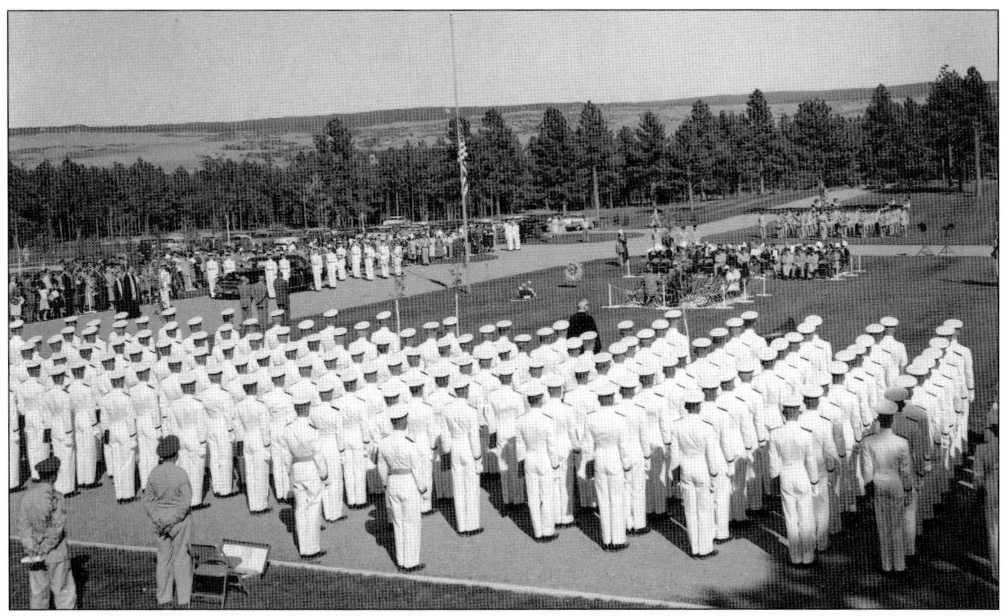

On Sunday, September 28, 1958, Lt. Gen. Hubert R. Harmon was laid to rest with full military honors in the first burial in the Air Force Academy Cemetery. Cadets wore their all-white parade dress uniform for this somber occasion. The first superintendent was beloved by the cadets who experienced his inspiring leadership, making him the first honorary member of the class of 1959 with an oversized proclamation in July 1956.

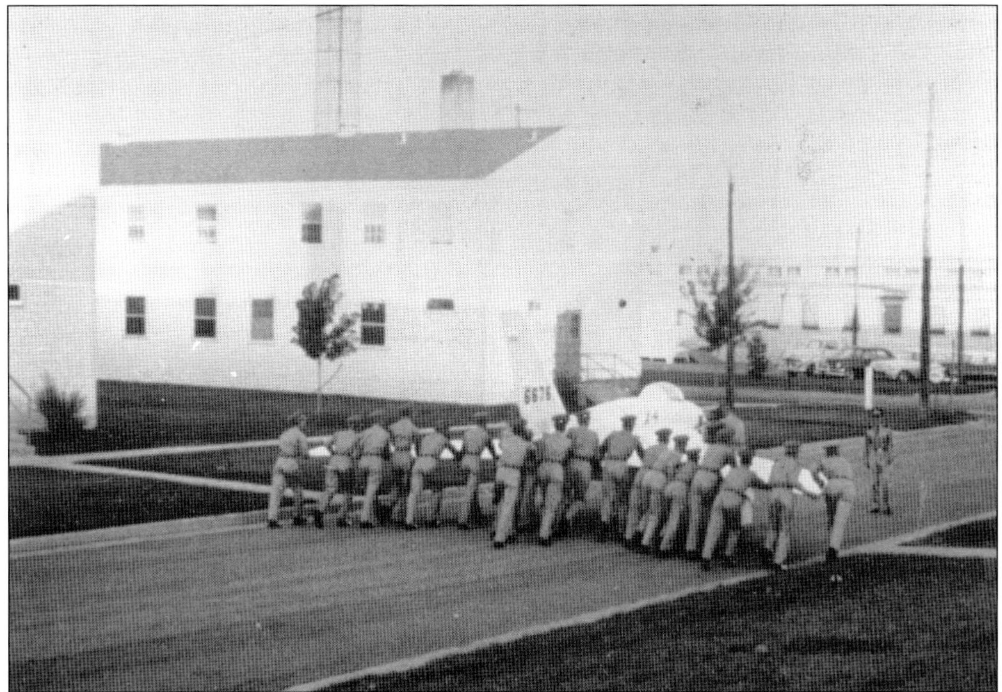

Spirit missions at the Air Force Academy take many forms, but a favorite among cadets from the beginning is moving the aircraft on static display around the campus. Here, cadets at Lowry are "borrowing" a display aircraft from the flight line to dress up their area of the base.

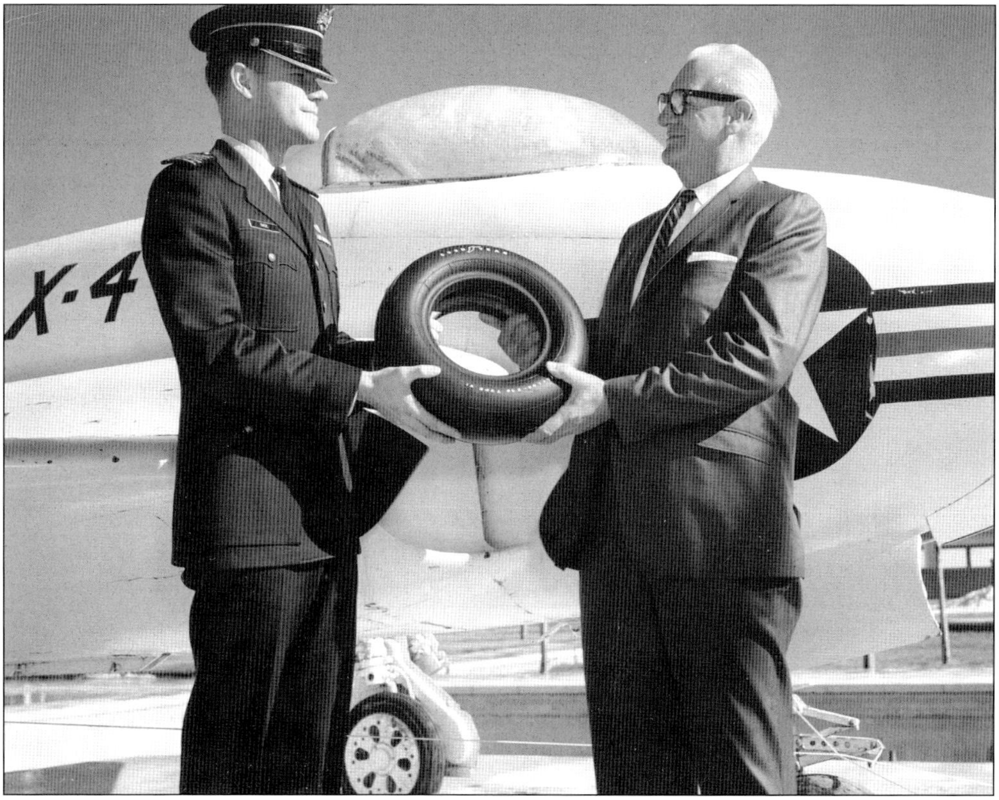

In December 1968, Walter C. Linke (right) of the Goodyear Tire Company presented Cadet Wing commander Thomas Case (left), class of 1969, with new custom tires for the X-4 static display. The one-of-a-kind tires of the small experimental jet aircraft had worn out after 12 years of mysteriously taxiing, albeit without an engine, to new locations around the academy grounds.

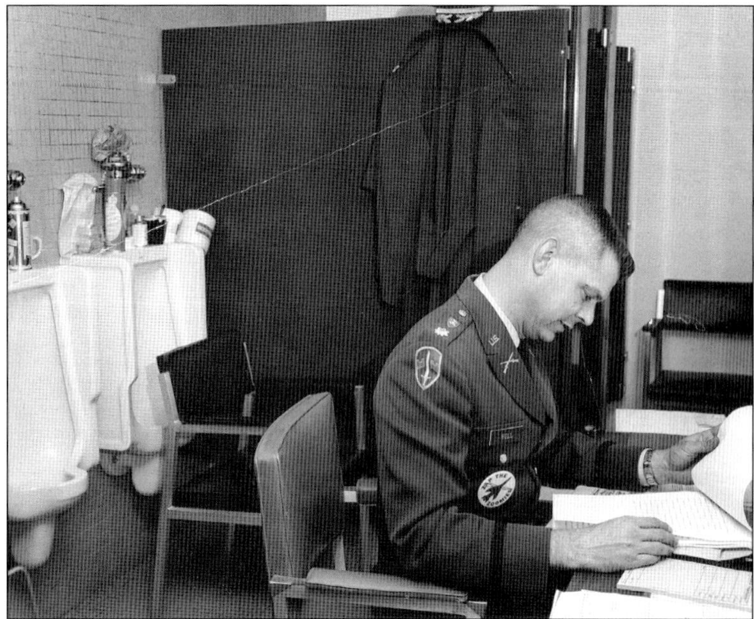

To relieve themselves of stress brought on by the challenging environment at the Air Force Academy, some enterprising mischief-makers relocated the entire office of this air officer commanding (AOC) into the latrine after hours. On November 3, 1967, Maj. Robert L. Hull, US Army, reported to his new duty station and went about his business, apparently unfazed.

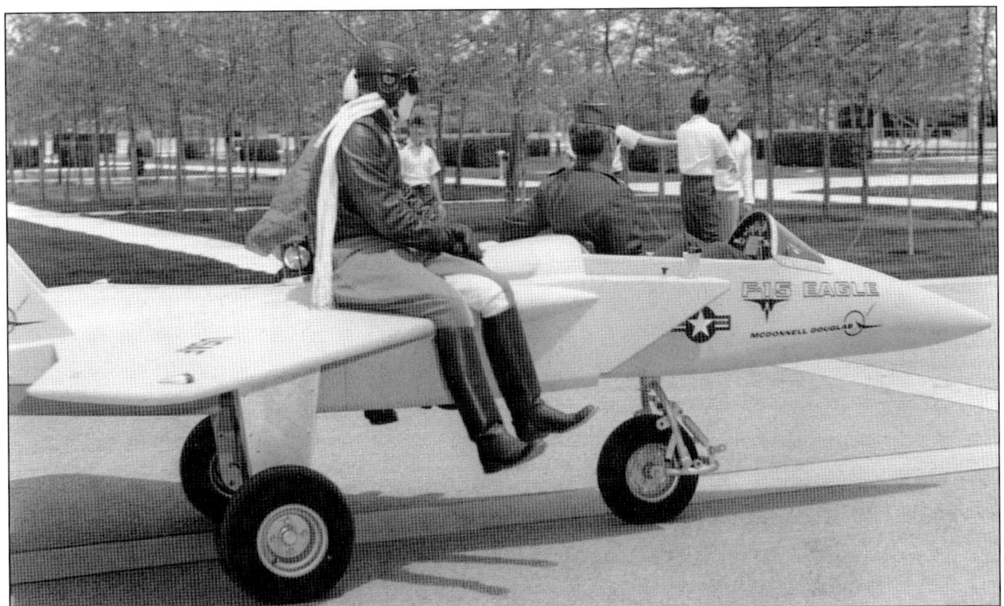

Sitting atop a miniature McDonnell Douglas F-15 Eagle, "Bedcheck Charlie" is taxiing through the Air Garden in this undated photograph. The ghost of a World War I flyboy, Bedcheck originated in the pages of the 1960s comic strip *Terry and the Pirates* by George Wunder in which two cadets are commanded to start an academy tradition. Bedcheck Charlie became the Air Force Academy's reminder of the spirit, energy, and passion of the flyers who came before.

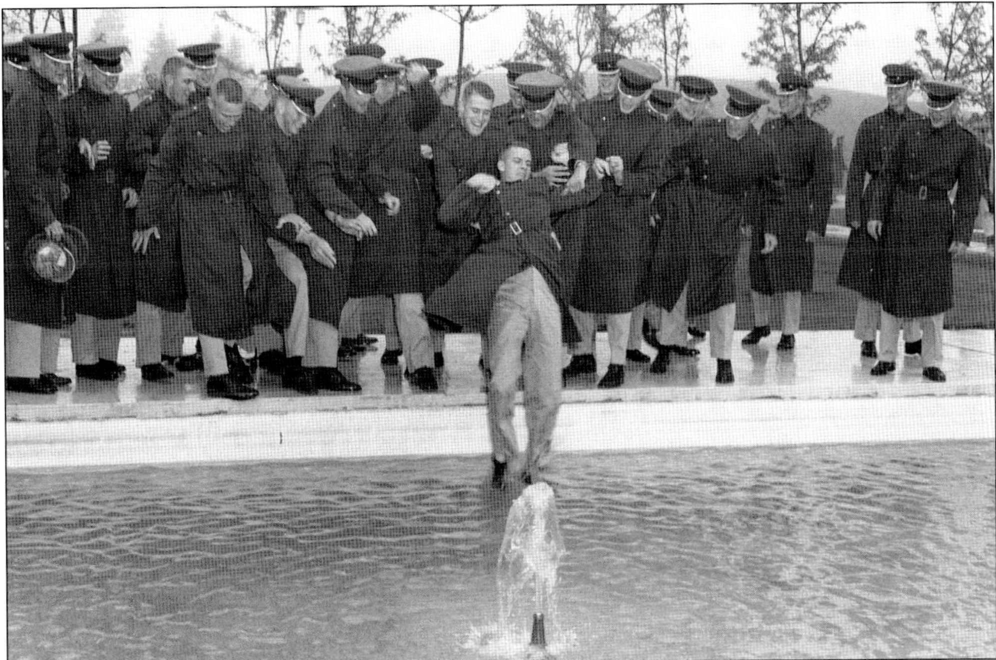

Dan Kiley likely envisioned the pools of the Air Garden as a serene retreat from the fast-paced life of cadet—a place to stroll with a date and enjoy the scenery. He probably did not foresee a horde of underclassmen chucking seniors into the fountains in celebration, as seen here. Now, senior cadets leap into the fountains themselves as a rite of passage upon completing their last final exam.

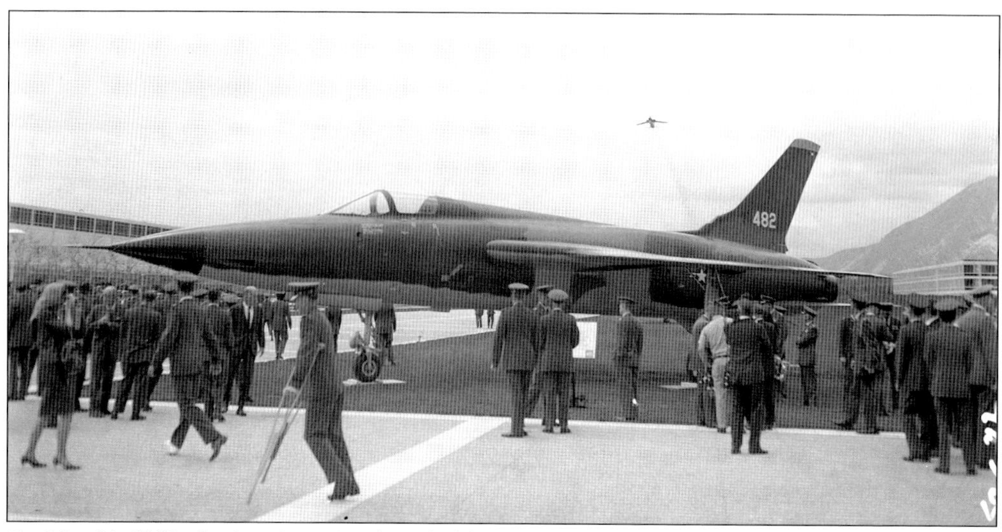

On May 31, 1968, the Air Force Academy held a ceremony on the Terrazzo to dedicate a new F-105 Thunderbird static display. A low-flying F-105, piloted by Lt. Col. James W. "Black Jack" Matthews, passed over the Cadet Area while breaking the sound barrier. The photograph above shows the inbound F-105 approaching from the south. (Photograph by Stanley Payne; courtesy of Special Collections, Pikes Peak Library District, 004-12081.)

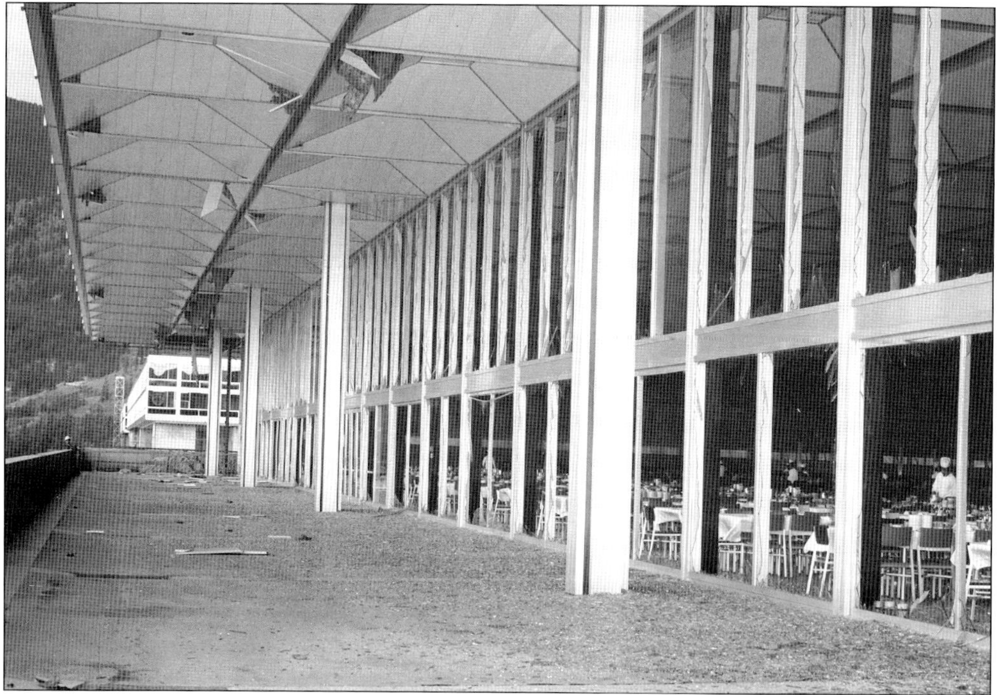

As a result of the sonic boom, more than 300 windows in Mitchell Hall, Vandenberg Hall, and the Cadet Gymnasium were blown out. Fortunately, most onlookers escaped without injury. However, 15 of the hundreds of visitors and cadets watching received minor injuries from the flying glass. Damages from the incident totaled more than $250,000. As seen above, the entire south wall of Mitchell Hall was damaged. It took several days to acquire enough plywood to cover the open window frames. Luckily, the Cadet Chapel was undamaged.

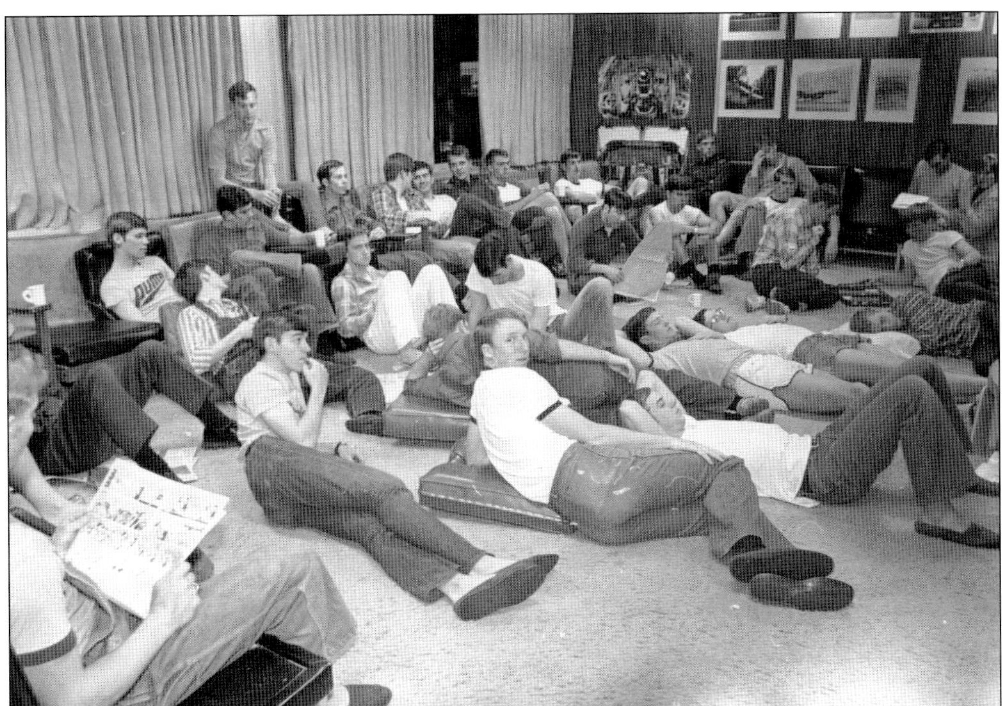

In February 1978, a group of cadets enjoys extra free time during the Russian flu outbreak that halted all Air Force Academy activities. This group is lounging comfortably in their squadron assembly room while 3,280 of their classmates who contracted the bug convalesce in their dormitory rooms. Luckily, only two cadets were hospitalized during the epidemic, and they made full recoveries. West Point and Annapolis experienced similar outbreaks on their campuses.

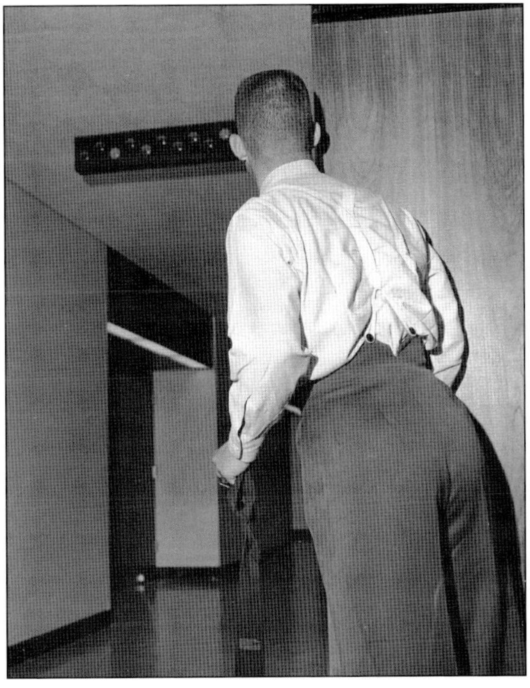

No cadet wants to be caught committing a fashion faux pas by being out of uniform. Although the use of minute-callers has continued to this day, in the 1960s, cadets could look to light panels on the hallway ceilings to find out the uniform of the day, which changed several times throughout the day. At Lowry, small colored flags were displayed on a flagpole outside of security flight to indicate the uniform to wear.

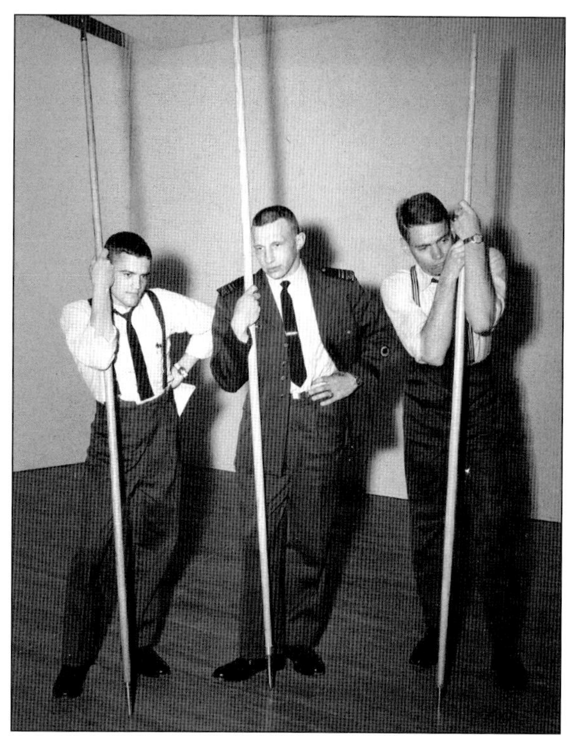

Rehearsing for the Arnold Hall theater stage, the cast of *Hey! Mr. Blue* looks downtrodden, and rightly so. In this scene, they are all candidates for walking tours on the Terrazzo. The amusing original caption lists four cadets: Nino Baldachi, John Haluska, Frank Karasienski, and Jerry Bowers. Nino Baldachi, a fictional cadet known for pranks, misdeeds, and never graduating, is probably to blame for the trouble these characters face.

The Flameouts were one of the many groups formed in the Cadet Music Club. In this photograph, the six-member band performs at the academy "Wing Ding" rock and roll show during the June Week festivities in 1966. Earlier that year, the group flew to California in a T-29 and laid down tracks at Columbia Studios for a 45 rpm record containing their hits "Fun Girl" and "I Won't Cry."

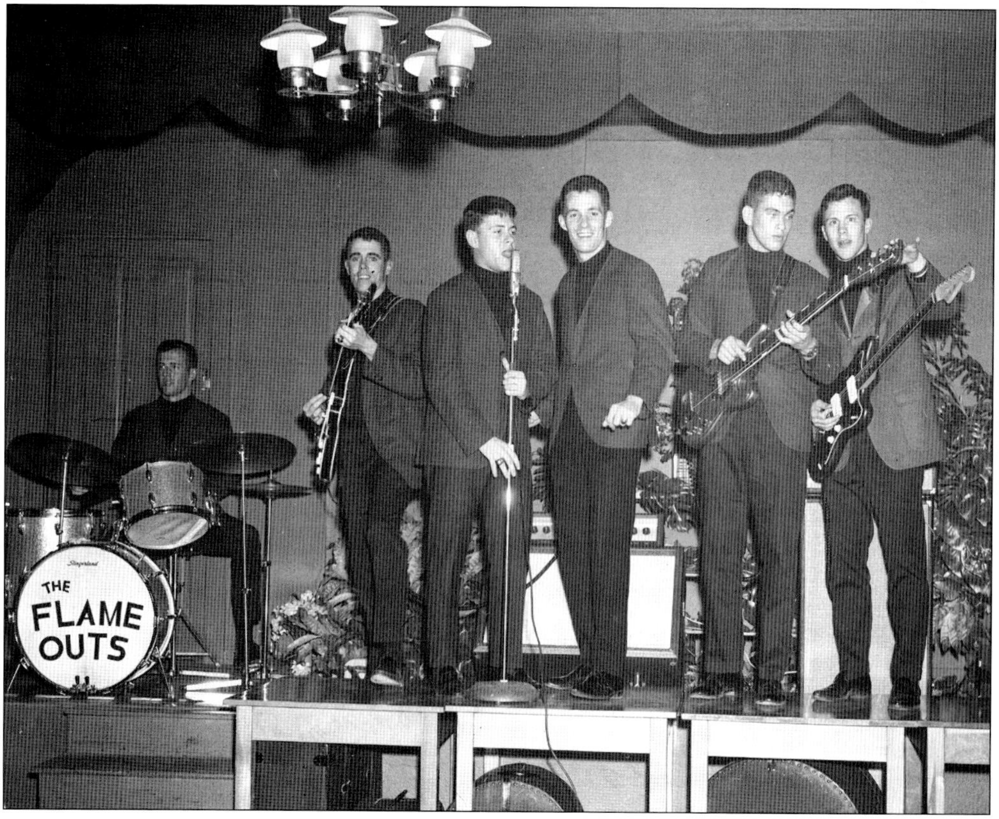

CADET FOOD ACCEPTABILITY REPORT | DATE 21 Sep 79

MEAL ITEMS REFER TO *(Check one only)*		BREAKFAST	✓	LUNCH		DINNER

	SERVICE OF FOOD *(Check one)*		WAITER SERVICE *(Check one)*		PORTION SERVED *(Check one)*
	SLOW		SLOPPY		SMALL
	AVERAGE		AVERAGE	✓	AVERAGE
✓	FAST	✓	NEAT		OVERSIZE
	PERSONNEL ATTITUDE *(Check one)*		BEVERAGES *(Check one)*		MEAL CONSIDERED *(Check one)*
	SOUR *(Explain under Remarks)*		UNSATISFACTORY *(Explain Remarks)*		UNSATISFACTORY *(Explain Remarks)*
	AVERAGE		AVERAGE		SATISFACTORY
✓	FRIENDLY	✓	GOOD	✓	GOOD

REMARKS *(Continue on reverse side)*

SUGGESTIONS *(Continue on reverse side)*

This checklist is for use by the Food Service Officer, and in no way will tend to reflect credit or injury to the Cadet completing the form.	SIGNATURE OF CADET	DUTY PHONE	ORGANIZATION
		4453	CS-18

USAFA Form 0-96, SEP 92 (CWXM) PREVIOUS EDITION WILL BE USED *U.S. GPO: 1992-676-418/65116

The Cadet Food Acceptability Report, Form O-96, was introduced in 1956. Cadets were required to complete six multiple-choice assessments of their dining experience in the cadet dining hall. Their answers, dictated by tradition, gave birth to the oft-heard academy phrase "Fast, Neat, Average, Friendly, Good, Good." This phrase became a way for graduates to identify each other; if one graduate offered "Fast, Neat, Average," another would reply "Friendly, Good, Good."

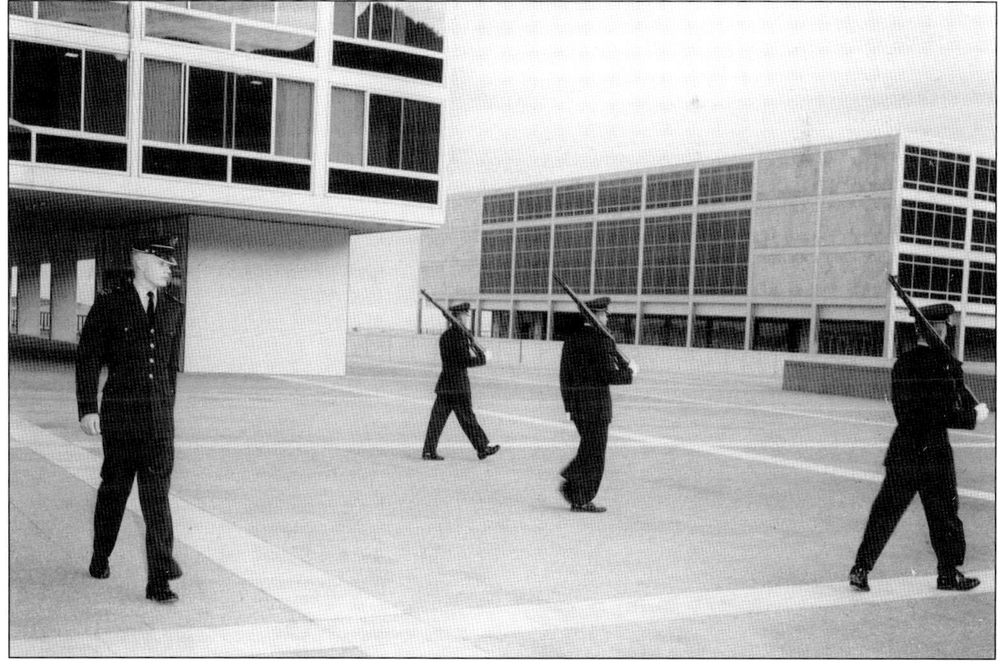

In a scene every academy graduate remembers, cadets are seen here walking off tours on the Terrazzo under the watchful eye of a member of the cadet staff. This hour-long punishment, during which cadets march with a shouldered M-1 rifle, is assigned when a cadet commits more serious infractions of Air Force Academy regulations.

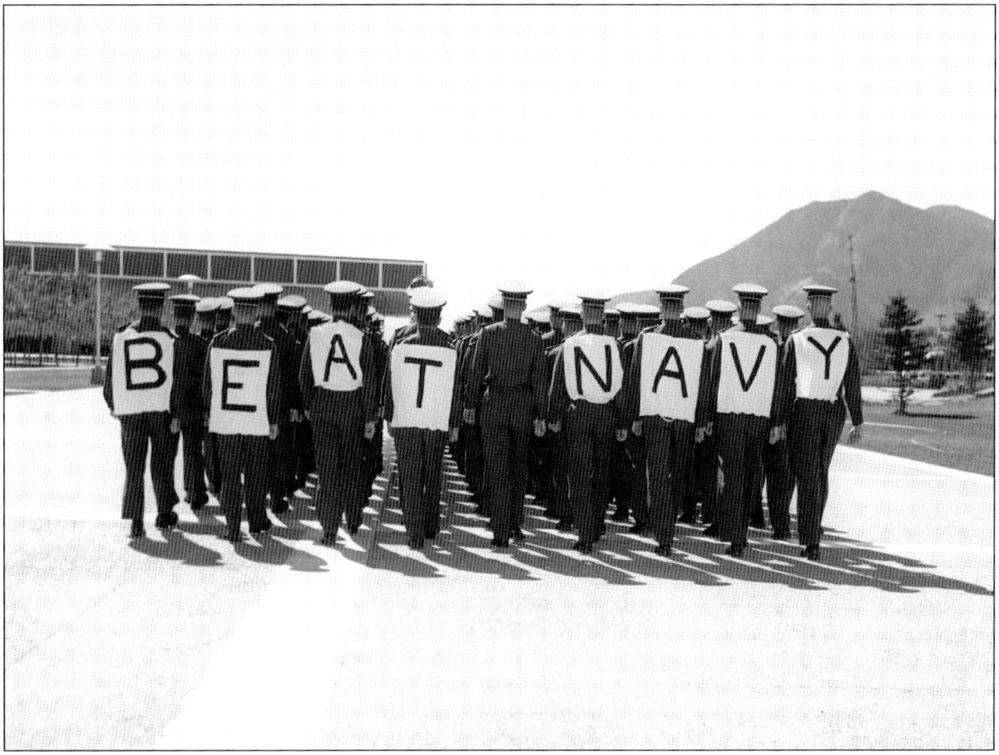

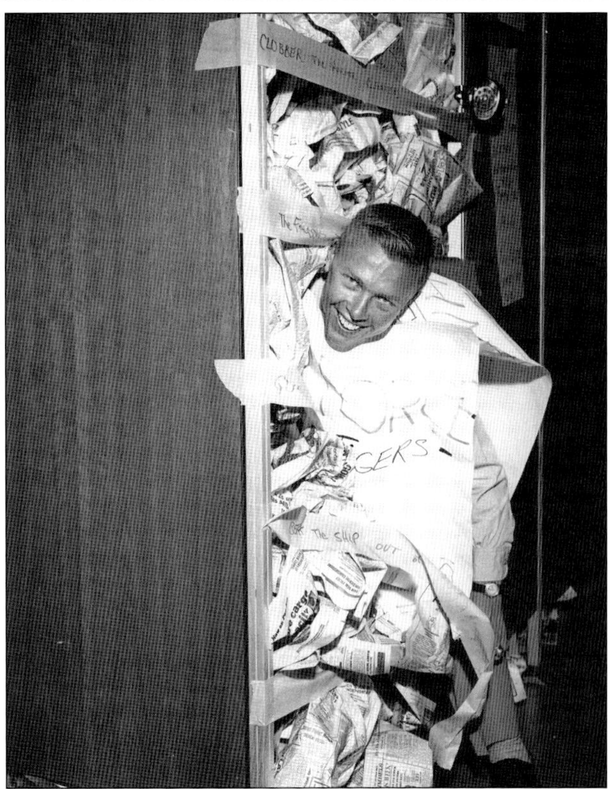

Col. George B. Simler, director of athletics, sought to schedule interservice academy games with West Point and Annapolis starting in 1958. However, neither school would agree to meet Air Force in Colorado due to the high elevation. As a result, the Falcons traveled to eastern cities to meet their interservice rivals until 1966, when they defeated Navy in Falcon Stadium 15-7. West Point first played at Air Force the following year. In the September 30, 1966, photograph above, Air Force Academy cadets use the noon meal formation to proudly display support for the Falcon football team prior to their first home game against Navy. At left, Lt. J.A. Butterfield, a Navy officer assigned to the Department of Political Science, reported to work the day before the game to find his office had been packed solid with crumpled paper and spirit signs.

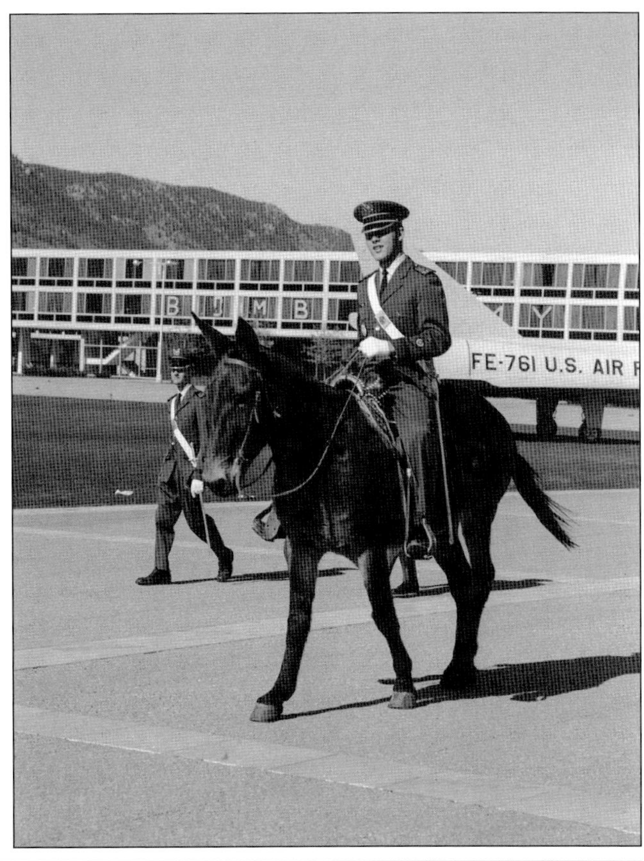

On November 2, 1963, the second Air Force Academy game against West Point was held at Chicago's Soldier Field in front of Pres. John F. Kennedy, along with all cadets from both academies. An excited Cadet Wing planned spirit events throughout the week leading up to the game. Here, the Cadet Wing commander, James C. Ingram, is riding a mule at the head of the noon meal formation.

Amid the spectacle of every interservice academy football game, a standout tradition is the "Prisoner Exchange." This ceremony, held before kickoff, features cadets participating in a semester-long exchange program with another service academy. Cadets from each side march to midfield, perform an about-face, and run back to their home academy to cheer for their team alongside their classmates.

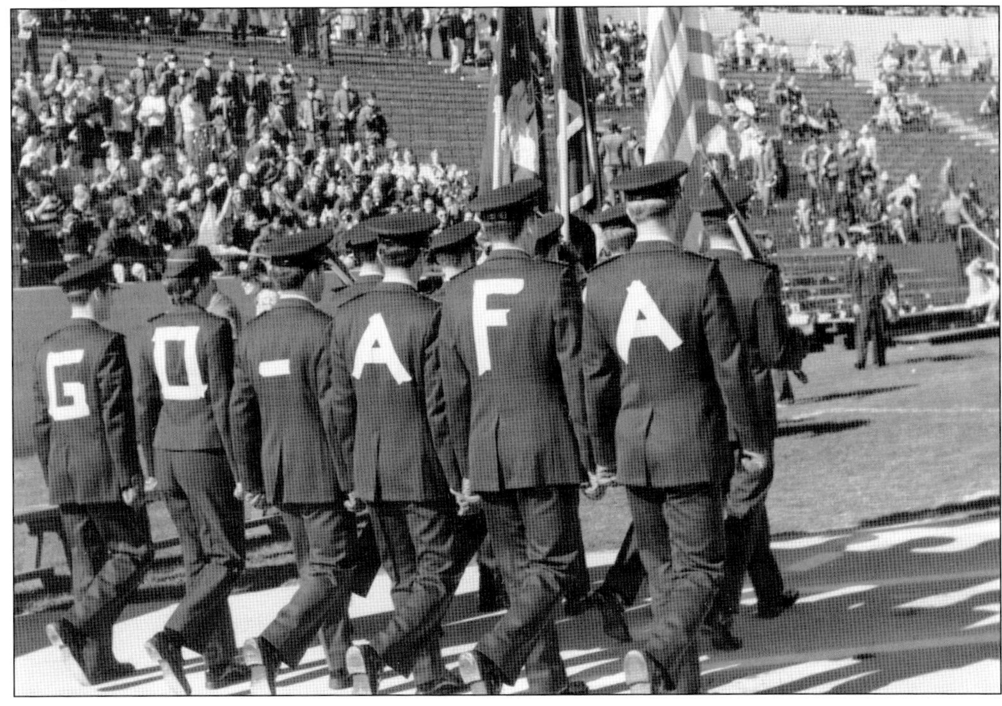

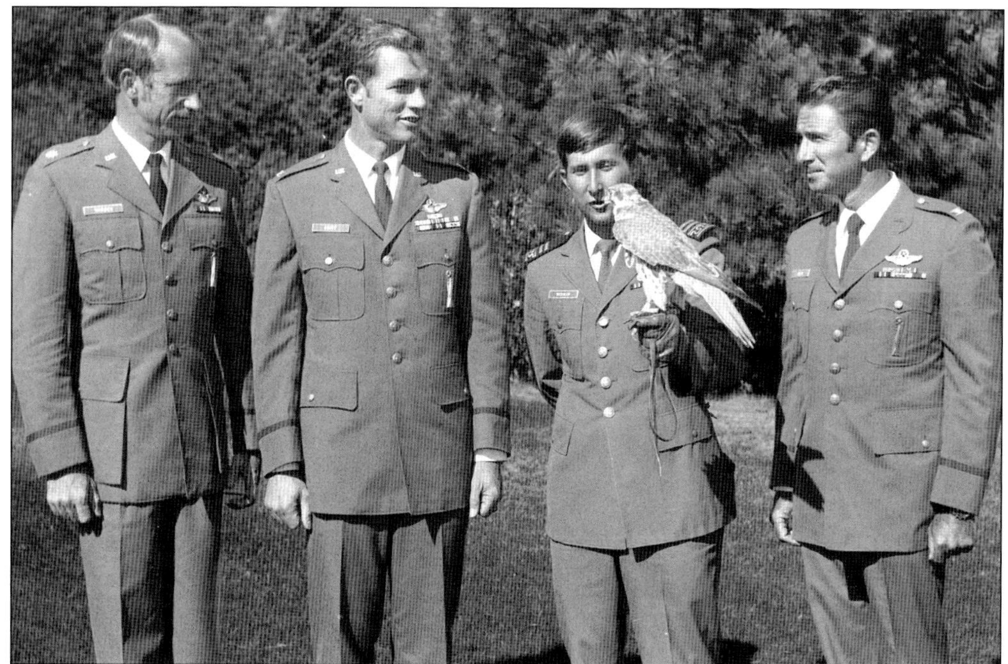

From left to right, Apollo 15 astronauts Lt. Col. Alfred Worden, Col. David Scott, and Col. James Irwin are shown here with Cadet Jim Wessler and a falcon named Hungry. Hungry provided a feather for the mission. During the last moon walk, Mission Commander Scott used the feather in a live broadcast, dropping it alongside a hammer to demonstrate that both would fall at the same rate in a vacuum. (Photograph by Stewarts Commercial Photographers, © Pikes Peak Library District, 013-9054.)

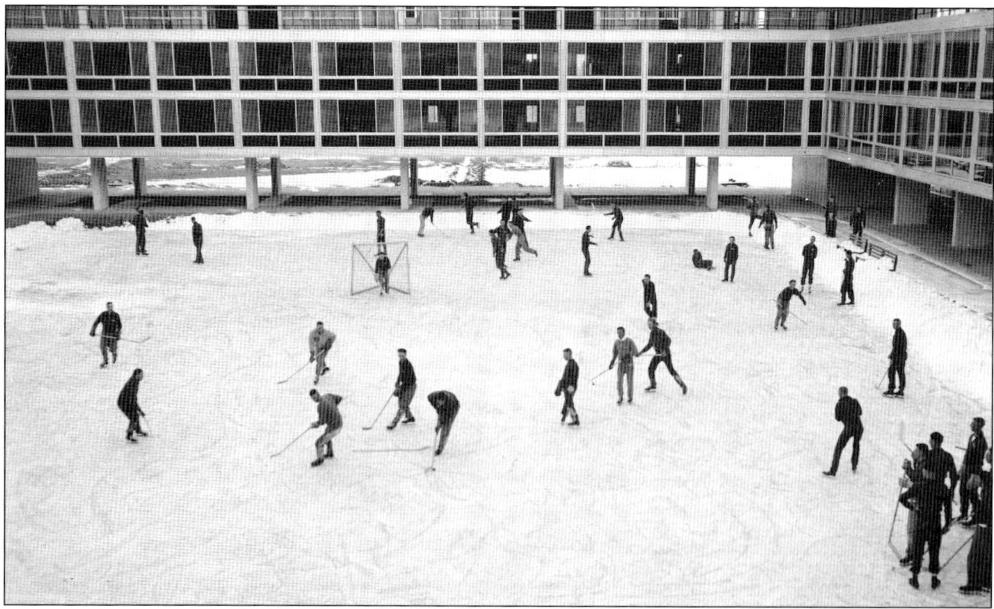

Cadets enjoy some time on the ice, skating in their makeshift hockey rink in one of the quads of Vandenberg Hall in this undated photograph. This scene captures the friendly and competitive spirit embraced by the Cadet Wing.

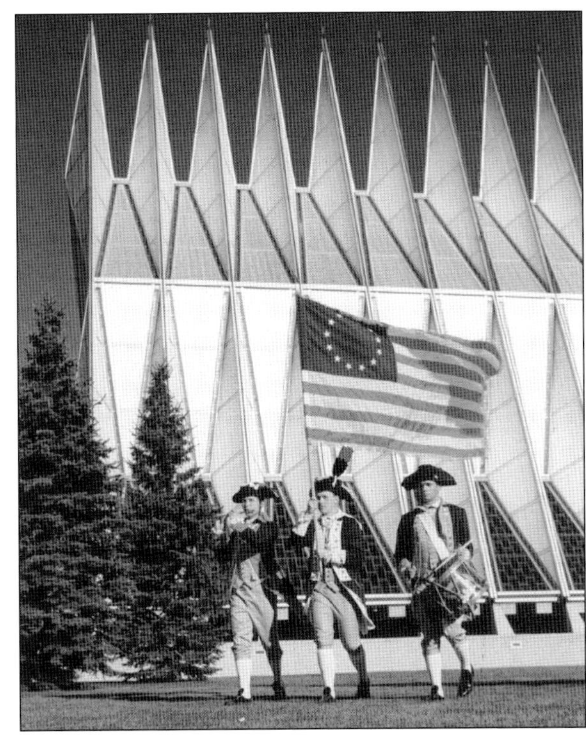

In 1976, the Air Force Academy was designated as a National Bicentennial University and a National Bicentennial Air Force Installation by the American Revolution Bicentennial Administration. Throughout the year, the Air Force Academy commemorated the anniversary with academic symposia and entertainment events. In February 1976, a large mural depicting the history of the Air Force Academy site was unveiled on the wall of the Arnold Hall Ballroom. Shown here, the Continental Color Guard, called "The Spirit of '76," was created by three cadets and performed at halftime of all home football games as well as at numerous other events. From left to right, Cadets 1st Class Steve Boyd, Peter Mapes, and Mike Byron wore authentic reproductions of Continental soldiers' uniforms and carried the original 13-star flag.

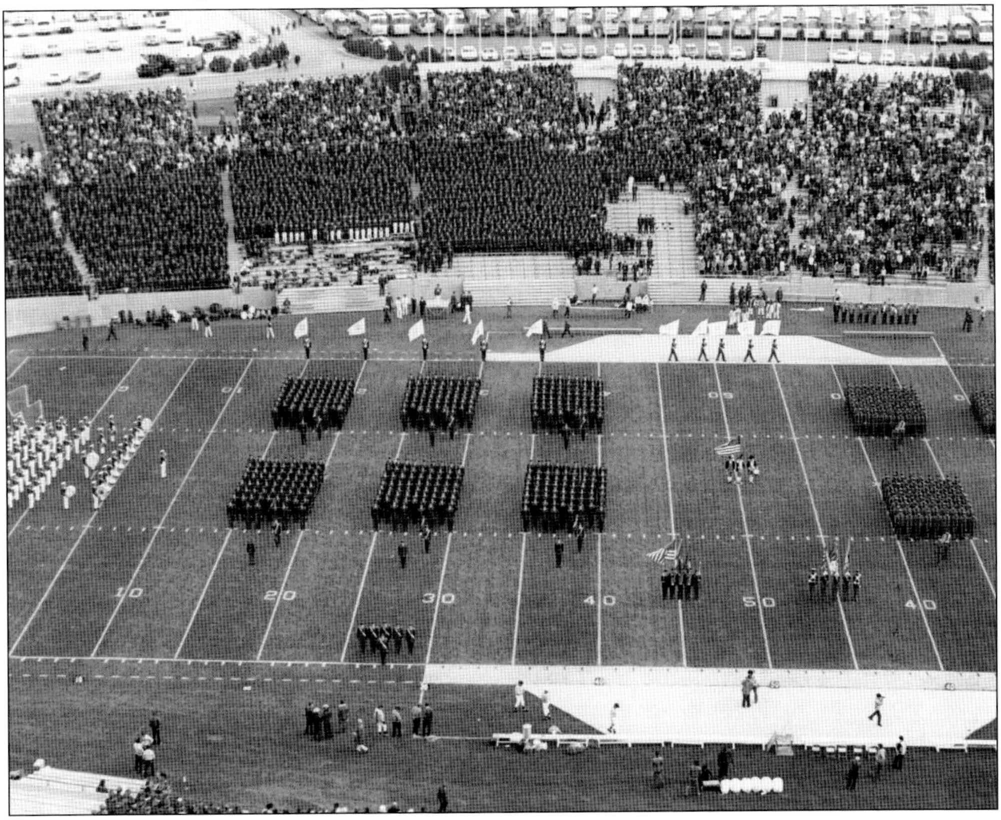

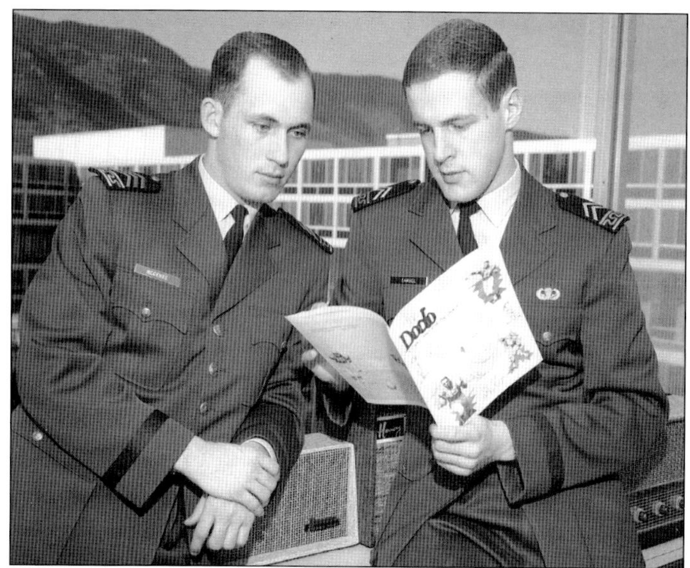

The *Dodo*, a satirical newspaper written by cadets, brought humor to the Cadet Wing from 1957 to 2004. The paper enjoyed support from the Air Force Academy's senior leadership, who saw it as a great morale booster. Here, Cadet Dave Samuel (right), class of 1964, discusses an issue titled "A Salute to the 1962 Falcons" with Cadet Jarrett McGeehee (left) in January 1963. Samuel was the editor-in-chief of the *Dodo* for the 1962–1963 academic year.

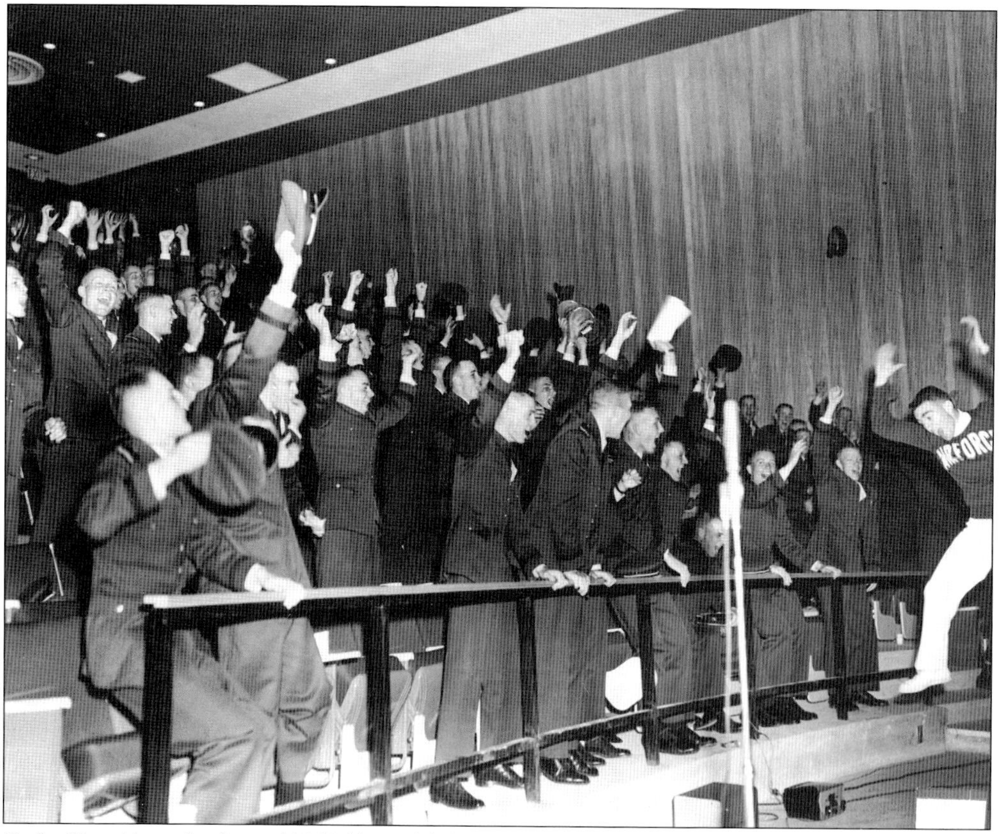

Cadet Ken Alnwick, class of 1960 (far right), leads the Cadet Wing in a cheer during an away game for the Falcon football team on October 24, 1958. Unable to travel to Stanford University, the cadets wanted their voices heard. Each cadet contributed 35¢ to lease a telephone line, allowing their cheers to be broadcast into the stadium via a loudspeaker system donated by the Tidewater Oil Company.

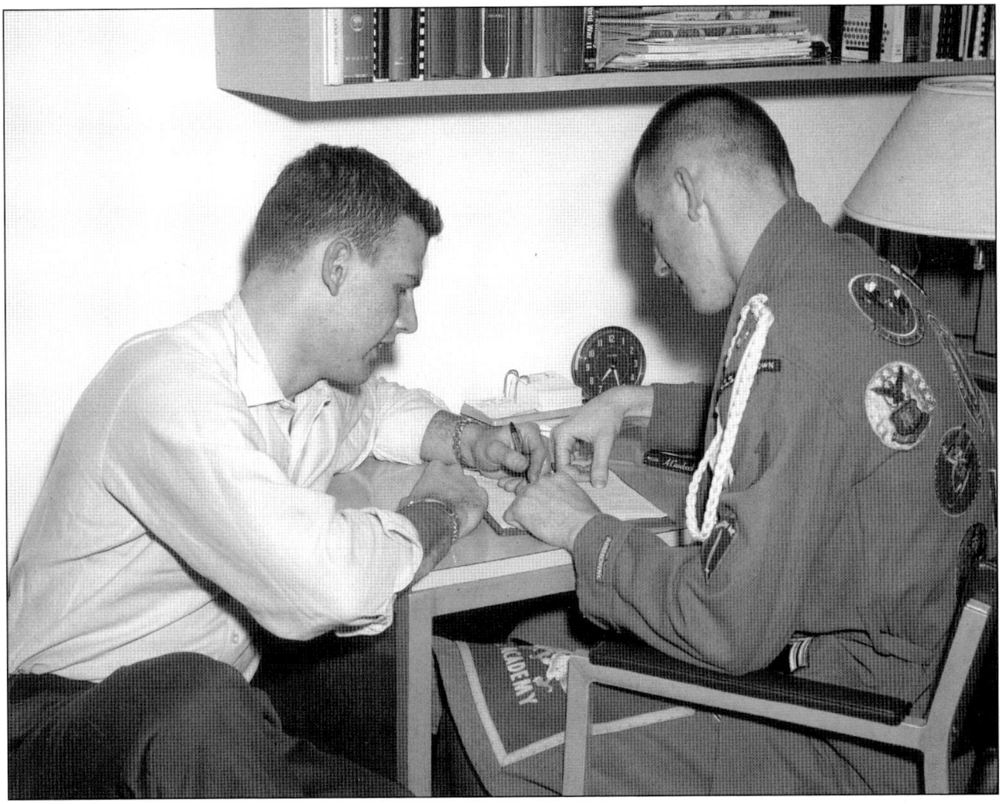

Bathrobes were vibrant expressions of individuality during the early years at the Air Force Academy, as shown by Cadet Bernard Cooney in this 1963 picture. Cadets decorated these informal uniforms with patches, rank insignia, and other emblems acquired throughout their time at the academy. Cadets from the 1980s recalled betting their bathrobes on interservice academy football games with exchange cadets, proudly sporting any winnings in the halls of their dormitories.

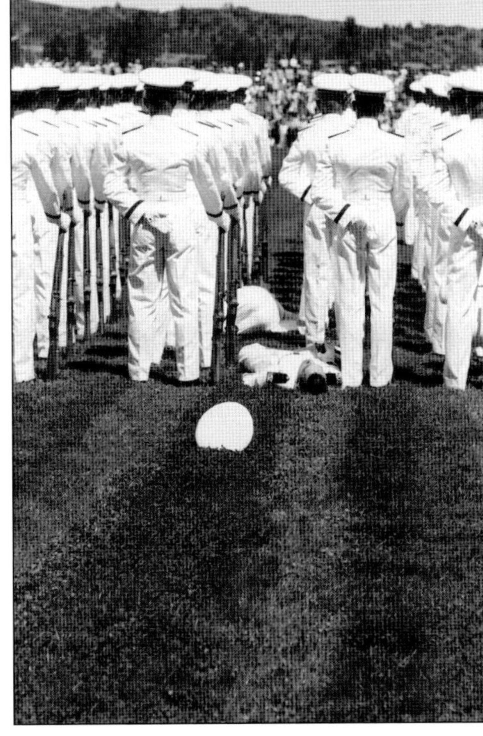

It is not uncommon to see a few cadets on the ground during parades. Underclassmen often faint from locking their knees while standing at attention for an extended period. The Air Force Academy's medical staff is always ready to assist. However, unimpressed fellow cadets will likely grade the fall and offer pointers on achieving a perfect 10 landing next time. (Photograph by Robert McIntyre; courtesy of Special Collections, Pikes Peak Library District, 045-7697.)

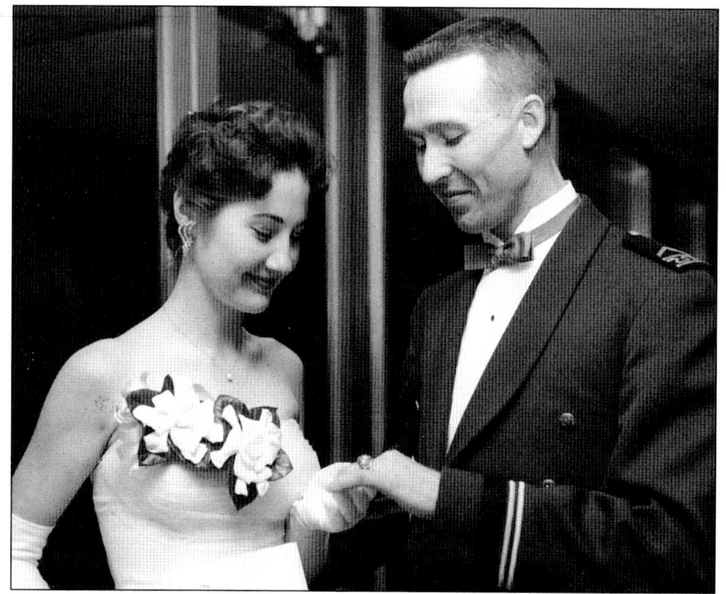

During Graduation Week, a formal ball is given in the Arnold Hall Ballroom for second-class cadets, signifying their transition to first-classmen. As part of the ceremonies during this "Ring Dance," the cadets unveil their Class Crest and receive their class rings. The rings are christened in a glass of champagne and are caught in the teeth following a toast. Here, a cadet's date admires his new ring at the Ring Dance in 1959.

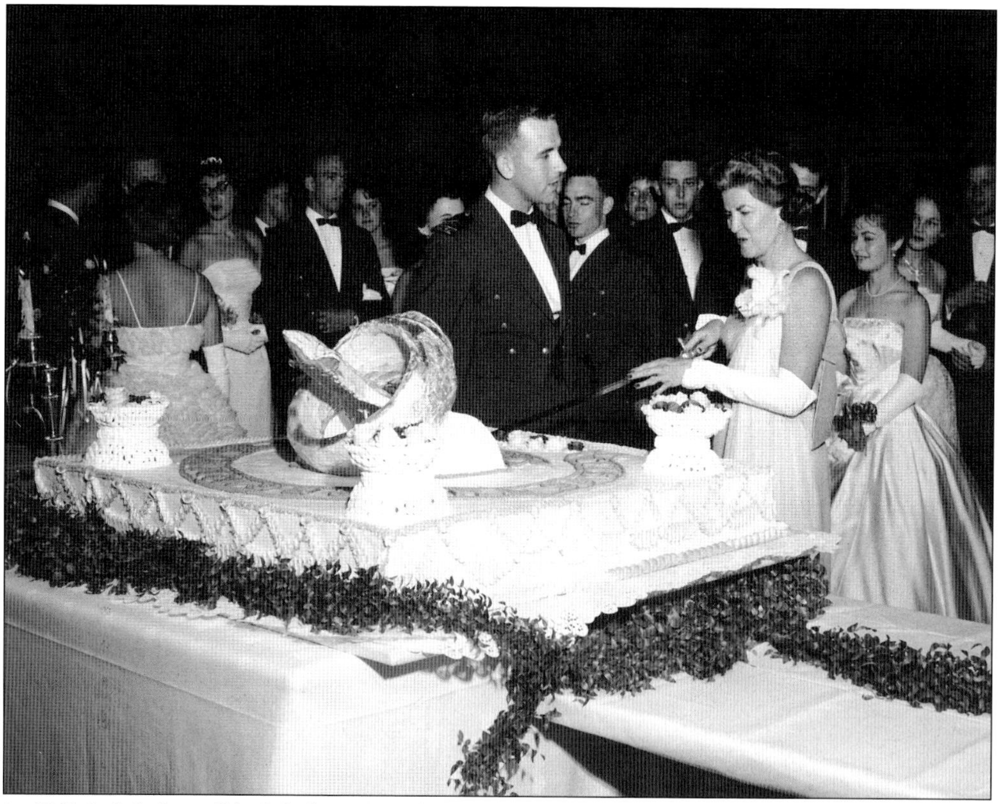

In 1962, Judith Seawell (right), the wife of the commandant of cadets, and Cadet John M. Hockemeier (left) use a saber to cut the traditional Ring Dance cake. The cake was decorated with an icing inscription reading, "The Beginning of the End." The Ring Dance, particularly in the Air Force Academy's early years, provided many cadets with a chance to present rings of their own as a proposal to their long-term girlfriends.

The Class Crest, designed by each class, is a symbol of camaraderie. The crest must include the Polaris star, a cadet saber, the class motto, an eagle, the class number, and the graduating year. Classes include additional design elements in their unique crest design to reflect their experiences, their inimitable bond, and the broader context of world events that mark their time at the Air Force Academy.

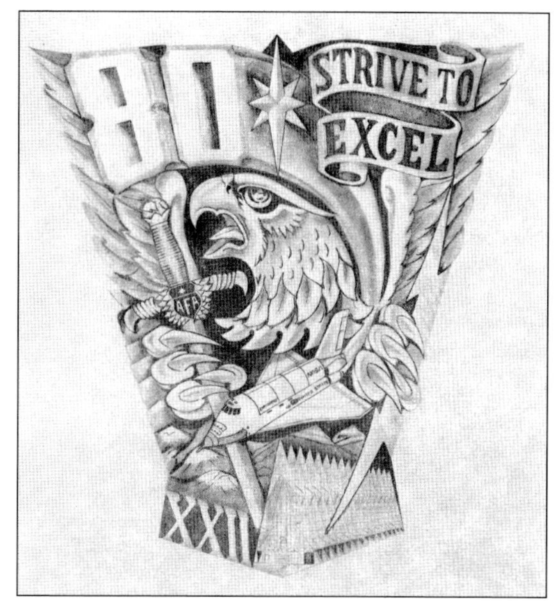

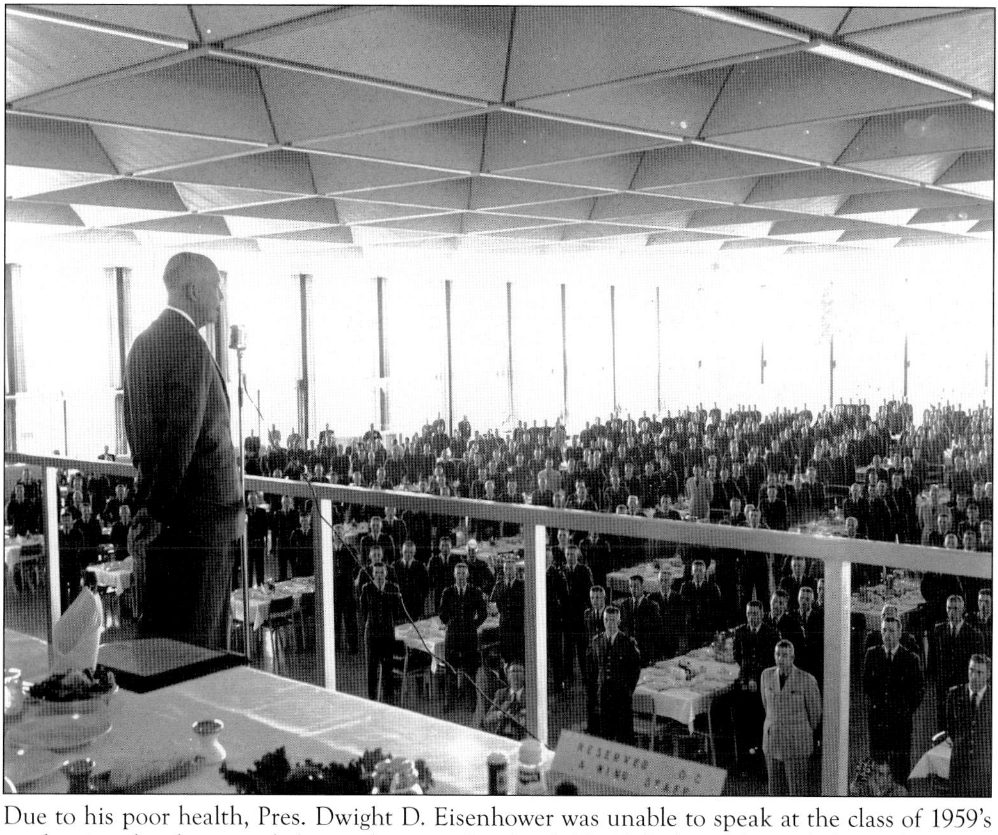

Due to his poor health, Pres. Dwight D. Eisenhower was unable to speak at the class of 1959's graduation, but he visited the week prior. On April 30, 1959, he addressed the Cadet Wing from the Staff Tower in Mitchell Hall, where he was presented with the first Air Force Academy diploma, honoring him as a member of the inaugural class. (Photograph by Stewarts Commercial Photographers, © Pikes Peak Library District, 013-491.)

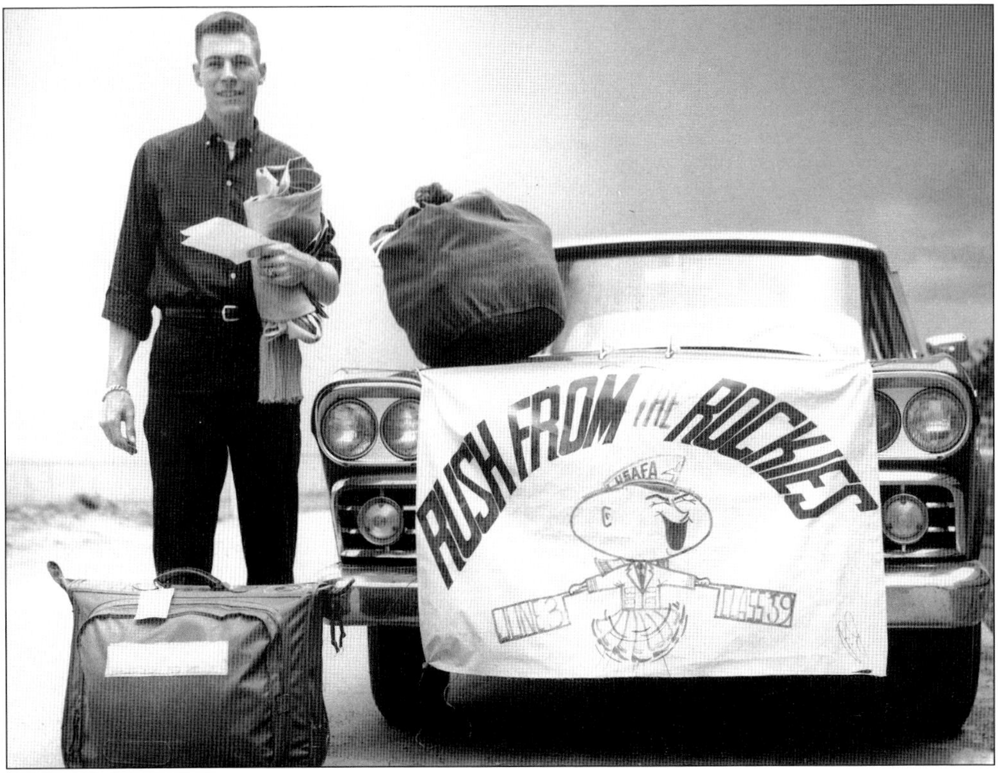

In the 1950s, the State of Colorado promoted tourism with the slogan "Rush to the Rockies." As he prepared to leave the Air Force Academy, John Gallo, class of 1959, humorously adapted this idea with a sign on his car featuring a cartoon cadet ready to "Rush from the Rockies."

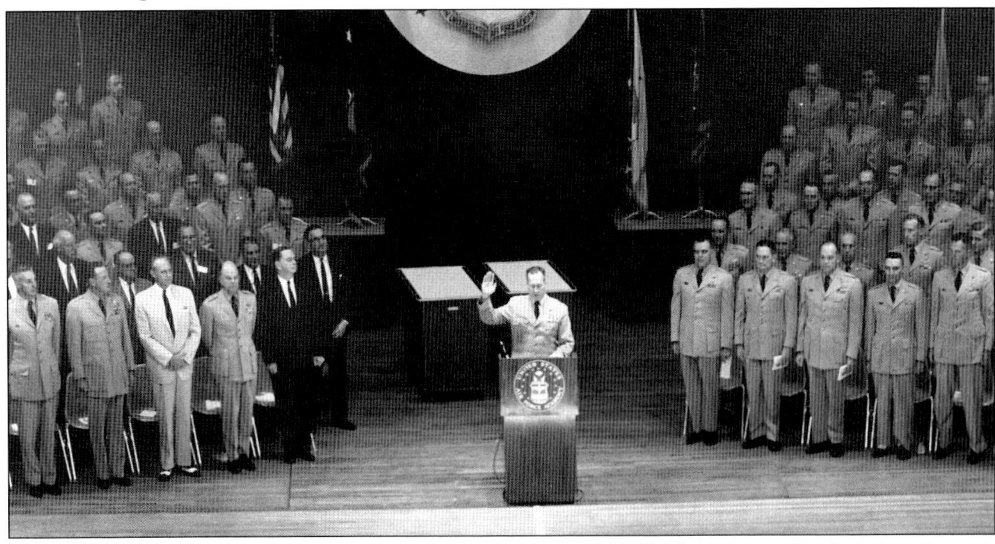

Graduation for the class of 1959 was held in the Arnold Hall Theater on Wednesday, June 3, 1959. Maj. Gen. Robert Stillman, commandant of cadets, is pictured here administering the oath of office to the 207 members of this class. The Honorable James H. Douglas, secretary of the Air Force, presented the diplomas, and Superintendent Briggs read a note from President Eisenhower congratulating the class on this historic event.

One of the most iconic representations of the Air Force Academy is the ceremonial tossing of caps at graduation in Falcon Stadium. The first cap toss, pictured here, was slightly smaller but still immensely significant for the graduates. Notably, the class of 1959 is the only Air Force Academy class to graduate indoors. The American tradition of tossing caps at graduation began at the Naval Academy in 1912.

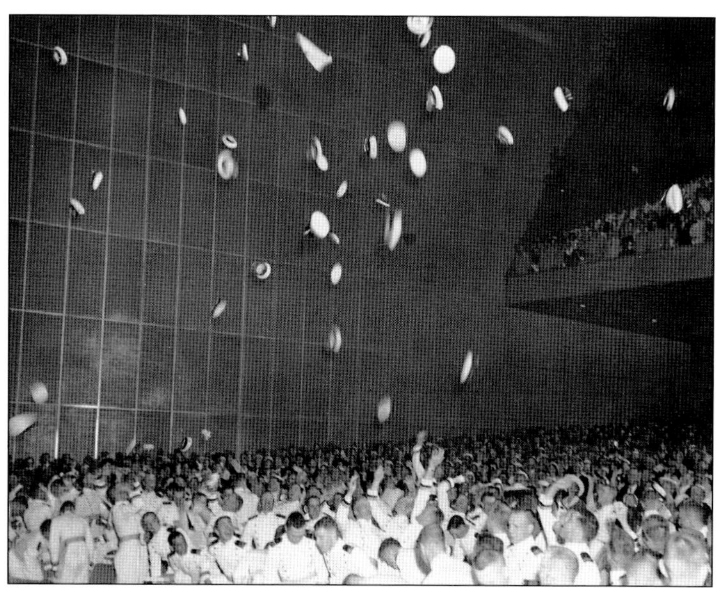

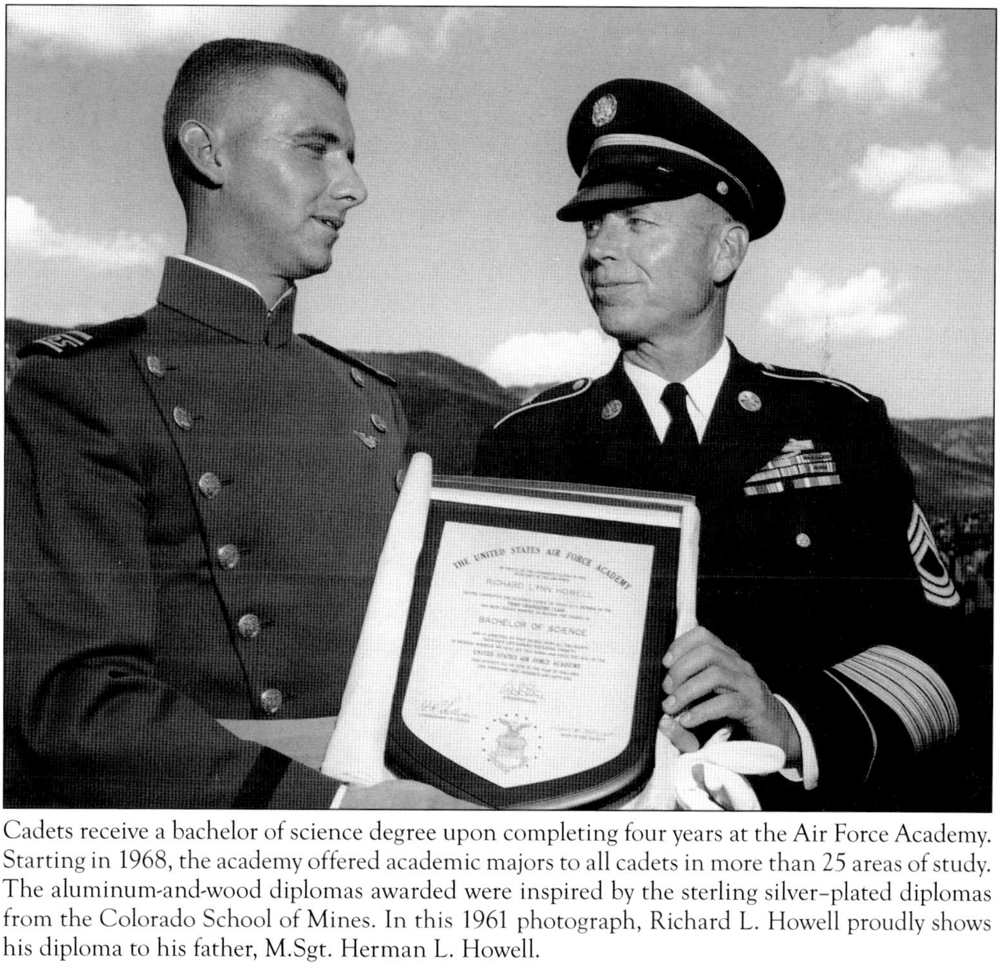

Cadets receive a bachelor of science degree upon completing four years at the Air Force Academy. Starting in 1968, the academy offered academic majors to all cadets in more than 25 areas of study. The aluminum-and-wood diplomas awarded were inspired by the sterling silver–plated diplomas from the Colorado School of Mines. In this 1961 photograph, Richard L. Howell proudly shows his diploma to his father, M.Sgt. Herman L. Howell.

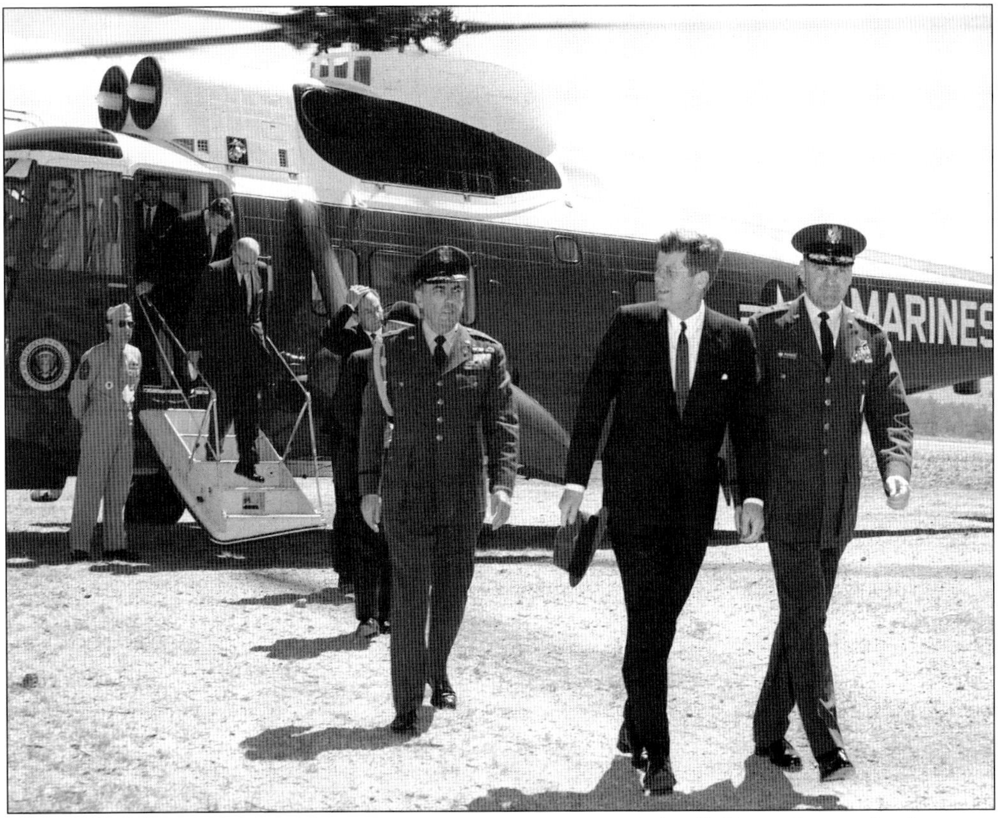

Pres. John F. Kennedy was the first president to attend an Air Force Academy graduation ceremony. Shown here, the president is departing a Marine helicopter outside the Talbott Portal of Falcon Stadium on June 5, 1963. President Kennedy was presented with a diploma and became an "instant graduate" of the class of 1963.

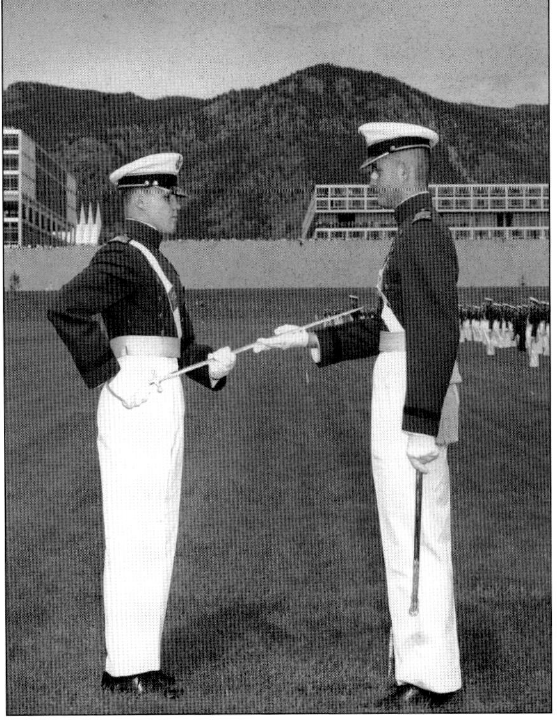

An important June Week tradition is the exchange of sabers between the Cadet Wing commander of the graduating class and the cadet selected to lead the first portion of the upcoming BCT program. Here, the 1963 Cadet Wing commander, Michael J.C. Roth (left), hands his saber, and the responsibility for the Cadet Wing, over to James C. Ingram Jr. (right).

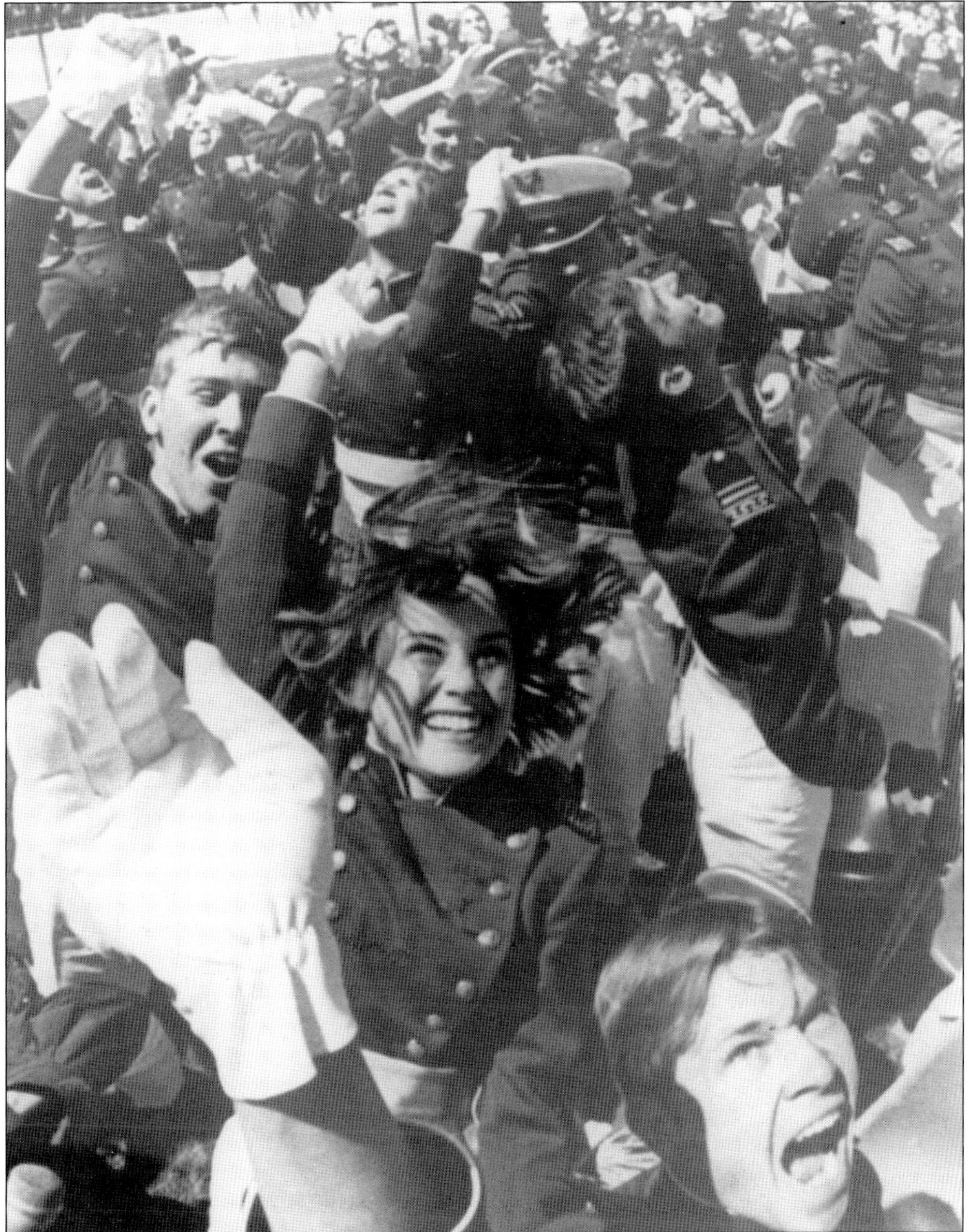

Kathleen Conley, the Air Force Academy's first female graduate, celebrates with her classmates during graduation on May 28, 1980. At the dedication of the Air Force Academy in 1955, the chief of staff of the Air Force, Gen. Nathan F. Twining, remarked, "From today on, the nation's interests will be in you cadets and those who follow. The Air Force Academy is not really important in itself. What is important is the product of the Academy. The graduates will be the measure of its success. In the final analysis, only you, the cadets, can make it a great school." Over the past 70 years, the Air Force Academy has graduated more than 56,000 men and women of character who have gone on to prove that the Air Force Academy has lived up to the great expectations set in 1955. The academy graduates have done themselves, the institution, and the nation proud.

Bibliography

Much of the information in this book is derived from photographs, newspapers, documents, and other materials found in Clark Special Collections Branch of the Air Force Academy McDermott Library. Additional information was provided by Jack Anthony, class of 1978.

Adams, Nicholas. *Skidmore, Owings, & Merrill: The Experiment since 1936*. Milan: Mondadori Electa SPA, 2006.

Barnes, Erinn, Time Morris, and Heather Jordan, eds. *Military Matters: Defense, Development, & Dissent in the Pikes Peak Region*. Colorado Springs: Pikes Peak Library District, 2022.

Brooks, Don L. *First Falcons: The Start of the Long Blue Line*. Morrisville, NC: Lulu Publishing Services, 2018.

Bruegmann, Robert, ed. *Modernism at Mid-Century: The Architecture of the United States Air Force Academy*. Chicago: The University of Chicago Press, 1994.

Cannon, M. Hamlin, and Henry S. Fellerman. *Quest for an Air Force Academy*. Colorado Springs: United States Air Force Academy, 1974.

Clement, Russell T., Robert Bruegmann, and Robert Allen Nauman, et al. *Walter A. Netsch, FAIA: A Critical Appreciation and Sourcebook*. Chicago: Northwestern University Press, 2008.

Cogswell, Hester Jane. *Pine Valley: A Window to the Early History of Colorado Springs and the U.S. Air Force Academy*. Bloomington, IN: iUniverse, 2011.

Fagan, George V. *Air Force Academy Heritage: The Early Years*. Golden, CO: Fulcrum Publishing, 2006.

———. *The Air Force Academy: An Illustrated History*. Boulder, CO: Johnson Books, 1988.

Kaplan, Edward A., ed. *High Flight: History of the U.S. Air Force Academy*. Chicago: Imprint Publications, 2011.

Kornahrens, Kathleen Utley. *"Bring Me Men . . ." Brought Women: Marching with the First Female Cadets at the U.S. Air Force Academy*. Jefferson, NC: McFarland & Company, Inc., 2023.

Landis, Lawrence C. *The Story of the U.S. Air Force Academy*. New York: Rinehart & Company, Inc., 1960.

Ringenbach, Paul T. *Battling Tradition: Robert F. McDermott and Shaping the U.S. Air Force Academy*. Chicago: Imprint Publications, 2006.

Witters, Arthur G., and J. Bryce Hollingsworth. *Off We Go! The Real Story of How the United States Air Force Academy Was Created, Designed and Built*. Chapel Hill, NC: Professional Press, 2009.

About the Friends of the Air Force Academy Library

I received personal and professional support from the Friends of the Air Force Academy Library, a tax-exempt charitable organization established in 1987 to promote the Air Force Academy as an outstanding educational, research, scientific, and cultural institution. Composed of alumni and friends, the group works with librarians and administrators to acquire, preserve, and publish materials that capture the rich heritage and traditions of the Air Force and the Air Force Academy.

To pursue these goals and improve the quality of faculty research and cadet education, the Friends help organize and catalog significant historic documents in the Clark Special Collections Branch. They digitize important document and photograph collections for preservation and accessibility. And they sponsor scholarly research fellowships to promote awareness and use of the rare original source materials available in the library with a view toward publications and presentations for colleagues and cadets.

Through these efforts, the Friends enhance the utility of the Air Force Academy's library as a resource for cadets, faculty, and other scholarly research dealing with aviation, military space, and Air Force and academy heritage.

Consistent with our mission to preserve history on a local level, this book was printed in South Carolina on American-made paper and manufactured entirely in the United States. Products carrying the accredited Forest Stewardship Council (FSC) label are printed on 100 percent FSC-certified paper.

MADE IN THE

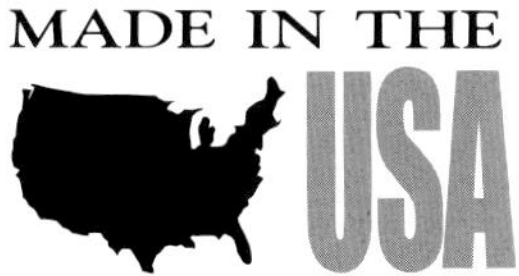